T0339839

IMPROVING EDUCATION IN THE US

IMPROVING EDUCATION IN THE US
A POLITICAL PARADOX

Rafael Yanushevsky

Algora Publishing
New York

Library of Congress Cataloging-in-Publication Data —

Yanushevsky, Rafael.
  Improving Education in the US: A Political Paradox/ Rafael Yanushevsky.
    p. cm.
  Includes bibliographical references and index.
    ISBN 978-0-87586-834-9 (soft: alk. paper) — ISBN 978-0-87586-835-6 (hard:
alk. paper) — ISBN 978-0-87586-836-3 (ebook) 1. Public schools—United States. 2.
Education and state—United States. 3. Education—Aims and objectives—United States.
4. Educational change—Government policy—United States. I. Title.
    LA217.2.Y37 2011
    379.73—dc22
                          2010053757

Front cover: ImageZoo

Printed in the United States

TABLE OF CONTENTS

The United States is a world power with a poor educational system — what a paradox! — and bickering over education reform may be a permanent feature of American society. In a further paradox, much of the problem lies outside the schools themselves but rests in the chaotic amalgam of competing bureaucrats, boards, associations, agencies and unions that make up the education "system," the broad social environment, and political divides.

In the past fifty years, despite all the wrangling between the two main political parties, the nation has been unable to develop a successful education strategy. Even among politicians there is a mindboggling lack of cohesion and consensus on public education. Although representatives of both parties advocate a good education for children, Democrats insist on increasing federal involvement in education accompanied with lavish federal funding while Republicans oppose the intensive involvement.

From elementary school to the university level, *Improving Education in the US* navigates readers through the confusing and often contradictory information about the problems facing education. The book shows the deficiency of the existing education system and compares it to more efficient, effective systems. It explains the basics of the organizational structure of education, the role of the federal government, state governments, and local governments in running school systems and how they are all different. The author considers various aspects of public education systems from elementary school through university, the genesis of public schools in the United

States, issues that still need to be addressed, trends in education and reform and analyses of what is working or not working.

Topics include:

- Problems schools are facing and reforms that have been implemented to address those problems
- How schools are financed
- How public schools compare to private schools

The main goal of this book is to explain the current American education system and why it is a failure despite ongoing efforts at reform. The author shows that the existing approaches to improve education are based on the same foolish idea that as long as government spending on education is great enough, improvement will follow. The author shows that multiple attempts to improve the functioning of the existing education system were unable to bring any tangible results because they dealt with separate, purely educational problems, rather than the global one, and were conducted by experts in education rather than experts in system analysis, operation research and optimal theory who are able to approach complex problems using the appropriate tools. He uses his knowledge in these areas to explain what should be done for progress in the US education system to become reality.

Bombarded by the unrealistic promises of politicians, parents want to believe them because the promises coincide with their desire to give their children a better education. But such promises have little chance for success, especially when any real analysis must inevitably show some portion of the huge educational bureaucracy and various educational organizations around the public school system to be redundant or dysfunctional, and by implication that means that some jobs would be called into question. Thus those responsible for doing the analysis have no incentive to do it well. Without any doubt, education is a national problem. Many or most Americans feel it is the government's obligation to resolve it, but it cannot be resolved without the active cooperation of all parties.

Everyone who cares about America's future must be armed with information related to the US public system of education. Is it not paradoxical that the richest and most advanced country in the world has an unsatisfactory system of public education that threatens the country's future prosperity? It is a dangerous sign of a possible future decline. The author hopes that this book will help readers to understand some of the difficulties in rebuilding the existing public education system. That being said, this book is his baby and he claims exclusive responsibility for any possible errors of fact and interpretation.

Chapter 1. The Wealth of a Nation

> "The most valuable of all education is the ability to make yourself do the thing you have to do, when it has to be done, whether you like it or not." - Aldous Huxley

When I first came to this country from the former Soviet Union, I had no idea what to expect. The year was 1987. What impressed me most about America was not the wealth of its economy, or its cars, but the libraries. I became a professor of engineering at the University of Maryland and of mathematics at the University of the District of Columbia and was astonished by the enormous range and volume of scientific information available. On the seemingly endless rows of library bookshelves were the latest, most cutting edge scientific journals and materials from all of the world's leading industrialized countries.

In the Soviet Union I had worked at the Institute of Control Sciences, one of the leading institutes at the Academy of Sciences. Yet despite the prestige of this world renowned institute, I had never had access to the kinds of information taken for granted at even small American universities. Yet to my great disappointment as an educator, my American students lacked mathematical skills entirely. There wasn't just a lack of knowledge of elementary algebra or calculus; my students didn't seem to have any deep understanding of mathematical procedures at all. Math, when it was used, was used mechanically and without any real comprehension.

As a teacher, I have found that students fear what they don't know or feel that they can't learn, and this leads to a negative attitude toward whatever subject it is they are deficient in or any other related field as well. Because math is an integral part of the study of other sciences, students tend to be scared away from technical or scientific study in areas such as physics, engineering, and earth sciences. Instead large numbers of students pursue liberal arts and business degrees or go into law. I found that most of the graduate level courses in math and science tended to be filled with foreign students from China, Greece, the Middle East, India, and other countries. It was as if the American students were content to get a bachelor's degree, avoid any serious study in rigorous math and science courses, and not go any further in pursuit of a university degree.

But people come here from around the world to get an education that may be unrivaled in quality and availability. America has attracted some of the world's most talented people from other lands who have earned degrees and become some of the greatest scientists, writers, doctors, and economists of our time. Nowhere in history has this been more evident than in the 19th century and 20th centuries when floods of immigrants reached America's shores and took advantage of the education offered them in its public schools, free of charge. With their help and intellect, the United States became a superpower capable of great achievements with a diverse, complex, flourishing, and productive economy that made it the richest country in the world.

THE GOLD STANDARD

For more than a century, American schools were the envy of the world and the US scientific and technological advances made this country a nation of innovators. Its schools turned out students whose genius made travel faster and cheaper than ever before, let their countrymen explore the heavens, and took them to the moon. But we live in the 21st century and the blessings of immigration, diversity, and an economic powerhouse are tempered by societal changes. America still has some of the finest schools and students in the world but the country has been lagging behind since the 1960s. In the last twenty-five years Americans have famously fallen behind many less wealthy or powerful nations. The reluctance to continue their education beyond a bachelor's degree — to get at least a master's degree, suggests that schools and parents have not instilled in children a love of learning. A bachelor's degree is considered essential to financial and social upward mobility; and most Americans who make it that far are satisfied with this minimal achievement; in fact for many, even this is not financially attainable.

The Race to Mediocrity

When my children were old enough to start attending school in a DC suburb in Maryland, I was confident because Montgomery County was known for having nationally ranked schools. These schools were modern and spacious. They had state-of-the art facilities and their classrooms were well equipped with computerized learning aids. But because of my experiences at the university level with students who lacked real math, science, and language comprehension I had a nagging fear that the curricula being taught weren't going to give my children the knowledge and skills necessary to succeed in life. Soon I became involved in their education and unintentionally compared the teaching in these schools with the teaching I had received in the Soviet Union's schools.

In 1957, the Soviet Union was still primarily a poor, underdeveloped society that had sustained heavy losses during World War II (which is why many Americans were shocked when the Soviets launched *Sputnik*). Politicians were at a loss to explain how the backward, war torn Communists had been able to accomplish what Americans had not. The space race and ramping up of education in the sciences that followed were an indirect admission of the superiority of the Soviet education system. So how is it that after fifty years of investing money in the US system of public education, Americans still cannot reach the desired results?

The education system of the former Soviet Union was extremely different from the kind found in the United States. In the Soviet Union education was centralized and was strictly controlled by the government at the national level. The ugly side of this centralized education system was that it suppressed local initiatives.

In that place and time, it was simply unacceptable for students to be shunted from one grade to the next without having achieved the requisite level of mastery in reading, writing, language, math, and science. The rigorous teaching methods used were rigid and autocratic, but the end result was that I had received a solid education. One benefit of the Soviet system was the government's ability to formulate goals and enforce their achievement. And the foundation in the basics that I learned made it possible for me to achieve a highly advanced level of training and move on to higher education successfully. So I expected nothing less from my children's schools here.

The Teacher Becomes the Student

Unfortunately, the more familiar I became with the curricula in my children's schools and how it was being taught, the more concerned I became. What my children were being taught wasn't challenging enough. The textbooks were handsome and well written, but didn't seem to stress the fundamentals of reading, writing, math, and science. And most students were either being taught *to the test* or learning just enough to get by and move on to the next grade level.

I discovered that many local schools weren't performing well and neither were others across the country. American schools were in crisis and had been for more than thirty years. But how could a country as wealthy and blessed with infinite resources such as the United States let this happen? I worried that my children's highly-ranked schools were lagging behind private schools and the public schools in other industrialized nations. And I knew that, if America didn't do something to change this, the country would not be able to compete in the global marketplace.

Education has always been a path to success, especially true for disadvantaged children. So what had changed? Why was the achievement gap for middle class children widening? Why were the children of poverty being almost entirely left behind?

When I tried to get information or guidance from the federal government, the state, or even my local school district, I was stymied. I dug into books in the library, searched online guides, and researched and read everything I could get my hands on about public education, its problems, and its reforms. And what I found wasn't reassuring.

As an educator at the university level, I had seen a range of problems and patterns of neglect or inadequate instruction among my students. Many of them had no real working knowledge, could only perform the mechanics of mathematics, and had little if any grasp of the sciences. I found out that many children had graduated from middle school without a real knowledge of their mother tongue and that English grammar simply wasn't taught properly at the middle school level. Once kids reached high school, English teachers often assumed that students already knew the basics in each subject so insufficient attention was paid to English composition; students graduated from high school without a real knowledge of sentence construction and grammar. They also knew little about algebra and so were unable to move on to higher levels of mathematical courses that are necessary to perform in any science, especially in physics-related subjects. It seemed to me that middle schools presented the weakest link in the education chain.

THE DEPARTMENT OF EDUCATION — MYTH OR REALITY?

Although Americans claim to have a proud lineage of public education going back to the Founding Fathers, the Constitution never mentions public education and a national system never existed. I began to research the history of public education, trends in school performance, what problems existed and what reforms had been put in place. Getting answers or getting involved hasn't been simple or easy. There are mountains of literature on the subject. But official information is difficult to digest because the American education system is not centralized at the national level. What then is the Department of Education?

Many people incorrectly assume that the Federal Department of Education is the head of education policy in the country. The Department of Education is a federal agency that doesn't set national policy and has little or no regulatory teeth. Virtually everything — from policy making to curriculum development, teacher certification, textbook selection, etc. — happens at the state, local, and even neighborhood level. Historically, there may have been free public schools in the United States for well over 100 years, but there has never really been a national public school system. At the Department of Education's website *www.ed.gov*, the second paragraph of the Policy page says:

> Please note that in the U.S., the federal role in education is limited. Because of the Tenth Amendment, most education policy is decided at the state and local levels. So, if you have a question about a policy or issue, you may want to check with the relevant organization in your state or school district.

To my surprise, the national public school educational system doesn't exist at all. The US system of public education is subordinate to the states' authorities, and is, in essence, locally centralized. There are local educational systems that consider themselves "the best" which operate quite independently, backed by money from state and local taxes but also seeking financing from the federal government. They want the federal government to pay for schooling but they certainly don't want the government telling them how to go about doing the teaching.

This lack of federal control over education and the different ways that national education policies are interpreted at the state and local levels are two key reasons why education still remains an unresolved problem.

Local schools also tend to be reluctant to use experts in math, science, and technical fields to design curricula. Combine this with a lack of parental involvement in children's learning and in curricula design, add political hot-button issues to the mix, and you have a recipe for disaster. In the last thirty to forty years, US progress in education has been marginal at best. Yet agreement on what is wrong with schools and how to fix them is virtually nonexistent.

First Response

> If an unfriendly foreign power had attempted to impose on America the mediocre educational performance that exists today, we might well have viewed it as an act of war." - excerpted from *A Nation At Risk*, The National Commission on Excellence in Education Report, 1983.

When *A Nation At Risk* was issued twenty-eight years ago, its condemnation of the US public schools must have been chilling for everyone, but especially parents. How did parents, teachers, reformers, and politicians respond to the crisis? The answer is astonishing.

People buried their heads in the sand. In all those years, few people with a stake in education came up with viable and realistic approaches to address the issues facing schools. Everyone, from parents to students, teachers, reformers, administrators, and politicians, seems to have suffered from the same paralyzing lethargy.

Asleep at the Helm

Because there was no centralized national public education system, there wasn't anyone at the helm to determine the course and change tack. The public education reform movement was rudderless and without direction. As a result, the status quo was maintained for far too long and public education in the United States is now in dire straits.

The lack of national consensus was compounded by monumental demographic changes over the last fifty years. Some of the issues schools needed to address, in varying degrees, across the country were:

- Schools had a hard time attracting and keeping good teachers
- Across the board, comprehension and test scores in the fundamentals of reading, writing, math, and science were either stagnant or had dropped to all time lows for middle class students
- High school graduation rates went down
- Dropout rates rose
- Parents, for whatever reason, were passive and not deeply involved in their children's education
- Achievement gaps for minorities and children living in poverty widened significantly
- Many schools fell into such disrepair that they were unsafe.

A Sinking Ship

That is why more recently people began questioning just how effective reforms such as the *No Child Left Behind Act* have been. In an attempt to get consensus on the status of education, the Department of Education issued a report in 2008 that reviewed how far Americans have come in the twenty-five years since *A Nation at Risk* was released. This new report was entitled *A Nation Accountable, Twenty-five Years After A Nation at Risk* and its conclusions were a real blow. Two of the Report's devastating findings were that:

> If we were "at risk" in 1983, we are at even greater risk now. The rising demands of our global economy, together with demographic shifts, require that we educate more students to higher levels than ever before. Yet, our education system is not keeping pace with these growing demands....

> Of 20 children born in 1983, six did not graduate from high school on time in 2001. Of the 14 who did, 10 started college that fall, but only five earned a bachelor's degree by spring 2007.

The real question is: What should parents, and not only parents — all who care for the country's future, do now?

To help educate readers about the situation, the following compass points are included that address the key aspects of public education.

Policy: Education and politics are inseparably linked. It's shown that, unfortunately, this bond only hinders progress in education. The following chapters deal with the genesis of public schools in the United States, government initiatives, trends in education and reform, analysis of what is working and why, and issues that still need to be addressed.

Operations: This compass point explains the basics of the organizational structure of education, the role of the federal government, state governments, and local governments in running school systems, and how they are all different. This lack of uniformity has created a patchwork of state and local systems that offer varying degrees of adequate funding, facilities and equipment, trained teachers, appropriate curricula, and school performance.

Research: Information is presented about public and private organizations, and governmental bodies involved in public education reform. As an expert in system analysis and optimization theory, and as a mathematician, believing that only what is *almost obvious* can be proven rigorously, the author explains persuasively *the obvious* — the deficiency of the existing education system and what should be done to improve it.

Students in the United States lag behind the rest of the world in math, science, and language and this lack of scholarship threatens the economic and political future of the United States. As Margaret Spellings, the former US Secretary of Education has said, "We live in a world where technological innovation and global competition are increasing at a pace never before seen. Now is the time to invest in our children to make sure they are prepared to succeed in the 21st century." While we need to look forward, we will be doomed to repeat mistakes if we do not learn from the past — which is why the next chapter is about the genesis and history of public education in America.

Chapter 2. The Founding Fathers and the History of Public Education

"The dogmas of the quiet past are inadequate to the stormy present. The occasion is piled high with difficulty, and we must rise with the occasion. As our case is new, so we must think anew and act anew." - Abraham Lincoln, addressing the Congress in 1866 regarding the formation of the Department of Education

In the Beginning

According to Webster's dictionary, education is defined as "the act or process of imparting or acquiring general knowledge, developing the powers of reasoning and judgment, and generally of preparing oneself or others intellectually for mature life."

This process begins shortly after birth, as parents start to teach the infant, through examples and instructions, how to behave, e.g., how to decode sounds and establish attitudes, values, skills, and certain knowledge that will govern him/her through life.

In the future, we will use the term *education* in a more narrow sense, meaning formal education or schooling, i.e., a deliberately planned and utilized process to help young people learn what is considered important for them to know. Schools are institutions that provide formal education. Educational goals relate to what is considered important to know. Public schools are funded by the society and serve the society in accordance with established educational goals.

The Founding Fathers of the United States understood that a stable and democratic society is impossible without its citizens accepting some common set of values and without a minimum degree of literacy and knowledge among most of its members. Education contributes to both. They also recognized the inherent danger an ignorant populace and electorate pose to their freedom. Ignorance makes the populace vulnerable to tyranny and breeds injustice.

In 1749, Benjamin Franklin wrote: "Nothing can more effectively contribute to the Cultivation and Improvement of a Country, the Wisdom, Riches, and Strength, Virtue and Piety, the Welfare and Happiness of a People, than a proper Education of youth, by forming their Manners, imbuing their tender Minds with Principles of Rectitude and Morality, [and] instructing them ... in all useful Branches of liberal Arts and Science."

About seventy years later Thomas Jefferson, who is recognized not just for his brilliant mind but for his creation of the University of Virginia, warned, "If you expect a nation to be ignorant and free and in a state of civilization, you expect what never was and never will be." In contrast to those who believed that education was a private matter and not a concern for the state, he understood that the gain from the education of a child would go not only to the child or to his parents but also to other members of the society.

The national system of education in the United States developed in the 19th century. But until the mid-1800s, in most parts of the United States schooling was still a privilege. Benjamin Rush, one of the leaders of the Revolutionary movement, believed, along with Franklin, Adams, Madison, and others, that a proper system of education was the only way to protect a republic. In 1768, in his essay *Thoughts Upon the Mode of Education Proper in a Republic,* he expressed the view that: "An education should be present that would give a thorough grounding in democratic principles, and at the same time would make for modification of instruments of society that would be necessary for progress toward greater freedom." Rush was against a dogmatic approach to education and believed that students "must be taught that there can be no durable liberty in a republic and that government, like all other sciences, is of a progressive nature." Rush, as well as the Founding Fathers, understood that the prosperity and future development of the

United States depended on the advancement of science. He paid special attention to a school curriculum suitable to American democracy. Rush outlined the following curriculum: "Let the first 8 years be employed in learning to speak, spell, read, and write the English language. Arithmetic and some of the more simple branches of the mathematics should be acquired between the twelfth and fourteenth years of his life. Natural history should find a prominent place early in the education, geography should be understood and mastered by age 12, and in place of the ancient languages should come French and German. Between the fourteenth and eighteenth years, the pupil should be instructed in grammar, oratory, criticism, the higher branches of mathematics, philosophy, chemistry, logic, metaphysics, chronology, history, government, the principles of agriculture, manufactures, and in everything else that is necessary to qualify him for public usefulness and private happiness."

However, the idea of universal public education remained only an idea, and up until around 1840, schools in the country were mostly private. Parents, not the government, paid for each child to attend school and there was no centralized body that established curricula or formal school systems. In the early days, education was usually for the elite. Most institutions only provided educational opportunities for boys from wealthy families, by tutoring and in small one-room schools.

After the Civil War, reformers demanded that education be available to all children. Congress enacted a couple of bills to encourage education for all children. The Land Ordinance of 1785 and Northwest Ordinance of 1787 (especially Act 3) set aside land for the building and operation of schools. They reflected the belief that education is necessary to become a good citizen and to have a strong government. But while schools were publicly supplied, they were not free of charge.

Horace Mann (1796–1859) in the 1840s called for the creation of an elementary public education system. At the time, he created what were called "common schools" — that is, schools commonly supported, commonly attended by all people regardless of race, class or sex, and commonly controlled. Free public education at the elementary level became available for American children only by the end of 19th century.

In the second part of the 19th century, the compulsory attendance laws were mandated by each individual state to ensure that the children were in school, receiving an education, and not working in industry. It was believed that the public school was the best means to improve the literacy rate of the poor and to help assimilate an immigrant population that was growing at a high rate. In the United States, compulsory attendance laws are statutes established by state governments that require parents to have their children attend school for a designated period. Each state by law determines when this period starts and ends. Modern compulsory attendance laws were first enacted in Massachusetts in 1853 followed by New York in 1854. Since 1918, all the states have compulsory attendance laws. Parents whose children don't attend school are considered to be breaking the law.

Public education means that the public controls education at schools so that the school serve the public's needs. The public schools inaugurated in the 19th century, called the "common" schools, charged no tuition. Common schools were open to all white children, were governed by local school committees, were funded by local property taxes and were subject to a modest state regulation. Common schools taught the basics of English literacy and arithmetic. They provided fundamental skills (reading, writing, reasoning, and oral communication), and the knowledge and the capacity for thought needed to pursue further learning in order to succeed in chosen fields, and to assume the responsibilities of informed citizenship.

However, later many jobs required higher levels of education. Public opinion increasingly saw value, both for the society and for the students, in graduating from high school. The first public secondary school in the United States was opened in Boston in 1821. The civic leaders of Boston voted to create the country's first public high school, open to boys 12 or older who could pass an entrance exam. By the end of the century, such secondary schools had begun to outnumber private academies, a form of secondary school that had existed since 1751. As the number of high schools grew, so did the quality of the education. Classes such as algebra, geometry, American history, bookkeeping, and surveying were added quickly to the meager curriculum, and towns with a population of 4,000 or more were even required to add general history, rhetoric, logic, Latin, and Greek. Three hundred high schools were added by the time of the Civil War. After a Michigan Supreme Court ruling in 1874 that the school districts must maintain a tax-supported public high school, the popularity of secondary education soared. By 1880, there were 800 high schools in the United States, and by 1890 their number reached 2,500.

The purpose of secondary schools has changed since those days. Secondary schools brought education closer to the needs of everyday life; they taught such courses as history, geography, algebra, geometry, modern languages, navigation, and astronomy. Their main intention went from preparing students for college to preparing students for life and non-academic jobs. There was a need for more teachers and the so-called principal teacher, a prototype of today's school principal, whose responsibilities weren't restricted to teaching. Eventually, as other duties became more time consuming, principal teachers stopped teaching and concentrated on managing the schools.

Educational administration was brought into being in the middle of the 19th century following the increase of principal teachers. This administration is an applied field that combines business and education. The trend in education to prepare immigrants for jobs in a growing industry required a centralized educational leadership. In 1837, the father of the American public school, Horace Mann, an adamant advocate of educational reforms, introduced the Act creating the Massachusetts state board of education. Later, similar boards were established all over United States. The creation of educational administration extended the responsibilities of principals who not only managed the school but also served as a liaison between the school and central administration. The first public school superintendent began directing the Buffalo, New York, school system in 1837. The term "superintendent of schools" came from the industrial terminology of the day (industrial plant superintendent). By 1900, the superintendent had replaced the school principal as the most influential and highest paid figure in public elementary and secondary education.

Schools have played a variety of roles in fostering the development of the United States. First they were needed to unify the country with its unstoppable influx of immigrants. Schools taught a common language (the basics of English) and developed patriotism, a primary allegiance to the United States. Primarily the public schools' mission was to assimilate the new immigrants into an English-speaking nation and to provide them with skills such as arithmetic that were needed for future employment.

Educational goals of the mid 19th century, influenced by the rise of industrialism and capitalism, changed not only the secondary school curriculum but also enlarged the curriculum of elementary schools which started to include such subjects as science and nature study, history, and geography.

Until the beginning of the 20th century, an eight-grade education was considered by most to be a complete one and high schools were mostly prep schools for colleges. Industrial progress and business development at the end of 19th century and in the beginning of 20th century set new requirements for education. Knowledge of mathematics, physics, and chemistry became important. The mission of high schools has thus changed. A prominent educational scholar, Elwood Cubberly (1868–1941), stated that schools should be like factories with students as the raw material to be turned into the product that was to meet the needs of the 20th century. Schools began teaching more than just reading and spelling. Sciences became a part of the new curriculum. Students began to see the real value of higher education because high school diplomas became tickets into good colleges and a more prosperous and satisfactory life.

Seven "cardinal principles of secondary education" were issued in 1918 by the Commission on the Reorganization of Secondary Education: "health, command of fundamental processes, worthy home membership, vocation, civic education, worthy use of leisure, and ethical character." The goals of education were much wider and included the development of high moral principles and an allegiance to the democratic traditions of the country.

A Missed Opportunity

America didn't have anything that even resembled a national policy until President Andrew Johnson and Congress created the Department of Education in 1867. The deliberations in Congress were rancorous as advocates and opponents argued for their own interpretations of the Constitution as it related to federal versus states' rights. States' rights advocates believed that federal interference in education matters was unconstitutional according to the Tenth Amendment, which provides that "the powers not delegated to the United States by the Constitution nor prohibited by it to the States, are reserved to the States respectively, or to the people." However, the concept of free public elementary education was accepted, and by 1870, all the states offered free elementary schools.

In the next one hundred years the United States made incredible leaps forward in industry, transportation — and population growth. The Industrial Revolution saw vast migrations from farms into the inner cities in search of work. Major social changes such as the end of slavery, the impact of segregation, and major waves of immigration from Eastern and Western Europe due to war placed enormous pressures on American public schools.

The rise in high school attendance was one of the most striking developments in US education during the 20th century, and the 20th century high school was a uniquely American invention. In 1900, only 10% of American adolescents aged 14 to 17 were enrolled in high schools. Most of these students were from wealthy families. From 1900 to 2000, the percentage of teenagers who graduated from high school increased from about 6% to about 88%. High school attendance grew because more and more students regarded secondary education as the key to succeed in an increasingly industrialized society. The *Fair Labor Standards Act* of 1938, which, among other things, placed limits on many forms of child labor, decreased the number of teenagers entering the workforce so that they were able to attend school. As the century progressed, most states enacted legislation extending compulsory education laws to the age of 16.

After World War II, the United States emerged as a superpower. America excelled other countries in many fields other than education. It had all the necessary resources to be the best in education as well, but it missed this opportunity. The after-war influx of qualified workers helped keep the economy healthy despite the local "educational insufficiency," but this medicine wasn't effective for long.

With the international expansion of the US economy, the decades of the 1950s and 1960s were periods of relative economic prosperity, with growth in employment and real wages. Young people saw the opportunity to get a job and to earn a living without higher education. Compulsory education laws were not rigidly enforced and were not observed. As a result, although high school attendance increased, it was not matched by an increase in the quality of education and it didn't produce the highly-qualified work force that was needed.

In his speech at the University of Michigan in 1964, President Lyndon Johnson said, "Today, 8 million adult Americans, more than the entire population of Michigan, have not finished 5 years of school. Nearly 20 million have not finished 8 years of school. Nearly 54 million — more than one-quarter of all America — have not even finished high school. Each year more than 100,000 high school graduates, with proved ability, don't enter college because they cannot afford it.... Most of our qualified teachers are underpaid, and many of our paid teachers are unqualified." This is a direct admission of failure of the government's education policy.

THE WINDS OF CHANGE

The launch of the Soviet's *Sputnik* changed America's perception of the efficiency of its education system. It started a race not only to reach the moon but to somehow catch up with the communist bloc in the areas of education and scientific and technical training. Despite government efforts, cracks were spreading in the foundation of the US education system, and the beginning of the crisis that plagues American schools today had already begun to take shape.

Americans really knew they were in trouble in 1983 when *A Nation At Risk* shocked everyone out of their stupor; but even so, since then the country has not really moved forward. Now, instead of being at the top, students in America have become complacent and education is on life support.

Sadly, states' advocates in Congress rehash the same old states' rights arguments used back in 1866. For those who oppose a federal education system, the argument is simple: education is not addressed in the Constitution, so it shouldn't be part of the federal system now. There is no role for a department of education. But if we follow that line of reasoning, then there are many modern advances or changes in beliefs that would have never taken place; the end of slavery and segregation come to mind. Whatever the reason behind their dispute may be, any reasonable person might argue that perhaps education wasn't mentioned in the Constitution because in 1787 there were more pressing issues for the Foundation Father's to contemplate!

The largest federal venture into local education came in 1965 with the *Elementary and Secondary Education Act* (ESEA). When President Lyndon Johnson signed the law, he declared that "all of those of both parties of Congress who supported the enactment of this legislation will be remembered in history as men and women who began a new day of greatness in American society." It felt as though the winds of change were finally blowing. However, four decades later, we have yet to witness that new day of greatness.

GOALS IN EDUCATION

If in the early days of common schools, students of various grades were taught in one room. The situation changed dramatically in the 20th century and continues changing. In most public schools education is divided into three levels: elementary school, junior high school (often called middle school), and senior high school. Grade levels vary from area to area. In most regions, grades 1 through 5 constitute elementary school; 6th–8th grade are considered middle school (or "junior high"); and grades 9 through 12 constitute high school. Middle schools or junior high schools are seen as the initial stage of secondary education and provide the transition to high school. In the United States, pre-school, elementary, and secondary education together are referred to as K–12 education. Almost all states require a child to begin attending school at an age ranging from five to seven years. Students may attend public schools, private schools, or home-school. The age when a child may stop going to school varies from 16 to 18. More states now require children to attend school until the age of 18. Some states have exemptions for students of the age 14–18.

The education system can function efficiently only if it has precisely formulated goals and all its components are focused on achieving these goals. The major goals of elementary education consist of achieving basic literacy and elementary mathematical skills among all students, as well as establishing foundations in science, geography, history and other social sciences. Now elementary schools provide knowledge in four basic subjects areas: language arts (reading, writing, spelling, and related language skills), mathematics, science, and social studies (usually history, geography, as well as some material from social and behavior sciences). The purpose of secondary education is to provide students with knowledge that can allow them to apply to a college or university to get the so-called higher education or in more general terms — with knowledge that enables them to use the opportunities and benefits of economic and social development. In most secondary schools, the basic courses are English, mathematics (algebra, geometry, pre-calculus, and calculus), social studies, science (biology, chemistry, and physics), foreign languages, and history. Schools are also responsible for social, emotional, moral, and physical development of students.

The goals of public schools in the 19th century and in the first half of the 20th century, the priority in teaching American cultural values, drastically changed after World War II. Reassessment of these goals was in the air in 60s and 70s. Starting from the second part of the 20th century, the educational goals and basic subjects of elementary and secondary schools have focused on preparing the young generation to participate actively in technological and scientific progress. It became clear that public schools should prepare for employment. Economic rewards of education became the main stimulus to get knowledge and the quality of education became one of the main public concerns.

In 1994, the *Goals 2000: Educate America Act* set the national goals for education to be achieved by the year 2000 as following:

(i) "All students will leave grades 4, 8, and 12 having demonstrated competency over challenging subject matter including English, mathematics, science, foreign languages, civics and government, economics, the arts, history, and geography, and every school in America will ensure that all students learn to use their minds well, so they may be prepared for responsible citizenship, further learning, and productive employment in our nation's modern economy."

(ii) "United States students will be first in the world in mathematics and science achievement."

(iii) "Every adult American will be literate and will possess the knowledge and skills necessary to compete in a global economy and exercise the rights and responsibilities of citizenship."

The United States has about 23–27 million illiterate adults. With such an army of unskilled workers, the future prosperity of the United States is at risk, and this fact is reflected precisely in Goals 2000. The above-discussed educational goals relate directly to the expected results from education for those who attend United States public schools. However, society is interested not only in providing education for those who want and/or are able to attend public schools. Its prosperity depends on the educational level of all its members. Poor people and minorities were among those who weren't embraced completely in the past and even now in the 21st century by the public education system. In 1987, more than a quarter of American high school children failed to graduate. That is why the national educational goals included also:

(iv) By the year 2000, "the high school graduation rate will increase to at least 90%."

Various reasons for the dropout rate were suggested: inadequate funding; inadequate teachers; inadequate school management; insufficient communication between teachers, administrators, and parents. To address these reasons and guarantee success in reaching the above-indicated goals the *Educate America Act* of 1994 contained also as the national goals:

(v) School readiness

(vi) Safe, disciplined, and alcohol-and drug-free schools

(vii) Teacher education and professional development

(viii) Parental participation

Goals (v) and (vi) assume "that all children will have access to high-quality and developmentally appropriate preschool programs that help prepare children for school, ...will receive the nutrition, physical activity experiences, and health care needed to arrive at school with healthy minds and bodies..." and students will be able "to study in a safe and secure environment that is free of drugs and crime, and that schools provide a healthy environment and are a safe haven for all children." According to Goal (vii), teachers should have access to programs for the continued improvement of their professional skills and the opportunity to acquire the knowledge and skills needed to instruct and prepare students for the next century. Goal (viii) foresees parental involvement and participation in promoting social, emotional, and academic growth of children.

Since Goals (i)–(iii) are global and their realization to some extent depends upon the realization of Goals (iv)–(viii), we will call Goals (i)–(iii) *the prime educational goals* and Goals (iv)–(viii) *the secondary educational goals*. Have these goals been accomplished?

The US education system is closely linked with local politics and dependent upon local decision makers and so is not uniform. Bending under the public pressure to improve the quality of education, politicians together with educators compete in rhetoric and disputes criticizing and praising the existing system. Choosing separate aspects of education, each group pursues its own goal. But local interests and preferences are always the number one priority.

In 1960, 86% of American schoolchildren attended public schools. By 1983, this amount had increased and reached 87% (the US population also increased). Currently, 89% of American schoolchildren attend public schools and a *complete education* means, at a minimum, a bachelor's degree from a college. If at the beginning of the 20th century American colleges were isolated and scientifically weak, now their number is great enough and the scientific level of most of them is high. Now more than 50% of high school graduates (grade 12) continue their education at colleges and universities; some form of college has become as common as high school had been in the 1960s.

Now we have entered a new century, an era where science and technology are dominant factors determining the development of its society. Is the education system equipping Americans to retain a leading position in the world? The following chapters will try to answer that question.

CHAPTER 3. DESTINY'S CHILD

> "Jails and prisons are the complement of schools; so many less as you have of the latter, so many more must you have of the former." - Horace Mann

AMERICA'S ACHIEVEMENTS

It's difficult to imagine that the Founding Fathers could expect that in less than 250 years of its existence the United States would become the only superpower, the richest country in the world. Its achievements are indisputable. It is a leader in science and technology, the country that created the atomic bomb, nuclear technology, semiconductors, and computers, sent a man to the moon, and opened the era of information technology. Does that mean that American education system is functioning well?

Appendix 1 contains a list of the post-World War II American Nobel Prize laureates in physics, chemistry, physiology or medicine, and economics, i.e., in the most important fields determining the technological progress and high living standards of the population. Only those who received both their elementary and secondary education in the US are included. These scientists attended public schools from states all across the country, from New York to California, including New Hampshire, Vermont, Massachusetts, Connecticut, Delaware, Maryland, Virginia, South Carolina, Kentucky,

Pennsylvania, Ohio, Indiana, Illinois, Wisconsin, Minnesota, Iowa, Kansas, Texas, Nebraska, Colorado, Utah, Oregon and Washington.

Several schools deserve to be mentioned specially. Five Nobel laureates from the list graduated from the Bronx High School of Science and Stuyvesant High School of New York. Two Nobel laureates studied at Abraham Lincoln High School and Technical High School in Brooklyn, New York City. New York City produced the largest number of Nobel laureates. Not to belittle the talent of the students, we should give credit to their parents for being in the right place and to the teachers and administration who created conditions for these gifted students to develop their talents.

Almost 100 years ago, Stuyvesant High School was founded as a manual trade school for boys. It was later established as a specialized high school for mathematics, science, and technology. The Bronx High School of Science was founded in 1938 as a specialized science and mathematics high school for boys. Initially its faculty included in part a contingent from Stuyvesant High School. When in 1963 the school celebrated its silver anniversary, President Kennedy hailed it as "a significant and path finding example of a special program devoted to the development of the student gifted in science and mathematics." Brooklyn Technical High School opened its doors in 1922. Together with Stuyvesant High School and the Bronx High School of Science, it's one of three original specialized science high schools in New York City. Abraham Lincoln High School, built in 1929, isn't considered a specialized high school. However, it too is noted for its famous alumni (not only in the fields that are embraced by the Nobel Price).

The experience of schools like these can be considered the best experiments when seeking to understand what works in education.

If we judge the level of education in the US based on the number of scientific publications in the leading scientific journals, no country in the world can compete with Americans. Scientific publications rates reflect the scientific productivity of various nations. The US superiority is obvious. However, over the last two decades, the United States has seen its share of world output of scientific papers steadily decrease, while the collective shares of nations in the European Union (EU) and the Asia Pacific region have increased. According to the National Science Foundation, the US share of world output dropped from 39% in 1986 to 33% in 2004, whereas during this period the share of Western Europe rose from 31% to 38% and the share of the Asia Pacific region rose from 13 to 25%. The US portfolio of scientific papers, an indicator of the priorities and emphasis of scientific research, dominated by life sciences (clinical medicine, biomedical research, and biology; 55% of publications). About 25% of articles were produced in the physical and environmental sciences (chemistry, physics, and earth and space sciences) and mathematics. Engineering and technology accounted for 6%. The European and Asia Pacific nations both produced a higher percentage share in chemistry, engineering, materials science and physics. For major European nations, the physical sciences shares are larger than in the US. In the industrialized economies of Asia (Japan, South Korea, Taiwan, Singapore, Hong Kong, India, and China), physical sciences account for more than 50%, and engineering and technical fields account for about 25% of the total publications output. These are countries that have a strong education system. If current trends continue, the Asia Pacific region will likely outstrip the United States in the next few years.

The level of education of many American universities, especially on the master's degree level, is very high. Many youngsters from other countries dream of getting a degree from an American university. For them this will open the doors of the most prestigious organizations. Indeed, more foreign students than Americans are enrolled in the advanced courses in many master's degree programs in important technical fields and mathematics. One reason, though hardly the only one, is the rising cost of higher education, which has certainly become a serious obstacle for many Americans. Unfortunately, there are many caveats when we compare the American education system with the education systems of other leading industrial countries.

DISPARITIES BETWEEN GOALS AND ACHIEVEMENTS

American society underwent dramatic changes in the second half of the 20th century. The 1960s and early 1970s have brought the emergence and expansion of the African-American civil rights movement, the movements dealing with students' rights and women's rights. As a result of the modern women's movement, women have made up an increasingly large percentage of the labor force. New immigrant groups, especially from Asian and Latin American nations, are a second factor causing social change. Economic opportunity has served as the primary lure.

However, the profound changes brought about by science and technology have led to other impacts — often unanticipated. Until about the middle of the 20th century, it was possible for people to earn a living, to meet their basic human needs, with low levels of academic achievement. Since then, scientific and technological advances have changed the nature of economy and increased the need for higher levels of academic achievement. Education has become more essential even as it has become more expensive. Many high school and college students began working after classes, reducing the amount of time spent on reading and studying. This contributed to declines in educational achievement. The march of scientific and technological progress, not supported properly by the US education system, has exacerbated economic inequality. Increased economic inequality has created additional problems for the public education system.

No parents want to think that their children perform below their potential or are less likely to succeed in life because of deficiencies in their upbringing. Yet, almost everything written about education reform or what makes some students more vulnerable than others contains the term *achievement gap*. If parents are to know how to address this gap, they need to know exactly what it means. In education it's a way of comparing disparities in academic achievement between different groups of students. It measures the difference between how well various types of students perform in school: minority students and white students, poor children and middle class children, urban and rural, or different minority groups. This gap is often measured by looking at test scores, dropout rates, graduation rates, course selections, and college graduation rates.

The US is at great risk of losing its competitiveness if it fails to increase the educational attainment levels of populations with low college participation and success rates. According to Harvard University professor of education and society Richard Murnane, "Within the lifetimes of today's teenagers, two of every five American workers will be black or brown, and the nation's economic and social future will depend critically on their skills. Projecting the status quo forward produces a frightening picture. One out of every three students of color fails to obtain a high school diploma. On the 2007 National Assessment of Educational Progress Grade 8 reading exam, 46% of black public school students and 43% of Hispanic students scored 'below basic.' Only 12% and 14% of these groups scored proficient or advanced."

Poverty and inadequate family resources are a part of the problem. One in four children of color lives in poverty. Two of three black children and one of three Hispanic children live in a single-parent family. The low resource levels available to support these children's initial development means that most come to school not ready to learn. The gaps between the achievement of students attending schools serving primarily students of color and the achievement of students in schools serving primarily non-Hispanic white students have increased steadily over the last decades.

As Susan Neuman, President George W. Bush's assistant secretary for elementary and secondary education. pointed out in a *Detroit Free Press* Op-Ed in July of 2008, "A child born poor will likely stay poor, likely live in an unsafe neighborhood, landscaped with little hope, with more security bars than quality day care or after school programs. This highly vulnerable community will have higher proportions of very young children, higher rates of single parenting, and fewer educated adults. The child will likely find dilapidated schools, abandoned playgrounds, and teachers, though earnest, ready to throw in the towel. The child will drop further behind, with increasingly narrow options."

The "Goals 2000" sounds good on paper. However, they haven't been achieved because they were not supported by a realistic, well thought-out plan of action. They still remain not more than a political slogan.

EDUCATIONAL STATISTICS

The high living standard in the United States is largely the result of its scientific and technological achievements. To sustain this level, American would need to continue to be at the top in all the most important areas of science and technology.

In the previous century, the US efficiently used the influx of educated, intelligent people from Europe and the Soviet bloc. Scientists, high level engineers, and managers from other countries still endeavor to get jobs in the US. However, improved living conditions in Europe, India and China will decrease the flow of talent and America urgently needs to develop its own resources — their young generation.

But America's bright past achievements contrast with a rather stark picture of the current education levels. Such giants of the new era of information technology as Bill Gates, Steve Jobs, James Gosling, Larry Ellison and some others offered a huge opportunity for computer science and biotechnology specialists. However, at the end of the 20th century the United States was unable to feed the information technology market with an appropriate work force. Thousands of people from other countries came to fill engineering positions requiring only decent mathematical skills. Many jobs related to programming were sent abroad; there weren't enough qualified Americans to fill these positions.

It's understood in sports that a star alone is unable to bring win first place for the team if the other players don't possess a certain level of skills. The same is true in industry and technology.

This isn't the first time when Americans feel that something is wrong with their system of education. A loud alarm sounded in 1957. The launch of the Soviet satellite *Sputnik* in 1957 ignited disputes about the need to improve the public school system. Have things improved in the last fifty years ago? The US is a leader in space exploration. It dominates in the area of information technology. Its achievements in science, technology, and medicine are very impressive and among the highest in the world. However, if the criterion we measure is the educational level of its young generation, America's gold reserve, the picture isn't very radiant. International assessments comparing achievements in various subject areas and comparing the performance of US students with that of their peers in other countries have shown that the quality of education in US schools is lower than in many other industrial countries.

Currently, the United States participates in three international assessments: the Progress in International Reading Literacy Study (PIRLS), which assesses reading performance of fourth-grade students; the Trends in International Mathematics and Science Study (TIMSS), which assesses mathematics and science performance in grades 4 and 8, both conducted by the International Association for the Evaluation of Educational Achievement (IEA); and the Program for International Student Assessment (PISA), coordinated by the Organization for Economic Co-operation and Development (OECD), which assesses the reading, mathematics, and science literacy of 15-year-olds.

The OECD is an international organization of thirty countries, each of which accepts the principles of representative democracy and a free market economy. The OECD headquarters staff collects data, monitors trends, and analyzes economic developments. It also researches social changes and evolving patterns in trade, environment, agriculture, technology, taxation and other areas. The OECD is known as a premier statistical agency as a result of comprehensive techniques used to gather and analyze data. Over a quarter of a million students in 41 countries took part in a test that assessed skills in mathematics, reading, science and problem solving. All thirty OECD member countries participated, as well as eleven partner countries, including Hong Kong and the Russian Federation.

US fourth-graders outperformed their counterparts in 23 of the 34 other countries participating in PIRLS 2001 in reading literacy, although they scored lower than students in England, the Netherlands, and Sweden. No detectable differences in scores are found between US students and their counterparts in eight of the remaining PIRLS 2001 countries. Although statisticians argue the rigorousness and validity of the results, the fact that US students are not the best is unquestionable. Moreover, a detailed analysis shows that on average fourth-grade students in private schools in the United States scored significantly higher than fourth-grade students in public schools on the combined reading literacy scale, and also on the literary and informational subscales.

TIMSS provides data collected in 1995, 1999, 2003, and 2007 on the mathematics and science achievement of US students of the fourth and eighth grades, respectively, compared to that of students in other countries. TIMSS participants include 13 industrialized countries, as well as middle-income and developing nations from around the world; 46 countries participated in TIMSS 2003. According to the 2003 assessment, the mathematics achievement of American students grades 8 and 4 are in 15th and 12th place, respectively: behind students from Singapore, Taiwan, Japan, Belgium, Netherlands, Latvia and the Russian Federation. The assessment in the separate domains, "knowing" (knowing facts, procedures and concepts), "applying" (applying knowledge and conceptual understanding) and "reasoning" (analyzing unfamiliar situations, complex contexts, and multi-step problems) and "cognitive" domains brings even more disappointing news. US eighth-graders are 14th, 17th and 14th and the fourth-graders are 7th, 14th and 12th for each of the mentioned domains, respectively.

According to the 2003 assessment of the science achievement results for eighth-grade students from 49 countries, US students were 9th (here we don't give the results for the fourth-grade students because, in our opinion, their level of science knowledge is low so that the comparative analysis doesn't present a reliable information) and showed significantly higher average science achievement in 2003 compared to the previous assessments in

1995 and 1999. However, the results of US students are worse than students from Singapore, Chinese Taipei (the designation under which Taiwan participated in the study) and Japan, Estonia, Hungary and the Netherlands.

PISA 2003 found that just under 20% of 15-year-olds in OECD countries are "reflective, communicative problem solvers" able to tackle difficult tasks. The students who score in the top category are not only able to analyze a situation and make decisions, they are also capable of managing multiple conditions simultaneously. They can think about the underlying relationships in a problem, solve it systematically, check their work and communicate the results. In Japan and Hong Kong, over a third of students rank within the top level.

Unfortunately, the results of the PISA 2003 study were even more disappointing for the United States than the assessment based on PIRLS and TIMSS. In mathematics and science, US students demonstrated scores below the OECD's average taken from the assessment of 44 countries and were in 28th and 22th place, respectively. In reading, the result was close to the OECD's average and corresponded to 17th place. The latest PISA 2006 results are not encouraging as well. In mathematics and science, US students were in 24th and 17th place, respectively.

Of course, the above-mentioned results are based on statistical analysis of data. The more comprehensible the data — the more reliable the results. Statistics may be distorted by the manner in which the data is gathered or by the manner in which the data is interpreted, which is eloquently expressed by the quote: "There are two kinds of statistics, the kind you look up and the kind you make up."

Difficulties in gathering representative data and not infrequently erroneous conclusions have given birth to other sayings: "There are three kinds of lies: lies, damned lies and statistics" and "Statistics will prove anything, even the truth." A more familiar quote is: "Figures don't lie, but liars figure." Even so, the TIMSS, PIRLS and PISA tests may fairly be considered to be strongly indicative of the real situation, although the results of the TIMSS tests often contradict the PISA test results. The main reason is the way the tests were prepared. The PISA tests are less formal than the TIMSS tests. The PISA mathematics literacy test asks students to apply their mathematical knowledge to solve problems set in various real-world contexts. This requires from students not only a broad range of mathematical content knowledge but also ability to apply them to concrete practical problems.

TIMSS measures more traditional classroom content such as an understanding of fractions and decimals and the relationship between them. It divides mathematical domains into two dimensions: first, the applied-knowledge *cognitive domains* and secondly, more traditional *contents domains*. The cognitive domains are "Knowing Facts and Procedures, Using Concepts, Solving Routine Problems and Reasoning," and the contents domains are "Number, Algebra, Measurement, Geometry and Data." It's no secret that most American schools teach students "how" to do something in a certain way rather than "why" it should be done in that way. PISA deals with education's application to real-life problems and life-long learning. It requires both "how" and "why" knowledge, so that its results, at a certain degree, are more informative and reliable than the results of TIMSS. In reading literacy, OECD/PISA doesn't measure the extent to which 15-year-old students are fluent readers or how competent they are at word recognition tasks or spelling. Instead, they assess whether students are able to "construct, extend and reflect on the meaning of what they have read across a wide range of continuous and non-continuous texts" (Chapter 2 of the publication *PISA 2003 Assessment Framework*). PIRLS, on the other hand, describes reading literacy as "the ability to understand and use those written language forms required by society and/or valued by the individual" (Chapter 1 of the publication *PIRLS 2006 Assessment Framework*). The literacy concept emphasizes the understanding of concepts, and application of knowledge in various situations. By focusing on literacy, PISA draws not only from school curricula but also from learning that may occur outside of school. Comparing the TIMSS and PISA results, we should take also into account that the TIMSS target population is all eighth-grade students, i.e., mostly 13-year-old students, whereas the PISA target population is all 15-year-old students, i.e., it reflects mostly the performance of US students who were in ninth or tenth grade.

As indicated earlier, depending upon slices of data chosen, we can draw different conclusions. For example, the results from TIMSS 2003 showed that US fourth and eighth-grade students perform above the international average for all participating countries in both mathematics and science. The PISA 2003 results showed that US 15-year-old students performed below the OECD average in mathematical literacy and scientific literacy. Both results are informative, but the TIMSS 2003 mentioned results sound as a positive statement because the study shows that US students at these two grade levels fare better than a "world" average. It's also possible to state that in eighth grade mathematics, for example, US students' performance wasn't measurably different from that of students in Australia, New Zealand, Scotland, the Slovak Republic, and Sweden; it was higher than that of students in Italy and Norway; and it was lower than that of students in Belgium, Hungary, Japan, South Korea, and the Netherlands. Such soothing statistics are used by those educators who try to defend the existing education system.

However, the PISA results showed that US 15-year-old students do not perform as well as their international counterparts in mathematics and science. Nevertheless, defending their position, the conservative educators believe that the TIMSS and PISA scores shouldn't be compared directly, and it would be incorrect to characterize the PISA low relative standings as a decline from TIMSS because of the lack of comparability of grade- and aged-based samples, methods of sampling, and goals of the assessments, the emphases on different content areas within the assessments (as described earlier), different sets of countries participating in each study, and other features. Without any doubt, the TIMSS, PIRLS, and PISA tests are not ideal and can be criticized in detail, but not to such a degree as to deny the overall results: American students demonstrated a low level of knowledge.

WHY ARE AMERICANS BEHIND OTHER LEADING INDUSTRIAL COUNTRIES IN EDUCATION?

For many countries, the first PISA 2000 results were a rude awakening. In Germany, for example, students performed better than Americans, but nevertheless scored comparatively low. Heated debates were ignited by the article "Miserable Noten für deutsche Schüler" ("Abysmal marks for German students", *Frankfurter Allgemeine Zeitung*, December 4, 2001). France, whose students also did better than their American peers, reacted with headlines like "La France, élève moyen de la classe OCDE" ("France, average student of the OECD class", *Le Monde*, December 5, 2001). In 2000, the *New York Times* highlighted the poor knowledge of American students in mathematics and science in a headline, *Students in US Don't Keep Up in Global Tests*. A *New York Times* article of December 7, 2004, was headlined "Economic Time Bomb: US Teens Are Among Worst at Math."

Many in the education establishment wrongly insist that more money would yield better schools and smarter students, that increased financial funding would lead to higher knowledge level outputs. Forty years ago, American sociologist James S. Coleman made clear that there is no reliable connection between the resources going into a school and the learning that comes out. Education problems are a fertile field for politicians who promise improvement without any clear understanding of what should be improved and how. "Increased school funding," "smaller classes," and "better teachers" are just slogans.

Spending on education has increased about three times since 1960s without significant improvement of test scores. Private funding of education is sometimes regarded as a way of making education more cost-effective. However, as it follows from the 2003 PISA report, although students in private schools usually (but not necessarily) perform better than in public schools (in Japan the picture is the opposite), effective funding isn't the factor that determines better quality of education in many private schools. No investor puts money in a project without analyzing whether it will likely bring a desired profit and examining the way to achieve the desired goal. Americans are investors in the education system because it is supported by taxpayers' money.

First, a sophisticated and detailed analysis of the existing education system must be done. It should be done by experts in system analysis applying to large scale systems. This is the way to find the system's bottlenecks and make decision how to eliminate them. However, Americans are still under the influence of empty political statements and accept obediently their increasing constantly local and property taxes with a hope that their children will be well educated.

To understand why the US is behind the other leading industrial countries in education, let us return to the TIMSS, PIRLS and PISA results. The United States is a huge country consisting of many states. Can US students be considered as a unified team in these tests? No. A uniform says nothing about a team; the team's actions, manner of behavior and technique, based on instructions and work of coaches, create the face of the team. US students in different counties, in different states, in isolated rural towns and in big cities, were coached differently — their studies were based on different curricula and they used different textbooks. Without an identical curriculum of the main subjects, it's impossible to have, for example, a team of eight-graders with the same potential level of knowledge in mathematics or science. Unfortunately, in the United States, in contrast to most countries, schools had no curricula of main subjects (English, mathematics, chemistry, biology, physics, etc.) defined at the national level and supported by directives, instructional guides, school inspections, and recommended textbooks.

The low performance can be eliminated only by rebuilding the whole structure to make it more efficient.

Like that of many other industrialized countries, the vast majority of the population in the US has completed secondary education and the rising number of college graduates now outnumber high school dropouts. As a whole, the population of the United States is becoming increasingly more educated. Post-secondary education is valued very highly by American society. While the TIMSS, PIRLS and PISA tests show that virtually all developed nations have caught up to or even passed the United States in elementary and secondary education, Americans show more interest to attain higher education than residents of most other countries. Just over a quarter of adult Americans (25 years or older) have completed college. More precisely, according to a 2003 study by the US Census Bureau, among the country's adult population, 85% have completed high school, 58% attended at least some college, and 27% have received a bachelor's degree or higher, compared with only 14% of Germans having completed college, 9% of Italians, and 19% of Canadians. The country has a reading literacy rate at 98% of the population over age 15, while ranking below average in science and mathematics understanding.

Although graduates from many American colleges and universities compare favorably with graduates of other industrial countries, high school students rank lower than many of those from Europe on mathematics and science tests. This is an alarming factor which cannot be ignored.

Information for Reflection

In Israel, 34% of the work force has higher education, 12% hold advanced degrees, and 25% are employed in technical professions. In its mere sixty years of its existence, Israel has become the third, after the United States and Netherlands, industrial nation in the world. Is this the best demonstration of the power of education?

The modernization of any system starts with an analysis of the existing system. Based on a detailed system analysis, how each component functions, their interaction and efficiency in performing functional requirements related to the separate units and the whole system, recommendations to rebuild the existing system are made. Following this approach we will analyze the structure of the US public school system, its creation, growth, and adaptation to new functional requirements at various stages of the US development.

Chapter 4. How the US Education System Works

> "In framing a government which is to be administered by men over men, the great difficulty lies in this: you must first enable the government to control the governed; and in the next place oblige it to control itself." - James Madison

Department of Education

In many countries, the public education system is highly centralized (state-financed and controlled) at the national level (e.g., France, Russia, Japan, South Korea, and Taiwan). The administrative control is usually decentralized and the managing responsibility is shared among the central (national), the local (regional) and institutional levels. Many countries have a Ministry of Education. Public education in different countries has some specifics reflecting their cultural, social, political, and economic needs. For example, in Australia there are so-called open and selective schools. The open schools accept all students, while selective schools are considered more prestigious; they select their students on the basis of academic ability. Although schools offer free education, many schools ask parents to pay a voluntary contribution. In the Netherlands, half of public education has become independent in the last ten years. Many state public schools, which were earlier under the auspices of municipal government, installed an independent board of governors; they receive government funding directly, instead of via the municipal channels. Since public education is provided and financed by government, the way educational instructions and funding reach schools and are utilized significantly influences the public education system's performance.

In the United States, about 5.9 million public school teachers and other school staff educate 48 million children in 96,000 public elementary and secondary schools (US National Center for Education Statistics, 2005). Although education in the United States is provided mainly by government, with control and funding coming from three levels — federal, state, and local, unlike the nationally regulated and financed education systems of most other countries, it is highly decentralized, and the federal government is not heavily involved in determining curricula or education standards. The United States Department of Education (ED) is a cabinet-level department of the United States government with about 4,200 employees and $68.6 billion budget. Created by the *Department of Education Organization Act* (Public Law 96-88), signed by President Carter into law on October 17, 1979, and started operating on May 4, 1980, it is administered by the United States Secretary of Education. Previously, its functions were in the Department of Health, Education, and Welfare that was created under President Eisenhower and officially came into existence on April 11, 1953. The US Department of Education was created in 1867 to gather information on schools and teaching that would help the states establish effective school systems but soon was demoted to an Office in 1868. The department plays a leadership role in the national dialogue over how to improve the existing education system. This involves such activities as raising national and community awareness of the education challenges confronting the nation and disseminating the latest information related to the innovative methods of teaching. The department administers programs that cover every area of education. The primary function of the ED is to collect data on America's schools that would help the states to improve their education systems, to focus national attention on key educational issues, to formulate federal funding programs involving education, as well as monitoring funds for these programs, and to enforce federal educational laws regarding privacy and civil rights. However, the Department of Education has no direct public jurisdictional control over the quality of educational institutions. The ED includes several offices; the most important is the Office of Innovation and Improvement and the Office of Elementary and Secondary Education. The Office of Elementary and Secondary Education is responsible for directing, coordinating, and recommending policy for programs designed to assist state and local educational agencies to improve the achievement of elementary and secondary school students and to foster educational improvement at the state and local levels. The Office of Innovation and Improvement makes strategic investments in innovative educational practices through discretionary grant programs.

BOARDS OF EDUCATION

American public education is primarily the responsibility of the states and local school districts. States set most education policy, have their own departments of education, raise the necessary revenue, determine the powers of school boards, create statewide education standards, and conduct assessments. Almost all state constitutions require the state legislature to establish the state board of education or create the position of the state superintendent of public instruction. The state board of education is the governing and policy making body for the public system of elementary and secondary education. It is responsible for the direction and operation of the state public school system. Its work touches all facets of education from accountability and evaluation to curriculum and teacher education. The staff members of the state board of education provide ongoing policy research and analysis of public education issues including instruction, student assessment, and funding. The board coordinates its efforts with the state department of education, which implements law and policies established by the board. Through its annual report on student, teacher and school performance, the board provides the legislature and the general public with information about the status of education in the state. The board also has the responsibility to study the use of state funds for public education.

The state superintendent of schools is the educational and administrative leader of the school system who oversees the functions of all schools and offices and serves as a link between the state department of education, the state board of education, and the state government. The superintendent works closely with the members of the board of education. His team performs duties and responsibilities required by law, implements the policies and decisions of the board of education and works together with the board's office staff. The superintendent supports the work of the board and provides its members with guidance and counsel on matters of education and public policy, including academic standards and accountability, public funding, land use, personnel, and legal matters. The superintendent and his staff also work closely with federal, state, and local elected officials, with local, regional, and national business leaders, with civic and community representatives, with regional and national professional associations, and also with the leaders of parent associations and school principals. The superintendent works with a staff of school district employees, who usually are responsible for hiring principals and other district staff, setting teacher and administrative salaries, administering teacher training, coordinating school transportation, allocating budgets among schools and school programs, and supervising school building construction and maintenance.

Most states employ the three-level educational model: state — local school district — school. As the twentieth century progressed, most states assumed a more active regulatory role than in the past. They consolidated school districts into larger units with common procedures. In 1940, there were over 117,000 school districts in the United States, but by 2000 the number had decreased to fewer than 15,000. The states also became much more responsible for financing education. They sometimes supported efforts to equalize local school district expenditures by using state funds and state laws to ensure more equitable per pupil expenditures regardless of the wealth or poverty of individual districts. In 1940, local property taxes financed 68% of elementary and secondary school expenses, while the states contributed 30% and the federal government contributed 2%. In 1999, state governments contributed 49% of elementary and secondary school revenues, local districts contributed 44%, and the federal government provided 7%. In 2005, along with the federal government's 8.3% of total funding, about 45.6% and 37.1% of funding came from the state and local governments, respectively.

A school district is a territorial unit within a state that has the responsibility for the provision of public education within its borders. These school districts vary tremendously in territorial size, enrollments, organization, legal powers, and status. School districts have their own boards of education, superintendents and staff that implement the state education policy at the local level and communicate with the state board of education, the state superintendent, and the state department of education. The school district board is the governing and official education policy-making body of the district. The board is responsible for the direction and operation of the district public school system. At the elementary, middle and high school levels, the district boards approve curricula, instructions, and assessments of student achievement, use students, staff, school, and system performance data to monitor and improve student achievement. Their superintendent is the liaison between the school board and state educational leadership. He is the key actor in curriculum policy. Upon recommendation of the superintendent the district board adopts a written district curriculum which describes, for each subject area and grade level, the content objectives which are to be taught in all district schools.

The district curriculum reflects the district's vision and goals for student learning, board policies, academic content standards, state and district assessments, graduation requirements, school and district improvement plans, and, when necessary, related legal requirements. The superintendent determines a process for curriculum development, selection, and/or adaptation which utilizes the professional expertise of teachers, principals, and district administrators representing various grade levels, disciplines, special programs, and categories of students as appropriate. The process also may provide opportunities for input from students, parents/guardians, representatives of local businesses and postsecondary institutions, and other community members. The board establishes a review procedure for the district curriculum in order to ensure its alignment with state and district goals for student achievement. Usually, the review is conducted whenever the state board of education adopts new or revised content standards for a particular subject or when new law requires a change or addition to the curriculum. In addition, the board may require a review of the curriculum in one or more subject areas in response to student assessment results, changing student needs, feedback from teachers, administrators or parents, state and federal requirements, and national standards.

In partnerships with local employee organizations the district boards resolve the problems of employees' salary and work conditions. They deal with such problems as hiring employees, school funding, and property taxes to support schools. Local districts raise about half the money used to support schools. The rest comes from the state budget. The federal government provides only the insignificant amount of money to schooling (several percent of its budget) as a help to implement some programs, but not more than that. The district school board may also exercise a quasi-judicial function in employee or student matters. Under certain conditions, its decisions can be appealed and considered by the state board. The district superintendent is appointed by the board and serves as the district's chief executive. The state law determines the size of the board, the terms of board members, how board members are selected, and how they may be removed. The majority of school boards are elected by the residents of separate school districts which operate the public primary and secondary schools within their boundaries. State laws and administrative regulations deal with: school district organization, elections, and governance; educational programs, instructional materials and testing; attendance rules; the length of the school day and school year; teacher credentialing, certification, tenure; school district finances and budgets; school safety; parents' and students' rights and responsibilities; and other aspects of school operations and policy.

Similar to school districts (the middle level of the educational structure) that can be considered as agencies of the state for the local operation of the state school system, school principals (the low level of the educational structure) are agents of the state school districts responsible for everyday school operations within the district.

The described three-level educational structure reflects the common features pertained to most states. Some states have a little bit different structure — more complicated or simpler. For example, Michigan created 57 intermediate school districts which provide various administrative and instructional services to local school districts assigned to their jurisdiction; the Hawaii State Department of Education functions as a single state school district.

BUREAUCRACY IN ACTION

A law passed by Congress sets down guidelines to carry out the new policies, which should be implemented, i.e., put into practice. Often, policy directives are not clearly defined, and bureaucrats must interpret the meaning of the law. As a result, the bureaucracy has flexibility, known as *administrative discretion*, in actual implementation. This "flexibility" multiplied by the number of levels of bureaucracy can not only diminish but almost erase the expected effect of the law. If the implementation of the law is accompanied by the federal funding, the federal money often fill the bureaucratic holes rather than reach the targeted recipients. Educational bureaucracy demonstrated its skills in this field.

The measures undertaken by the United States government to improve the level of education in the country reflect the policy of the president and its administration concerning the existing system of education. The Acts of Congress related to education are assumed to be implemented in practice by the states. Governors' education policy should reflect the federal education policy. But how close should states follow the federal government directions? On the one hand, many educational acts are formulated in such a general and diffused form that they give governors a lot of room for maneuvering. On the other hand, the federal education initiatives are usually accompanied with financial support; to get money from the federal government states should show how they are going to spend them, how they are going to implement the governmental education programs. As mentioned earlier, the state boards of education are the governing and policy determining bodies for the state systems of public education; they are responsible for the direction and operation of the state public school system. As a rule, the state boards formulate their mission in realizing the national educational goal (to provide a high-quality, world-class education that ensure success for every student through excellence in teaching and learning) and the related goals in tune with the governmental education policy (ensure success for every student; provide an effective instructional program; strengthen productive partnerships for education; create a positive work environment; provide high-quality business services that are essential to the educational success of students). The main problem is how these goals, which contain many adjectives, are decoded by each state and how they can be achieved.

The state boards of education set education policy in the areas of standards, instructional materials, assessments, and accountability. They adopt academic content standards, adopt most of textbooks, support professional development for teachers on the adopted instructional materials that are used in the classroom, ensure rigorousness of curriculum, maintain the assessment and accountability system, and adopt regulations to implement legislation. This policy is carried out by the various divisions of the state education departments. Although the structure of many state departments of education is different, as well as their names, we will present the most common and important units and names. Usually, the assessment and accountability division (or assessment and accountability separate units) collects data from schools, oversees the calculation and reporting of schools accountability data, develops, coordinates, and administers state testing programs; the curriculum and instruction division develops curriculum frameworks, oversees the adoption of instructional materials, produces and distributes them; the professional development division provides resources to support educators to gain content knowledge and to increase their range of effective teaching; the school improving division provides fiscal resources and assistance to improve student achievement (especially, in low-performed schools); the special education division provides information and resources to help individuals with disabilities; the partnership development division develops corporate and other partnerships.

As indicated earlier, the boards of education exist also in the local school districts. They implement the state education policy, have divisions similar to the state department of education and are subordinate to the state board of education.

The state education policy is backed up by the state laws. The state education code contains the laws related to all aspects of education passed by the legislature and signed into law by the governor. The state board of education adopts the legislative platform for the state legislature that presents the board's positions on priority education issues. Various education initiatives, proposed by politically controlled boards of education and approved by the legislature, find their place in the state education code.

As mentioned above, districts are governed by local boards in accordance with the state's laws. Such decentralization of the public school education system is the reflection of the United States' structure and its traditional approach — to prefer executive power at the local level rather than the central government. But that means the quality of education is a slave of local conditions. Different districts may have more or less ability to provide schools with appropriate buildings, classrooms, technology, and teachers. The inability in some districts to pay teachers a decent salary obliges them to hire less qualified teachers, especially in mathematics and science; these schools have also higher dropout rates.

The highly decentralized system of public education can be efficient only under certain conditions, which will be discussed later.

EDUCATION AND ITS ENVIRONMENT

The foundation and development of the main blocks of the educational structure were accompanied by the creation of related organizations which can be called the educational environment. These organizations don't participate directly in the education process and don't support it with money. However, they influence it indirectly providing certain services to public school systems.

One of the oldest of these is the National Teachers Association (now called the National Education Association, NEA), the largest public organization of school educators, founded in 1857 by forty-three educators in Philadelphia. NEA was a part of the fight to make education freely available for all children. Initially, NEA led the effort to expand and enhance public education, to professionalize teaching, and to improve educational achievement and attainment for all students. Now NEA has 3.2 million members and defends mostly the interests of education employees, assists them in bargaining matters, using news media and advertising, lobbying congressional representatives and state legislators to improve their economic conditions.

The American Association of School Administrators (AASA), founded in 1865, is a professional organization for more than 13,000 educational leaders across the United States. The AASA members are chief executive officers and senior-level administrators from school districts, superintendents of schools. They are responsible for the education policy, oversee its implementation, and represent school districts to the public at large. Should they be answerable for America's stagnation in education?

The American Educational Research Association (AERA), a national research society, was founded in 1916. Its primary goal is to improve the educational process by encouraging education research and promoting the practical application of research results. There are twelve divisions within AERA, ranging from administration and curriculum to teacher education and education policy and politics. However, their efforts haven't brought noteworthy results in improving education.

In about the same year, the American Federation of Teachers (AFT) was founded. It is an affiliated international union that represents the economic, social, and professional interests of teachers. AFT states its mission as follows: "to improve the lives of our members and their families, to give voice to their legitimate professional, economic and social aspirations, to strengthen the institutions in which we work, to improve the quality of the services we provide, to bring together all members to assist and support one another and to promote democracy, human rights and freedom in our union, in our nation and throughout the world." AFT now has more than 3,000 local affiliates nationwide, 43 state affiliates, and more than 1.4 million members. Although AFT states that the quality of the services provided by its members is one of its concerns, its main priority is in protecting the economic interests of its members. NEA and AFT have begun a merger, which has already been accomplished in some states.

The National Council for Accreditation of Teacher Education (NCATE), an official independent accrediting body responsible for accreditation in teacher education, was founded in 1954. NCATE serves as the profession's mechanism to help establish high quality teacher preparation. Unfortunately, it hasn't got much to show for its efforts.

The Council for Basic Education (CBE) is an independent non-profit organization that promotes a curriculum for the basic subjects. Founded in 1956, CBE develops and establishes programs that support teachers, administrators, and policymakers to reform and improve the quality of education. However, in the more than fifty years of its existence, the problem of a curriculum for the basic subjects has not been solved.

Among many educational organizations the most influential voice belongs to the National Academy of Education (NAE). Founded in 1965, the Academy has sponsored a variety of commissions and study panels that addressed key issues in education and have published influential proceedings and reports with recommendations concerning the education policy. It consists of up to two hundred US members and up to twenty-five foreign associates who are elected on the basis of their outstanding contributions to education. Unfortunately, we still don't see any progress.

The Educational Testing Service (ETS), a nonprofit organization that offers consulting services, technical assistance, educational research and assessment, and other solutions for school districts, institutions, businesses and government agencies, was founded in 1947 when the American Council on Education, the major coordinating body for all the nation's higher education institutions, the Carnegie Foundation for the Advancement of Teaching, and the College Entrance Examination Board contributed their testing programs, a portion of their assets, and key employees to create it (see also Chapter 14).

Founded in 1985, the National Center for Fair & Open Testing (NCFOT), a nonprofit organization, provides information, technical assistance and advocacy on a broad range of testing concerns, focusing on three areas: elementary and secondary schools, university admissions, and employment tests. It publishes a regular electronic newsletter, *The Examiner*, and a catalog of materials on testing to help teachers, administrators, students, parents, and researchers.

The National Board for Professional Teaching Standards (NBPTS) is a nonprofit organization founded in 1987 to advance the quality of teaching and learning by developing professional standards for accomplished teaching, creating a voluntary system to certify teachers who meet those standards. The efficiency of this organization can be fully implemented only if there would have existed a national system of education with a solid set of requirements, standards for both students and teachers all over the United States. The current local curricula and standards diminish significantly its role.

One more public non-profit organization, founded in 1993, is the Center for Education Reform (CER). Its sources of funding include contributions from foundations, businesses, and private individuals. Through publications and its website CER advocates reforms that produce high standards, accountability and freedom, such as school choice programs for children most in need, common sense teacher initiatives, and proven instructional programs. *Mandate for Change* (The Center for Education Reform, Washington, D.C., January 2009) is an effort led by CER to set a bold agenda for the government (see *www.edreform.com*).

Among the narrowly focused professional organizations there are two organizations that are linked with the weakest parts of American education. Founded in 1920, the National Council of Teachers of Mathematics (NCTM) is a nonprofit organization focused on mathematics education and providing professional development to support teachers of mathematics. It is engaged in political and public advocacy to focus decision makers on improving learning and teaching mathematics. Through its publications, conferences and workshops NCTM promotes standards for school mathematics as an important part of knowledge that students should acquire. NCTM has published a series of *Standards for School Mathematics* outlining a vision for school mathematics in the USA and Canada. NCTM developed the *Curriculum and Evaluation Standards for School Mathematics* (1989) followed by the *Professional Standards for Teaching Mathematics* (1991), and the *Assessment Standards for School Mathematics* (1995). In 2000, NCTM released the updated *Principles and Standards for School Mathematics*.

Founded in 1944, the National Science Teachers Association (NSTA) includes science teachers, science supervisors, administrators, scientists, business and industry representatives involved in various aspects of science education. The Association publishes a professional journal for each level of science teaching, a newspaper, *NSTA Reports*, and many other educational books and professional publications. NCTM and NSTA conduct conferences to enhance professional development and provide forums for science and math educators.

Founded in 1959, the American College Testing Program, Inc. (ACT) is a nonprofit organization that provides assessment, research, information, and program management services in the broad areas of education and workforce development (see also Chapter 6) .

Here we have mentioned only the most influential educational organizations, which present only a small part of organizations associated with education whose life cycle depends upon the educational problems they are involved in and related funding.

In addition, there are hundreds of advocacy groups that come out with various proposals on education. While *advocacy groups* often assume an adversarial posture, they also work in partnership with governments and the *private* sector to achieve mutual goals. Lobbying is the practice of *private advocacy* with the goal of influencing governmental officials to support its efforts and to get funding for their future activity. To be absolutely fair, we should mention that some of them consider their activity as a way to earn a living. Their proposals are entirely idealistic and exploit parents' desires and hopes rather than offering something concrete that can bring tangible results. Maybe that is why the country has so many advocacy groups, which consume millions of dollars for empty research and useless efforts?

For example, according to *Baltimore Sun*, February 19, 2009, "More than 20 advocacy groups have banded together — calling themselves the Baltimore Education Coalition — to protest possible state funding cuts to city schools. The money that schools will receive as part of the federal stimulus package signed this week by President Obama isn't good enough for them...." It is obvious that the above advocacy groups don't understand or don't want to understand that simply pumping money into education, which didn't bring any results in the past, cannot be an effective measure in the future without drastic changes in the educational process. Unfortunately, the authors of the above proposals, as well as the representative of the Baltimore Education Coalition, propose band-aids instead of a radical operation. Efficient systems are built from the top, based on precisely formulated functional requirements rather than on rhetoric and unsubstantiated financial demands.

The organizations and groups mentioned are just a drop in the Education sea, where the profit motive has distorted all the incentives and created a many-headed Hydra that continues to defy those who would tame it.

Chapter 5. Education and Politics

> "Mothers all want their sons to grow up to become president, but they don't want them to become politicians in the process." - John F. Kennedy

Education has become a major political issue. Public polls during presidential election years rank it as one of the most important problems facing the nation. In the 1980 election education was rated 23, but by 2000 it was considered the most important problem facing the nation. According to the CNN/Opinion Research Corporation Poll, October 30–November 1, 2009, education was in fifth place (behind the economy, health care, the wars in Iraq and Afghanistan, and the federal budget deficit).

A History of Government Initiatives

Those who state, based on the Tenth Amendment to the Constitution ("The powers not delegated to the United States by the Constitution, nor prohibited by it to the States, are reserved to the States respectively, or to the people"), that Congress has no authority to appropriate and spend federal funds on education should admit that the federal government has been acting without constitutional authority, i.e., unconstitutionally, for a very long period of time, following a pattern that began before 1787 when the Constitution was adopted. Before the Constitution, *The Land Ordinance* of

1785 established a mechanism for funding public education in the United States.

Even before creation of a federal body to handle education problems, the United States government demonstrated its determination to support and promote education. We have mentioned the latest government acts to improve education. But the history of such initiatives goes way back.

The *Morrill Act* of 1862, also known as the *Land-Grant Act*, provided grants in the form of federal lands to each state for the establishment of a public institution to fulfill the Act's provisions, for the "endowment, support, and maintenance of at least one college where the leading object shall be, without excluding other scientific and classical studies and including military tactics, to teach such branches of learning as are related to agriculture and the mechanic arts, in order to promote the liberal and practical education of the industrial classes in the several pursuits and professions in life." The second Morrill Act of 1890 provided annual funding. Many prominent state universities were created by this wise legislation.

The *Smith–Hughes Act* of 1917 was the first major legislation providing federal aid for public elementary and secondary education.

In 1919, the Commission on the Reorganization of Secondary Education issued the document *Cardinal Principles of Secondary Education*, in which the commission called for extensive modifications of secondary education to match changes in society: "the substitution of the factory system for the domestic system of industry; the use of machinery in place of manual labor; the high specialization of processes with a corresponding subdivision of labor; and the breakdown of the apprentice system.... the character of the secondary-school population undergoes modification; and the sciences on which educational theory and practice depend constantly furnish new information." As indicated in the commission's findings, "secondary education, however, like any other established agency of society, is conservative and tends to resist modification." This commission emphasized the seven cardinal principles of secondary education mentioned in Chapter 2. A secondary school should encourage good health habits, give health instruction, and provide physical activities; should increase proficiency in fundamental processes (writing, reading, oral and written expression, and mathematics) and teaching "must go hand in hand" with practice; should develop "those qualities that make the individual a worthy member of a family, both contributing to and deriving benefit from that membership"; should develop an understanding of the relationship between the vocation and the community in which one lives and works; should provide knowledge of social organizations and a commitment to civic morality; should give the student the skills to enrich his/her body, mind, spirit and personality in his/her leisure; should teach high ethic standards, personal responsibility and initiative, the standards that the entire school, including its principal and teachers, must follow.

During the Great Depression (1929–1939) the federal government established the emergency educational program and made some direct grants to school districts in extremely depressed areas to keep schools open. World War II led to a significant expansion of federal support for education. The *Lanham Act* of 1941 and the *Impact Aid* laws of 1950 eased the burden on communities affected by the presence of military and other federal installations by making payments to school districts. The *GI Bill* of 1944 authorized postsecondary education assistance to veterans of World War II. As a result, many veterans who would not otherwise have been able to afford it attended undergraduate and graduate school after World War II.

The Soviet *Sputnik* in 1957 symbolized a potential military threat to the US security as well as a blow to American national pride. Heated discussions were launched about the need to improve the public school system; science and science education were in the center of these discussions. President Eisenhower used *Sputnik* to pass in Congress the *National Defense Education Act* (NDEA) of 1958 to provide aid to all levels of education in the United States for four years (it was extended in 1961 for two more years), primarily to stimulate the advancement of education in science, mathematics, and modern foreign languages; but the NDEA also provided aid in other areas, including technical education, geography, English as a second language, counseling and guidance, school libraries and librarianship, and educational media centers. The Act authorized increased funding for scientific research and science education. It provided institutions of higher education with 90% of capital funds for low-interest loans to students. NDEA provided federal support for improvement and change in elementary and secondary education.

The dubious title of the Act, admitting various interpretations of the phrase *national defense* — to defend education, the intellect or, in a more general sense, to defend America's future? — underscored, nevertheless, its national importance. However, the Act (Title I) contains statutory prohibitions of federal direction, supervision, or control over the curriculum, administration, or personnel of any educational institution, thus essentially declining any government responsibility for actually improving the education system.

The *Educational Television Act* of 1962 authorized grants to educational institutions or non-profit organizations to build educational television stations. The *Civil Rights Act* of 1964 provided technical and financial aid to local public school districts to help with desegregation. Discrimination was barred under federally assisted programs. Many schools that were racially segregated before 1954 still remained racially segregated afterward, despite the Supreme Court *Decision on Segregation* of 1954 that legally terminated racial segregation in the United States. Now, those public schools that aggressively refused to desegregate were forced to do so by means of desegregation busing in the affected parts of the country.

The lack of tangible progress in education brought to life the *Elementary and Secondary Education Act* (ESEA) of 1965, focused on strengthening secondary and elementary education programs for children of low-income families. As a part of President Lyndon Johnson's *War on Poverty*, it provided federal funds for additional school textbooks, various instructional materials, and resources to support educational programs, educators' professional development, and necessary educational services in low-income areas. Federal aid to elementary and secondary schools had been a subject of discussion after World War II. However, nothing had been done until ESEA increased federal funding for "compensatory education" programs for children in low-income areas from 4.4% in 1964 to 8.8% in 1968 and up to 9.8% in 1980. The Act was originally authorized through 1970; however, the government reauthorized the Act every five years since its enactment.

The *Higher Education Act* (HEA) of 1965 provided financial assistance to students in postsecondary and higher education. Altogether with ESEA, they created better conditions to get an appropriate education for a wider spectrum of Americans. As a part of this Act, the National Teacher Corps was authorized to provide teachers to poverty-stricken areas of the United States. Similar to NDEA, HEA contained the section *Federal Control of Education Prohibited*, so that the government provided resources but demurred from controlling how efficiently they would be spent.

The *Bilingual Education Act*, part of the 1967 amendments to the *Elementary and Secondary Education Act*, authorized federal funds for school districts having substantial numbers of students with limited mastery of English. (Estimates of such students range from 2.5 to 4.6 million, 7–10% of the US student population.)

The *Education Professions Development Act* (EPDA) of 1967 was designed to help school systems, state educational agencies, colleges and universities training "persons who are serving or preparing to serve as teachers, administrators, or educational specialists in institutions of higher education."

In 1972, in order to ensure that female students were not discriminated against in any way, Congress passed Title IX of the *Education Amendment*.

The *Family Educational Rights and Privacy Act* of 1974 (FERPA) was designed to protect the privacy of student education records. It states clearly that educational agencies and institutions that receive funding under a program administered by the U. S. Department of Education must provide students and/or their parents with access to their education records, an opportunity to seek to have the records amended, and some control over the disclosure of information from the records.

The *Education for All Handicapped Children Act*, also known as *Individuals with Disabilities Education Act* (IDEA), of 1975 mandated that schools provide a free and appropriate education, individualized instructional programs, to students identified as having disabilities. It also called for placing such students, whenever possible, in regular classrooms rather than separating them from mainstream students. In 1990, the *Education for All Handicapped Children Act* (EAHCA) was renamed the *Individuals with Disabilities Education Act* (IDEA). IDEA of 1991 ensures services to children with disabilities. IDEA has been reauthorized and amended a number of times, most recently in December of 2004. It was amended the *Individuals With Disabilities Education Improvement Act* of 2004, now known as IDEIA, which provides that students with disabilities should be prepared for further education, employment and independent living. The Act requires that public schools create an *Individualized Education Program* (IEP) for each student who is found to be eligible under the both the federal and state eligibility/disability standards. As of 2006, more than 6 million children in the US receive special education services through IDEA. With the passing of the *American Recovery and Reinvestment Act* of 2009 (ARRA) on January 28, 2009, IDEA was granted $12.2 billion in order to provide funding for the implementation of this act.

Part of the expansion of federal involvement in education was the planning and development of a national student assessment system during the

1960s. The US Commissioner of Education from 1962 to 1965, Francis Keppel, a former dean of the Harvard School of Education, believed that one could hardly determine the quality of academic performance in the schools without information about the academic achievement of the students, and that progress educational would be impossible without a reporting system providing state or federal authorities with data on student educational achievement. In 1969, the *National Assessment of Educational Progress* (NAEP), a federal testing program to assess the level of students' knowledge in the main academic subjects (English, mathematics) was introduced. Since 1969, assessments have been conducted periodically in reading, mathematics, science, writing, US history, civics, geography, and the arts. The implementation of the testing program faced opposition from those who saw the tests as an instrument to increase federal power over state education and a road leading to a national curriculum. Proponents of the testing program offered a compromise — to create the Education Commission of States, which would help states develop effective policy and practice for public education by providing data, research, analysis and leadership. In addition, to dissipate the considerable concern that federal funding for assessment would deprive the NAEP of its independence and autonomy, the US Office of Education assured the Education Commission of States (which was to set up the policy oversight of NAEP) that it wouldn't interfere with the policy or analytic aspects of the assessment.

A CALL TO ARMS

In 1979, based on the *Department of Education Organization Act*, the Department of Health, Education and Welfare was reorganized in the US Department of Education and the Department of Health and Human Services. The new Department of Education began operation in 1980 at the Cabinet level. Education Secretary Terrel Bell organized the National Commission on Excellence in Education which, after an eighteen-month study, presented the report *A Nation at Risk: The Imperative for Educational Reform*, 1983.

The report was shocking: "What was unimaginable a generation ago has begun to occur — others are matching and surpassing our educational attainments...." And "The educational foundations of our society are presently being eroded by a rising tide of mediocrity that threatens our very future as a nation and a people."

The report concentrated primarily on secondary education. Secondary schools curricula were found to be unsuitable to the requirements of the time, given the high demand for highly skilled workers in scientific and technological fields. The report warned about the economic consequences, indicating that the country was losing its competitive edge in the world economy. At an even more fundamental level, the report showed that the nation was at risk of losing its global position because "Some 23 million American adults are functionally illiterate by the simplest test of everyday reading, writing, and comprehension. About 13% of all 17-year-olds in the United States can be considered functionally illiterate." The document also indicated the role of schools in developing "the intellectual, moral and spiritual" qualities of the young generation.

The report called for broad reforms in public education and teacher training. It recommended a curriculum including four years of English, three years of math, three years of science, three years of social studies, and half a year of computer science, and it established the goals to be achieved.

> The teaching of English in high school should equip graduates to: (a) comprehend, interpret, evaluate, and use what they read; (b) write well-organized, effective papers; (c) listen effectively and discuss ideas intelligently; and (d) know our literary heritage and how it enhances imagination and ethical understanding, and how it relates to the customs, ideas, and values of today's life and culture. The teaching of mathematics in high school should equip graduates to: (a) understand geometric and algebraic concepts; (b) understand elementary probability and statistics; (c) apply mathematics in everyday situations; and (d) estimate, approximate, measure, and test the accuracy of their calculations. In addition to the traditional sequence of studies available for college-bound students, new equally demanding mathematics curricula need to be developed for those who don't plan to continue their formal education immediately.

In addition to these new basics, it was also proposed that the study of foreign languages should be begun in elementary schools.

As for teachers, the report indicated that many were not academically qualified. "The teacher preparation curriculum is weighted heavily with courses in education methods at the expense of courses in subjects to be taught." The report ascertained a high demand for teachers of mathematics, science, foreign languages, and specialists in education for gifted and talented, language-minority, and handicapped students; it pointed out the need of increasing teachers' salaries in order to attract and retain qualified teachers. Many recommendations of *A Nation at Risk* were the seeds for the education reform movement. Among them was the need for states to develop curriculum standards determining what students should know and be able to do in each academic discipline and a testing program to measure student achievements. As a result, by 2001, all of the states had federally approved state curriculum standards in the areas of language arts, mathematics, and science and developed tests to measure student achievements..

In 1983, the federal government decided to shift management of the NAEP program from the Education Commission of States to the Educational Testing Service. The 1990 NAEP publication *Accelerating Academic Achievement* indicated: "Across all three ages assessed (9, 13 and 17) overall reading performance in 1988 was as good if not slightly better than it was nearly two decades earlier... In 1986, mathematics had changed very little from the levels achieved in 1973." The need of a decisive government involvement in education became obvious.

The *Improving America's Schools Act* (IASA) of 1994, that amended the *Elementary and Secondary Education Act* of 1965, focused on encouraging a comprehensive and systemic school reform, improving instructional and professional development to meet high standards, strengthening accountability, and promoting the coordination of resources to improve education for all children. It was linked closely with the *Goals 2000 Education Program*, the pivot of the *Goals 2000: Educate America Act* of 1994, which provided resources to states and communities to improve significantly the level of education so that children would be able to realize their potential.

The Goals 2000 established the basis to identify world-class academic standards, to measure student progress, and to provide the support that students may need to meet the standards. The *Educate America Act* of 1994 codified in law the six educational goals concerning school readiness, school completion, student academic achievement, mathematics and science, adult literacy, and safe disciplined and drug-free schools; it includes also two goals encouraging teacher professional development and parental participation (see Chapter 2).

The passing of the Goals 2000 allowed the federal government a new more active role in its support for education. The federal government provided not only financial support but offered a comprehensive approach to help students succeed in life and encouraged local school systems to meet high education standards. Nevertheless, as in the previous acts related to education, the government assured that it wasn't going to invade the sphere of local education. Section 318 of the *Goals 2000 Act* states "Nothing in this Act shall be construed to authorize an officer or employee of the Federal Government to mandate, direct, or control a state, local educational agency, or school's curriculum, program of instruction, or allocation of state or local resources or mandate a state or any subdivision thereof to spend any funds or incur any costs not paid for under this Act."

The Act established the National Education Standards and Improvement Council (NESIC) within the Department of Education for the purpose of providing an independent review of the model of National and State Academic Standards. NESIC should examine and certify national and state content, student performance, opportunity-to-learn standards, and assessment systems voluntarily submitted by states. The National Council of Teachers of Mathematics developed standards in mathematics. The US Department of Education funded the development of standards for sciences, English and foreign languages, geography, and history.

The *National Skills Standards Act* of 1994, incorporated as Title V of Goals 2000, established the National Skill Standards Board to facilitate development of rigorous occupational standards and to oversee a system for certification of attainment of skill standards. The board should identify broad occupational clusters and create a system of standards, assessment, and certification for each cluster. The *School-to-Work Opportunities Act* of 1994 required states to coordinate school-to-work plans with the educational reforms required by the *Goals 2000 Act*. The *school-to-work* term characterizes an approach that combines the work-based learning component with the school-based learning component, i.e., provides opportunities for students to learn about and experience work while being in school. The School-to-Work Opportunities program under this Act should integrate school-based learning and work-based learning, integrate academic and occupational learning, and establish effective linkages between secondary and postsecondary education. The Act included the finding that "three-fourths of high school students in the United States enter the workforce without baccalaureate degrees, and many don't possess the academic and entry-level occupational skills necessary to succeed in the changing United States workplace." Unemployment among US youths is "intolerably high and earnings of high school graduates have been falling relative to earnings of individuals with more education." At the same time, "a substantial number of youths in the United States, especially disadvantaged students, students of diverse racial, ethnic, and cultural backgrounds, and students with disabilities, don't complete high school," and "the United States lacks a comprehensive and coherent system to help its youths acquire the knowledge, skills, abilities, and information about and access to the labor market necessary to make an effective transition from school to career-oriented work or to further education and training." The law was introduced with a hope that "the work-based learning approach, which integrates theoretical instruction with structured on-the-job training, combined with school-based learning, can be very effective in engaging student interest, enhancing skill acquisition, developing positive work attitudes, and preparing youths for high-skill, high-wage careers."

The above acts assumed restructuring, rescheduling, and rethinking educational practices and were intended to change the ways teachers teach and students learn.

The 1998 *Reauthorization of Higher Education Act* (its short title is *Higher Education Amendments* of 1998) that amended the *Higher Education Act* of 1965 to extend the authorization of programs under the act of 1965 was also a part of the governmental policy to improve education and to make it easier for millions of Americans to get higher education.

Over the last three decades per-pupil spending has more than doubled (taking inflation into account) without bringing any tangible results. Students are learning and achieving at about the same level as in the 1970s. According to the NAEP data, the average reading score for 17-year-olds on a 0–500 point scale was 285 in 1971; in 1999 it was 288. The average math score was 304 in 1973; in 1999 it was 308. The average science score was 305 in 1969; in 1999 it was 295. In addition, according to the study of graduation rates (Jay Green, *High School Graduation Rates in the United States*, Manhattan Institute Report, November 2001), if in 1969 the graduation rate peaked at 76%, it dropped to 70% in 2001. According to a recent US government report, *The State of Literacy in America*, released by the National Institute for Literacy (NIL), there has been a significant growth in illiteracy in America. Over 90 million US adults are functionally illiterate or near illiterate, lacking the minimum skills required in a modern society. With such an army of unskilled people for a work force, the future prosperity of the United States is at risk, and it is obvious that the previous system of pumping money into education has not brought the needed results.

Under President George W. Bush, government education policy was focused primarily on elementary and secondary education. In contract to the above-indicated laws related to education, the *No Child Left Behind Act* (NCLB) of 2001 became the first federal law that made federal funding dependent upon the achieved educational progress. It reauthorizes the *Elementary and Secondary Education Act* of 1965, holds schools accountable for student achievement levels, provides penalties for schools that don't make adequate yearly progress toward meeting the goals of NCLB and gives parents greater choices in choosing schools for their children. The NCLB law requires every school to do its best to improve student achievement and each state to set academic standards and yearly goals. According to the goals of NCLB, by 2014 all children should be achieving at their state's proficiency level in reading, language arts, math, and science. Adequate yearly progress is the minimum level of improvement that school districts and schools must achieve every year to meet this goal. Every state should test students in grades 3–8 and in high school on what they know in English and math; by 2007–2008 students in 4 and 8 grades and in high school should be tested also in science. To have a realistic picture of how various children are doing in a school district, the test scores are reported in eight different subgroups: white, black, Hispanic, American Indian, Asian or Pacific Islanders, students eligible for free or reduced lunches, students with limited English proficiency, and students qualifying for special education services. The Act requires school districts to hire qualified teachers and offers new resources for teacher training. It states clearly, "teachers must be well prepared. Today, some school districts employ teachers who are not well prepared to teach the grade level or subject they are assigned. This is a serious problem in schools that are struggling to meet their academic goals."

In 2002, the Education Sciences Reform Act established within the US Department of Education the Institute of Education Sciences (IES) that should provide rigorous evidence on which to ground education practice and policy. The Institute of Education Sciences operates through its four subdivisions, the so-called centers. The National Center for Education Statistics (NCES) is the primary federal entity for collecting and analyzing data related to education. Under the current structure, the Commissioner of Education Statistics, who heads the National Center for Education Statistics in the US Department of Education, is responsible by law for carrying out the NAEP project. The National Assessment Governing

Board appointed by the Secretary of Education but independent of the Department, which is a bipartisan group whose members include governors, state legislators, local and state school officials, educators, business representatives, and members of the general public, sets policy for NAEP and is responsible for developing the framework and test specifications for the assessments. NCES annually produces three major publications designed for general audiences: *The Condition of Education, Digest of Education Statistics, and Projections of Education Statistics.* These publications are used in diverse ways by policymakers, researchers, and the general public. NCES produces other publications that draw upon a variety of data sources, such as *Trends in Educational Equity of Girls & Women,* a series on the educational status and progress of racial/ethnic minorities, and annual indicators of school crime and safety. As part of its congressional mandate, the National Center for Education Statistics is required to report on the state of education in the United States and other countries. To carry out this mission, NCES engages in a number of activities designed to gather information and produce indicators on how the performance of US students, teachers, and schools compares with that of their counterparts in other countries. NCES and other offices within the US Department of Education work with foreign ministries of education and international organizations, such as the Organization for Economic Cooperation and Development, the International Association for the Evaluation of Educational Achievement, and the United Nations Educational, Scientific and Cultural Organization (UNESCO) to plan, develop, and implement reliable and meaningful measures across countries. The National Center for Education Research (NCER) supports rigorous research that addresses the nation's most pressing education needs, from early childhood to adult education. The National Center for Education Evaluation and Regional Assistance (NCEE) conducts unbiased large-scale evaluations of education programs and practices supported by federal funds. The National Center for Special Education Research (NCSER) sponsors a comprehensive program of special education research designed to expand the knowledge and understanding of infants, toddlers, and children with disabilities.

In 2003, the *Higher Education Act* of 1965 and 1998 was again amended and reauthorized expanding access to higher education for low and middle-income students. To encourage growth and change, it must be reauthorized by Congress, generally every five years. In addition, Congress also considered bills directly or indirectly linked to HEA. The Act and subsequent government's steps followed the publication of the White Paper *The Future of Higher Education* by the Education and Skills Secretary Charles Clarke, which set out the government's plans for radical reform and investment in universities and colleges.

When the time came to reauthorize the *No Child Left Behind Act* of 2001, discussing the future amended NCLB, US Secretary of Education Margaret Spellings said, "Five years ago with *No Child Left Behind*, we shifted our national education dialogue from how much we are spending to how much children are learning. Today, we need a new conversation about how to strengthen and improve this law....*Bringing well-qualified math, science, and critical foreign language professionals into our nation's secondary schools as adjunct teachers will help prepare students for life in the 21st century, not only by helping fill teacher shortages in high need subjects, but also by helping kids learn more about some real-world applications from those with first-hand experience* [emphasis mine]." President George W. Bush has proposed a $500 million Teacher Incentive Fund for states and school districts that choose to reward effective teachers and a $25 million initiative to create the Adjunct Teacher Corps, which should encourage professionals to teach part-time middle and high school courses in the core academic subjects, particularly in mathematics and science.

A school failing to meet yearly progress established by the NCLB law faces various remedial actions. Among them are tutoring programs. Parents may select from state approved tutorial services. The provisions of NCLB force schools to pay more attention to the needs of students who have historically lagged behind on test scores and provide tutoring for such students. When schools do not meet state targets for improving the achievement of all students, parents are given the option to send their child to another school. The promise of *No Child Left Behind* was accompanied by an education plan that would allow poor students at chronically failing public schools to use federal vouchers to attend private schools. The *Public School Choice* guidance of the ED (January 14, 2009) contains the public school choice provisions and updates the *Public School Choice Non-Regulatory Guidance* of February 6, 2004. The *Voluntary Public School Choice* program of the ED supports states and school districts in efforts to establish or expand a public school choice program. The Department makes competitive awards to state education agencies, local education agencies, or partnerships that include both, and other public, for-profit or nonprofit organizations.

The *Charter Schools Act* of 1998 (amended on July1, 2005) was one more attempt of the federal government to increase student achievement by establishing public schools that operate independently from the existing educational structure. The Act also designated the parameters within which the schools must operate and the conditions by which their charters can be renewed (see details in Chapter 11).

Of course, NCLB of 2001 didn't receive a unanimous approval and support. The process of amending this Act is accompanied with criticism of its separate sections. The discussion of the reauthorization of NCLB allows various educational organizations and politicians to attract attention of public not only to the Act under consideration, but in many cases, mostly to themselves. Education and politics are inseparably linked. Unfortunately, this bond only hinders progress in education.

POLITICS AND EDUCATIONAL PROGRESS

The question of federal aid for education was always a political hot potato. Any educational initiative on the federal level is labeled by its opponents as an assault on local school control; they refer to the Tenth Amendment to the Constitution as reserving education as an issue for the states. When considering the education policy of the Democratic and Republican parties, we should remember that they both came from the Democratic Republican Party, founded in 1792 by Thomas Jefferson, James Madison and other influential opponents of the Federalists, supporters of a strong federal government. The Democratic Republicans, whom Alexander Hamilton labeled as the Anti-Federalists, presented themselves as a party of liberty and states' rights, of "government rigorously frugal and simple," in the words of Jefferson. Nowadays, the philosophy of the Republican Party fully corresponds to Jefferson's words. In contrast, the Democratic Party, especially in such areas as economy, business and finance, health and education, supports the substantial governmental regulations and control. However, policy is like weather; it changes from time to time, and representatives of both parties change their positions on many issues, including education.

In the Party's early years, the Republicans were among the first US politicians who proposed significant federal aid for education. In 1870, Republican President Ulysses S. Grant urged Congress to support primary education with grants, making him the first president who advocated federal aid for education. As the Republican platforms of 1880 and 1884 and the Republican presidents of 1880 and 1888 endorsed national support for education, the Democratic platform maintained that the establishment and support of the public schools belonged exclusively to the states. Then during the earlier part of the 20th century, the Republican Party shifted its policy, limited aid for education and stated that the federal government shouldn't interfere with state and local control of schools. This statement accompanies constantly all governmental education acts. The Democratic Party also shifted its policy, now favoring federal aid to education. After World War II, the Republican Party's position fluctuated between limited backing and denial of all support. In the election of 1952, the Democratic and Republican parties took opposite positions. The Democratic Party called for federal aid for teachers' salary increase, school construction, reconstruction and maintenance. The Republican Party countered with the following platform statement: "The responsibility for sustaining this system of popular education has always rested with local communities and the states. We subscribe fully to this principle."

Nevertheless, the postwar era signified the period of an increasing federal involvement in education. With the next presidential elections of 1956, the Republican Party turned toward supporting education, lessening some of its differences with the Democrats, who continued promoting vast money for educational programs. However, as shown earlier in this chapter, in response to events that demonstrated the weakness of the education system and undermined prestige of the United States, and brought concerns over the country's rate of scientific advancement, the Republicans strongly supported federal involvement in education. The Eisenhower administration urged Congress to approve the *National Defense Education Act* that signaled an expanded role for the federal government in education.

Since the 1960s, the two major parties both support federal aid in principle. The disagreement is over the extent of such involvement. Earlier, politicians liked to talk about declining enrollment and the dropout rate and were focused on providing special programs for students with particular needs rather than on improving the academic quality for everyone. Mixing middle-class and low-income children was supposed to improve schools for the poor. In 1964, a publicly funded preschool program for low-income children was created. The various studies focused, for example, on establishing how middle-class white students were better prepared than low-income and black students; they weren't directly linked with the global educational problems the nation faced. Since education became a spicy political issue, this type of research was popular and consumed significant federal funds without noticeably improving the level of education. The Democrats called for generous financial support for various education grants, teachers' salaries and construction of classrooms and other facilities. The Republicans believed that vast financial support would only lead ultimately to federal domination and control of schools, subordinating state and local governments to administrative divisions of the federal government.

Later the Republicans softened their position; they backed grants, loans, and work-study programs for students, advocated expanded programs for preschool children and suggested the establishment of a commission to study educational quality and other programs. The *No Child Left Behind Act* drew the positions of both parties nearer. However, this Act included accountability requirements based on results, a significant difference from previous education proposals that emphasized the Republican position on how money should be spent.

Election campaigns are the hottest period for political debates, and slogans concerning education are used often as hollow promises for political gain. Public officials say what their constituents want to hear, and in many cases they address local rather than global problems. But when the election is over and the limited time, funds and other resources are parceled out, these objectives often fall by the wayside.

In recent years, the discussion has shifted from the necessity of governmental help to the amount of federal aid and its specifics. In general both parties agree on the need to: create an educated and skillful workforce in the vital areas of science, math, engineering, and information technology; guarantee affordable access to broadband technology for all Americans within the next five years; and guarantee school readiness and security.

But when the discussion touches specifics, their differences are substantial. The Democrats want the government to help students from poor families, minorities, to provide grants for various education research programs, to support financially increasing teachers' salaries, vocational and training programs, small school classes, programs for gifted/talented students, etc. They suggest this is the only way to raise the overall quality of education in the country and enhance student achievement. Reducing class size is one specific objective that appeals to parents without its usefulness having been proven. The Republicans call the Democrats squanderers and say that government investment in education and its allocation should depend upon school performance. They are more cautious in their concrete proposals and link them with accountability. Some educators assert that accountability is a political concept rather than an educational one, and it shouldn't be applied to education. Accountability relates to the justification of expenditures of public funds, i.e., it's an important economic concept linked directly to money rather than the educational achievement. However, to take federal money to spend locally, without achieving the expected educational goals, is inadmissible, and accountability establishes a certain mechanism (far from perfect) to control federal aid for education.

As mentioned above, opponents of federal aid to public schools contend that federal involvement in education interferes with states' rights under the Constitution. States are eager for federal handouts but resist federal control of spending. In its report of 2005, *Delivering the Promise: State Recommendations for Improving No Child Left Behind*, the National Conference of State Legislatures (NCSL), a bipartisan organization that backs the interests of state governments before Congress and federal agencies, wrote:

> Congress should acknowledge that states have the authority over education and are committed to the same goal of improving education and allowing every child to succeed; Congress should create a revitalized state-federal partnership that focuses on results, not on processes, and ensures accountability without stifling state and local innovation; Congress should amend NCLB in a way that eliminates direct federal regulation of local education agencies and limit its direct interaction to states; the US Department of Education should fulfill its role as a national center for diagnostic data collection and scientific research and dedicate more resources toward those services; Congress should create clear, unambiguous conditions that are placed on federal education funds, and limit the punitive financial consequences on states if they choose not to participate, thus, eliminating the use of coercion.

By ordering such reports, states aim to remind the central government about their constitutional rights.

But the argument that federal aid for education interferes with states' rights has little legitimacy. To help with good intentions doesn't mean to take under control. Moreover, even providing financial aid and checking how money was spent is not the same as imposing one's will. If we provide money for medicine to sick people, we have the right to check whether the money was spent as intended, but we do not get to decide which medicine they take.

Information for Reflection

President Andrew Johnson and Congress created the Department of Education in 1867 after extensive debates with those who stated that federal interference in educational matters was unconstitutional. In 1866, Congressman Rogers indicated that the formation of the Department of Education was not among the enumerated powers granted to Congress under the United States Constitution, declaring that "there is no authority under the Constitution of the United States to authorize Congress to interfere with the education of the different states in any manner, directly or indirectly" (39th Congress, 5 June 1866, The Congressional Globe, 2968).

Similar statements are used now by the opponents of federal involvement in education. Their argument is simple: education is not found among the enumerate objects of the Constitution. A reasonable counterargument is: maybe education was not mentioned in the Constitution because in 1787 it was not an urgent item to be included!?

It seems appropriate to remind these "strict constructionists" of President Lincoln's words in his message to Congress in 1862: "The dogmas of the quiet past are inadequate to the stormy present. The occasion is piled high with difficulty, and we must rise with the occasion. As our case is new, so we must think anew and act anew" (Collective Works of Abraham Lincoln, ed. Roy P. Basler, Rutgers University Press, 1990).

Neither the Democratic nor Republican party looks uniform. There are radical and moderate members in both parties. Despite their different views on separate educational issues, they cannot deny the fact that federal aid for education and the government acts did influence the state and local education programs, i.e., the government did interfere, at least indirectly, in state and local education programs and policies. Nevertheless, both parties continue repeating that the federal government must in no way interfere with state and local education policy, as if they returned to their origin — the Democratic–Republican Party.

Information for Reflection

"The new political movement that now controls much of the Republican party, the so-called Leave Us Alone coalition, is one of Americans who simply wish to be left alone by the government, who want the government out of their lives and pockets. Directly opposed to this coalition is the descriptively titled Takings Coalition, which is at the heart of the tax-and-spend left — the Democratic Party, big unions, trial lawyers, basically anyone who wants a European style nanny government (Grover Norquist, Leave Us Alone, HarperCollins Publishers, New York, 2008)." Many political analysts believe that the widely-used dichot-

omies of left vs. right or liberal vs. conservatives are less informative than the leave-us-aloners vs. the takers, and it is perhaps more important to understand these new coalitions than the Republican or Democratic parties themselves; they will battle for control of America's future over the next fifty years.

Unhappiness with the quality of public education motivated the leave-us-aloners to advocate homeschooling; instead of sending children to public schools, parents educate them at home. Homeschoolers became a growing phenomenon mainly through the leadership of Michael Farris, a lawyer in Washington State, who was the son of a public school principal. Today homeschoolers are about one percent of the population.

Some reasonable questions are: What level of education should parents have to teach their children the courses that meet high school requirements? Can a middle-class family afford to hire tutors to teach high school courses at home?

Stating that they do not ask for the government's money, time, or attention, the Leave Us Alone Coalition nevertheless recognizes the necessity of the government to guarantee a strong national defense and security. The National Defense Education Act of 1958 was the first serious warning that without a strong system of public education the United States was at risk. The Founding Fathers never considered education a private matter. The compulsory attendance laws show that we consider education compulsory, i.e., education required by law for children to receive and governments to provide. The leave-us-alone theory is not applicable to education.

Trade Unions and Educational Progress

Education, particularly in primary and secondary schools, is one of the most highly unionized sectors of the US labor market. Teachers' trade unions, representing the interests of teachers, exist in all states. They are affiliated with the two largest education trade unions ("duopoly"), the American Federation of Teachers and the National Education Association, described in Chapter 4. Each local teachers' union is largely responsible for actually bargaining with the boards of education concerning teachers' salaries and representing the teachers' interests in day-to-day-affairs and local problems. In turn, AFT and NEA speak for their membership with respect to various national problems.

The difference between these organizations is that the AFT, being affiliated with AFL-CIO, a national union labor organization that represents a "united labor movement," goes beyond K–12 public education. The union represents higher education faculty (including professors, non-tenure-track faculty, and graduate student employees), nurses working in private sector hospitals, state public employees, school nurses, school librarians, and education paraprofessionals such as bus drivers and cafeteria workers.

The increasing unionization of educational workforce in 1960s did not improve the education system. NEA, representing more than 90% of public school teachers, gradually transformed itself from a professional association to a collective bargaining agent for teachers. The American Federation of Teachers allied itself with the labor movement and naturally supported all means including strikes to protect teacher's interests (salary increases, work conditions, etc.) rather than the quality of education. Although both organizations assert that they don't support a particular political party, that they are "non-partisan" and make decisions based on the evaluation of candidates' attitude toward public education, in reality they have endorsed and provided support for every Democratic Party presidential candidate starting with Jimmy Carter. Most of their political contributions go to the Democratic Party. Local teacher unions lead aggressive campaigns to elect pro-union supporters to the city council, mayor's office and school boards in order to help the unions in collective bargaining.

To demonstrate their concern for the state of education in the country rather than the pursuit of goals such as higher salaries and improved working conditions, AFT and NEA undertook campaigns discussing the goals of *A Nation at Risk* and *No Child Left Behind*. They supported measures to strengthen curriculum and graduation standards, school security, and smaller class sizes and called for increased funding for education. The American Federation of Teachers report (*Building Minds, Minding Buildings: Turning Crumbling Schools into Environments for Learning*, Washington, DC, 2000) attracts attention to the deplorable physical conditions in public schools. Various reports produced by AFT and NEA conclude the necessity of increasing federal support for education. As to the requirement for children to meet state test standards, NEA, for example, believes this shouldn't be applied to poor, disabled or minority students, or to students not proficient in English. The NCLB standards became the main subject of criticism. According to the NEA's Director of Education Policy and Practice Joel Packer, to meet the criteria NCLB sets, 44% of districts cut time spent on science, social studies, art, music, physical education and even lunch. Before the bill is reauthorized, both NEA and AFT agree the new act must use more than test scores to measure student learning and performance, reduce class sizes to boost learning, and increase the number of highly qualified teachers in schools. Criticizing the *No Child Left Behind Act*, the AFT President Edward McElroy said, "According to the Forum on Educational Accountability the law's emphasis needs to shift from applying sanctions for failing to raise test scores to holding states and localities accountable for making the systemic changes that improve student achievement." AFT believes that the school choice in accordance with NCLB, supplemental educational services and other "school improvement" provisions "are punitive, ideological, not logically sequential and neither research nor evidence based." NEA states that "the federal accountability measures deem schools as successes or failures on the basis of student scores on annual standardized math and reading tests." A national campaign launched by AFT and NEA, as if to improve the NCLB law, in reality was a political campaign against the Bush Administration, the campaign for uncontrollable federal aid for education. "AFT consistently has called for greater accountability and higher standards of learning. That has not changed," said the AFT Executive Vice President Antonia Cortese. "We believe that to help all children succeed, schools need good curricula, better assessments, professional development for staff, intensive interventions for struggling students and fair accountability." "We're standing up for children, whose parents are saying, 'no more' to costly federal regulations that drain money from classrooms and spend it on paperwork, bureaucracy and big testing companies," says the NEA President Reg Weaver. "The principle of the law is simple: If you regulate, you have to pay."

By paying only lip service to the NCLB's use of an accountability system, rigorous standards and testing of teachers, AFT and NEA only make matters worse. These unions stand for teachers rather than for children. It is not the union leaders' job to care about education. Their functions are different. They do care about their leadership positions, the source of their wealth. They are not interested in changing their power structure and the education system.

According to *The Washington Post* of May 19, 2010, "The proposed new D.C. teachers' contract, which could boost some salaries well over $100,000, is causing tremors in the city's non-unionized charter school sector, where officials view the pact as only the latest inequity in District policies governing the funding of its two school systems." Given that the District's public schools remain among the most troubled in the nation, this is an example of "excellent" performance by union leaders who have demonstrated their ability to protect the interests of those who pay them.

Another example of a fruitful trade union activity is the including of the cosmetic procedures (plastic surgery, chemical peels and other skin treatments) in the Buffalo schools teachers contact. According to *The Buffalo News* of October 31, 2010, "Last year, about 500 schools employees took advantage of the benefit, costing the district as much as $9 million, all at taxpayer expense."

It is clear why trade union leaders dislike the word "accountability."

Information for Reflection

> *A growing threat to the teachers' unions is the Association of American Educators (AAE), the largest national, non-union, professional teacher association, which neither spends any of its members' dues on partisan politics nor supports or opposes controversial agendas unrelated to education. AAE believes that professional educators should be free from all forms of involuntary membership and endorsements and that strikes and walkouts are detrimental to students and to the reputation of teachers. Its over three hundred thousand members are dedicated to improving education through cooperation, rather than confrontation. AAE endorses more local control of education, greater parental involvement, and higher standards of excellence and accountability for all stakeholders — teachers, students, administrators, and parents.*

> *Why do educators join AAE? AAE provides its members with the low-cost liability insurance and legal assistance on job related issues. And what is most important, its members do not like the fact that union dues are used to promote a controversial social agenda and political candidates. They believe a professional educational association should be concerned only with education.*

DEMOCRATS AND REPUBLICANS ON EDUCATION

The Gaither Report, a government paper produced after the launch of Sputnik in 1957, gave the Democrats a chance to recast themselves as the true hardliners. In 1958, when the Soviet leader Khrushchev vowed to "bury" the United States in a race involving impressive scientific achievements as well as arms, President John Kennedy vowed "to get America moving again." This was interpreted as an intent to direct federal resources to the military and educational fields. He emphasized the need of federal support for schools and attempted to make it a major issue in the election. The Kennedy–Johnson administration's advocacy for education resulted in several major measures that provided schools with federal aid.

In his book *Rewriting History* (Regun, New York, 2004) Dick Morris describes how Hillary Clinton tried to help her husband, Arkansas Governor Bill Clinton, get reelected by coming up with "the idea of a commission that would travel around the state holding hearing and bringing attention to the low quality of Arkansas schools." Arkansas was fiftieth in the country in education, and Hillary's political instinct prompted her to believe that the public would accept the tax increase only if it came with serious educational reforms. The commission, which she would lead, would then recommend fundamental reforms in education standards, standardized test for students, mandatory testing of teachers and big salary raises for teachers who passed the test. A part of Hillary's program was a decision to test every teacher, tenured or not, to see whether he/she was able to teach professionally. According to the original plan, the teachers were to be tested on their basic knowledge and skills. But the test results showed that half of the teachers failed miserably, and these results, if released, would have infuriated the teachers' union, minority groups (minority teachers did extremely poorly), so the Clintons asked Morris to poll Arkansas voters to determine the politically acceptable level of failure for teachers. The real fifty percent passing grade for teachers was changed to ten percent, the level determined by the poll. US historian Henry Adams (1838–1915) was right when he said, "Practical politics consists in ignoring facts."

Morris praised Hillary Clinton for "her foresight and courage in her efforts to reform schools." He wrote that "Hillary adopted a distinctly moderate tone, combining with a liberal generosity toward education with an insistence on high standards." However, the above episode happened about thirty years ago. Twenty years later Hillary Clinton changed her position and opposed testing teachers "unless they are the new ones, fresh out of school" (Lazio vs. Clinton, NBC Debate, October 27, 2000).

In 2007, discussing the education problem during the presidential debates, Senator Hillary Clinton said, "I really believe that it takes a village to raise a child and the American village has failed our children. I have fought for more than 35 years for early childhood education, for more mentoring, for more parent education programs, to get our children off to a good start. I have fought to make sure that schools were fair to all children. That's the work I did in Arkansas, to try to raise the standards particularly for the poorest of our children, and most especially for minority children. And certainly in the White House years, and now in the Senate, I've continued that effort because I don't think there is a more important issue." In his book *My Life* (Random House Inc., New York, 2004) Bill Clinton wrote: "I proposed a large package of education reforms, arguing that we should change the way we spend the more than $15 billion a year of education aid to 'support what works and stop supporting what doesn't work,' by requiring states to end social promotion, turn around failing schools or shut them down."

In 2000, running for the presidency, George W. Bush said, "As President, I will fundamentally change the relationship between the states and federal government in education. I strongly believe in local control of schools and curriculum. We will grant unprecedented freedom and flexibility in return for high standards and results. In my administration, federal dollars will no longer follow failure. We will ask states and local school districts to set their own standards to achieve excellence in the core areas of math, English, science, and history, and hold them accountable for results. I oppose a national test because it would undermine curriculum developed at the state and local level."

Senator Chuck Schumer, who claims to be the brain trust of the Democratic Party and is considered its main ideologist, in his book *Positively American* (Rodale Inc., New York, 2007), showed his understanding of the need of tough government standards for all schools which differs him from many Democrats, including Edward Kennedy, the Democratic Party's leader on education. He believes that the time came "to revamp large parts of public educations" and wants "the federal government to be far more involved in solving this problem... The federal government needs to take control in three ways that really matter: standards, money, and teachers." He supports a rigorous national standard by which each school will be judged, supports regular yearly student testing and wants to "triple federal education spending" which should be given to schools that agree to certain conditions, and "enhance salaries of qualified teachers in the most critical subjects, like math and science." In addition, districts that agree to participate should "make one promise: They'd have to freeze property taxes that go to education, so that in effect property taxes are cut by 50% within ten years." After four years, the schools should be reevaluated and funded "only if they enact prescribed requirements and programs." Emphasizing the necessity of the federal education reform he writes: "We wouldn't ask fifteen thousand localities, or even fifty states, to be responsible for national defense — and then underfund them!... Improving our K-12 educational system is at least as important to our country's future as maintaining our world's best military." However, Senator Schumer's mathematics demonstrates his poor knowledge of this subject.

It's unclear why he wants to triple the education budget and how he is going to cut property taxes by freezing them. It's easy to make promises by operating with integers (increase three times, decrease two times) since it's easy to understand simple mathematical operations; but it doesn't make them realistic. Perhaps sensing that his position could be criticized by many members of his party, the Senator blames President George W. Bush: "And thanks to the Bush administration's knee-jerk hatred of anything federal, there isn't a single national test — each state is allowed to design and score its own tests." If the Senator based his assertion on the above-given quote of the President's speech, he is absolutely right. However, we should take into account that the President's statement was made during his presidential campaign; it sounded similar to Al Gore's statement and reflected the opinion of many Democrats and Republicans. Now the attitude toward a national test has changed; it finds more support than it did ten years ago. The Senator's proposal to create "a new National Commission on Education" to develop a national standard can be considered as an option since the Department of Education has enough inner resources to resolve this problem. However, we cannot agree with his desire to finance school districts in advance and to give a new chance to localities helping them with financial resources before establishing the standards. As if the Senator forgot what comes first — the chicken or the eggs.

In his book (with Mark Salter) *Hard Call. Great Decisions and the Extraordinary People Who Made Them* (Twelve Hachette Book Group, New York, Boston, 2008) Senator John McCain writes: "Unless we systematically reform our education system so that our children acquire more proficient or unique skills, we are going to find it increasingly difficult to compete for jobs with the Chinese and Indians....The resource-consuming administration of education bureaucracies, politically influent unions that serve the interests of teachers and not students, and timid school boards all resist real change ... But the impediments within the system are so averse to change that the most effective agent of change, the person who understands the reality and forces progress toward a new idea, will have to come from within." Although the Senator doesn't offer any concrete measures to improve the situation, his gloomy picture of the current system of education shows his dissatisfaction how this problem was handled in the past. His hope in "the person ... within" looks a little bit naïve; this problem needs a "hard call" from the top.

President Barack Obama promised to recruit an army of new teachers, especially high quality math and science teachers, pay them higher salaries and give them more support. In return, he expects higher standards and more teacher accountability. Obama said, "I will provide funds for states to implement a broader range of assessments that can evaluate higher-order skills, including students' abilities to use technology, conduct research, engage in scientific investigation, solve problems, present and defend their ideas....Despite resources that are unmatched anywhere in the world, we have let our grades slip, our schools crumble, our teacher quality fall short, and other nations outpace us." However, admitting that the US government overspends on education, compared with the rest of the world, and for many years the government had been pumping more and more money in without getting any substantial results, Obama merely offers the same medicine — additional funding. The $789 billion economic stimulus package included $115 billion in new education funding, dollars that will be used for things like school construction and renovation, special education teacher incentives and technology. Time will tell whether it works.

Chapter 6. I Learn Therefore I Am

> "Let us think of education as the means of developing our greatest abilities, because in each of us there is a private hope and dream which, fulfilled, can be translated into benefit for everyone and greater strength for our nation." - John F. Kennedy

It is impossible to evaluate any result without establishing first a certain criterion. *A Nation At Risk* recommended for the states and local high schools to create minimum standards of proficiency in the basic subjects. Before they could graduate, students would have to show that they have attained these levels by taking standardized tests. The aim was to raise the standards and the level of difficulty in English, social studies, language, math, and science classes and get students to perform better. Educators pointed out that without a firm grasp of the basics, students are not just unfit for college, they are not able to compete as qualified employees in a global marketplace that relies heavily on a skilled labor pool. According to *A Nation Accountable*, "It is a national shame that nearly a third of our high school students still do not take the rigorous program of study recommended in 1983 for all students, regardless of whether they intend to enter the workforce and college after high school."

Sadly, little was done to turn things around after both *A Nation At Risk* and *A Nation Accountable*.

This chapter reviews the different kinds of tests used to evaluated performance, shows that the mess in the testing and grading system is one more indicator of disorder in the US education system.

TESTING AND GRADING SYSTEMS

In the United States, students are continuously assessed throughout the school year by their teachers, and report cards are issued to parents usually at the end of each quarter. Generally, the scores for individual assignments and tests, along with the maximum number of points for each assignment, are recorded for each student in a grade book, which in many schools can be accessed by using the Internet.

The concept of grading students' work quantitatively was developed by William Farish, a tutor at Cambridge University, and first implemented in 1792. Farish had borrowed his system from factories, where it was used to classify quality of products. Similar to many other countries, the United States schools use classical five-point discrete evaluation. However, Americans operate with letter rather than number grading, and there are many variations in different school districts. Each school district approves the grading and report policy for its schools accompanied by the description of grading procedures.

Here are the grade symbols used in American report cards and an example of their qualitative definition and correlative level of performance on a 100-point scale:

A = Outstanding level of performance; or top 10% (90 to 100) = 4.0

B = High level of performance; or second 10% (80–89) = 3.0

C = Acceptable level of performance; or third 10% (70–79) = 2.0

D = Minimal level of performance, minimum passing grade (60–69); or fourth 10% = 1.00

F (or E) = Unacceptable level of performance; or bottom 60% (0–59) = 0.00.

(Whether the failing grade is called "F" or "E" usually depends on school districts. "F" comes from the simpler two-point grading system — Pass and Fail.)

In contrast to many countries with the five-point discrete evaluation, where the last two symbols signify an unacceptable level of knowledge and are insufficient for a student to move to the next grade, in the United States the grade D is a pass to move forward.

The qualitative definition is:

A = Superior; 4 Quality Points

B = Above Average; 3 Quality Points

C = Average; 2 Quality Points

D = Below Average; 1 Quality Point

F (or E) = Unsatisfactory; 0 Quality Points

To recognize and encourage the additional effort and learning required in classes beyond the usual level of difficulty for high school courses, a weighted grade scale is used in some school districts for certain courses (the so-called Advanced Placement [AP] program, as well as Honors, Advanced-level, and International Baccalaureate [IB] courses [see Chapter 7]) if a student completes successfully the course. In addition, a student may earn college credit and /or advanced placement if he/she passes successfully the AP exam. AP tests are scored differently from the A–F (or E) grading scale. As in many other countries with the five-point discrete evaluation they are scored on a numeric scale 1 to 5, with a score of 3 and above considered passing, so that the quality points are: A = 5 Quality Points; B = 4 Quality Points; C = 3 Quality Points.

AP tests are administered by the College Board, a non-profit membership association that develops and maintains college level courses in various subject areas and offers the AP program since 1955. These activities are funded through fees charged to students taking AP exams. The indicated quality points are not supported by all states, and leading universities don't recognize these quality points. However, many schools add a certain percentage to the value of the class if a student completed the course successfully. Many schools add 0.5 to the value of an AP class (thus, an A would be a 4.5, a B would be a 3.5, etc.). Percentage ranges may vary even from one school to another. The A range above 4 is inconsistent with the highest numeric *grade point average* (GPA) score 4.0 that a student can achieve in most American schools. The AP, Honors, Advanced-level, and IB courses are reflected in the so-called *cumulative weighted grade point average* WGPA, which may be above 4.0.

Similar inconsistencies and improvisations with points and grades travel from one school to another. In parallel with the B grade, some schools use B- (80 to 83), B (84–86) and B+ (87–89); analogously the C grade is modified. The grade point average is computed by taking the mean of all grades. In schools, the grade point for each quarter is computed based on grades for individual tasks/assessments. For these grades teachers use points or percentages. Teachers never assign a grade lower than 50% to the tasks/assessment; a zero means a student didn't show any work at all or didn't attempt to meet the basic requirements. Grading becomes a grey area.

Although they are required to exercise their professional judgment in assigning grades, within the parameters of required procedures, the procedures are fuzzy and teachers have a lot of latitude in evaluating tests, quizzes and various assignments. To raise student grades for reporting purposes, some teachers give significantly more points for home projects than for tests which demonstrate a real level of knowledge. Some teachers with low-level math skills evaluate various assignments on different scales and incorrectly calculate final grades.

Although the grading system has been used for more than a hundred years, schools continue experimenting with various ways of grading. As in the case with curricula, school districts and/or schools seem to be experimenting with grades just to attract public attention.

Information for Reflection

Are AP exams that give potential university credits a useful initiative? The answer depends on how we interpret "usefulness." Without doubt, AP courses enrich students' knowledge. Schools are interested in promoting these courses, since this increases the school's rating. Moreover, students attending these courses increase their cumulative GPA. The obvious inference is in favor of these courses. However, it's very important who teaches them and how the students' knowledge is evaluated. The proliferation of AP courses was fueled by government subsidies and by the College Board's aggressive promotion, which resulted in a tripling of the program since 1990 alone; more than 30 courses are offered now. Many schools have no teachers who are able to teach AP courses. But the desire overweighs the ability and, for example, a teacher of history teaches the course on macro economics. This occurs as a result of bureaucratic zeal. In such cases, students are taught to the future test; they learn the principal statements by heart, without understanding, and their knowledge is far below the expected level. This is the main reason why many universities don't trust the quality of knowledge determined by AP exams, which are checked mostly by school teachers rather than college professors.

There are two types of students who take AP courses. One set are ambitious students who have established high goals, who want to succeed and contribute to the society. Others are students with more moderate goals who want to finish college as soon as possible, and they use the opportunity to get a college credit for free by taking AP courses.

"College" in America can mean a lot of different things, from some of the highest quality private institutions to what are essentially local trade schools. Some of them are hunting for students; other have too many applications and, as a result, a rigorous admission policy. Most such colleges don't get credits based on AP exams. Colleges also don't want to lose the money which comes to the College Board and the Educational Testing Service which conducts AP tests.

In addition, it is possible to assume that a more liberal testing policy (diminished test requirements) would attract more students to take AP exams, i.e., it would bring more money to the College Board and the Educational Testing Service. Even assuming that the best students deserve the college credit and, as a result, they shorten their study at a college and, hence, pay less money for their higher education, this indirectly increases the financial burden on other students.

Students should take the AP courses to demonstrate their high level knowledge rather than to attempt to earn university credits. These credits should be earned at colleges and the level of students' knowledge should be evaluated by college professors.

THE TRUTH OF THE TEST

The *No Child Left Behind Act* is an attempt to establish national education standards. In recent years, standardized multiple-choice tests have become the main performance criteria of students and schools and the whole education system. Tests are used to assess the effectiveness of both teaching and learning.

In their enthusiasm many accountability reformers made outrageous claims about how effective the *No Child Left Behind Act* would be, but in hindsight we know that NCLB has had mixed results. In many cases there were other factors that impacted how well students performed on these standardized tests. But at least the tests provided the Department of Education with scores in rudimentary subjects so that policy makers and educators could see which schools were doing better than others and then try to determine why.

This was the first time in American history that students in all fifty states had taken tests on reading and math from the same grade levels. The tests were revealing because they showed how different grade levels in different regions performed, how urban schools fared against rural, minority versus white, English speaking versus non English speaking, as well as many other variables. More importantly, the results of these tests by grade level have been made available to parents, teachers, students, and the public — reformers, politicians — and they have been published on the Internet for everyone to see. For the first time, everyone had the same information, was able to engage in a more equitable debate process, and make more informed decisions about how to respond to the results of tests by grade level.

The states independently developed and adopted standards for public school students and tests to measure student performance. The tests measure a student's performance against the state content standards, which outline what all students should know and be able to do. The contents and format of standardized tests determine the shape of curriculum and the style of teaching. Although these tests measure only a limited range of knowledge and skills, nevertheless, if they are well designed they can be a useful and objective measure of basic student achievement in the most important subjects. Unfortunately, mediocre education standards set by some states mislead the government, as well as their own residents, about student performance. These states regularly inflate student achievement by setting low standards and giving easy tests.

As part of standards-based educational reform efforts, some states require students to achieve passing scores on standardized exams in order to obtain a high school diploma. Still many states are struggling with the design of their examination systems, debating such questions as which subjects should be tested, what should be the minimum passing scores. In 1980, eleven states set the minimum passing scores on their standard tests to receive the diploma. By 1997, seventeen states enforced such a requirement (National Center for Education Statistics, 1999, Table 155). Now more and more states (Alabama, Alaska, California, Delaware, Florida, Georgia, Hawaii, Indiana, Louisiana, Massachusetts, Maryland, Minnesota, Mississippi, Nevada, New Jersey, New Mexico, New York, North Carolina, Ohio, South Carolina, Tennessee, Texas, Utah, and Virginia) have laws authorizing high school graduation exams. Most of these states require students to pass tests to graduate, others plan to implement this requirement in the future. However, each state develops its own exams based on state curriculum standards, so the test requirements and student pass rates vary among states, i.e., the standards differ notably from state to state. Moreover, the conditions for receiving a high school diploma based on these tests are also different. For example, the Maryland High School Assessment (HSA) is a graduation requirement beginning with the graduating class of 2009, i.e., in order to earn a Maryland High School Diploma students are required to earn a satisfactory score on the HSA, which, in addition to the high school testing requirements of the *No Child Left Behind Act* based on tests in algebra/data analysis and English, include also tests in biology and government. The graduation requirement is accompanied with specifications that look too tangled and questionable. The passing scores are calculated with "high accuracy": algebra/data analysis (412), English (396), biology (400), and government (394). As an option, a student can earn passing scores on state-approved substitute tests and substitute one or more of those scores for passing scores on the HSA or earn at least the minimum score on each HSA (algebra/data analysis (402), English (386), biology (391), and government (387)) and earn a combined score of 1602. As explained by the Maryland board of education, "This combined-score option benefits students because it allows higher performance on one test to offset lower performance on another test." It is reasonable instead of a HSA's test to take into account a similar or more complicated test. But how are these calculations linked with the existing grading system? All these minimum and passing scores look fuzzy and are based on fuzzy mathematics.

As mentioned above, some states try to embellish their educational achievement, so that the results of state assessment tests cannot serve a reliable estimate of the quality of education in the US. Nevertheless, despite a certain weakness of the tests, their implementation was a move in the right direction and the source of reliable statistics concerning educational progress. The issue for discussion remained whether measures of academic learning, usually, tests scores, are broad enough indicators of what students have gained in school. It's impossible not to agree with those who believe that a standard test cannot be the only reliable estimate of a student's level of knowledge of a certain subject. The final assessment should take into account (in accordance with the existing grading practice) the student's grades in this subject as well. Nevertheless, in no way this fact belittles the importance of the tests.

Since *A Nation At Risk* was written, there have been hundreds, maybe thousands of reports written about the importance of standards for achievement in public education. In an effort to impose higher standards and force students to take more difficult class work many colleges raised admission standards. Any student wanting to go to these schools would have to show that they had achieved what the Commission called "authentic accomplishment."

The SAT and ACT tests, given to high school juniors who plan to attend college to test their level of knowledge, do a better job of measuring the level of knowledge of school graduates than state assessments do. Colleges use the ACT and SAT tests to compensate for the substantial imbalances in curricula and assessments among US secondary schools; SAT/ACT scores are used, in addition to the secondary school records, to evaluate students applying to colleges/universities. The ACT is more widely used in the Midwestern and Southern states, while the SAT is more popular in the Northeastern and Mid-Atlantic states; recently, the ACT has been becoming more popular in the Western states. The SAT is administered by the College Board and is developed, published, and scored by the Educational Testing Service. The ACT test was developed by the American College Testing Program, Inc., now known as ACT, Inc.

The SAT test was first introduced in 1901, when it was known as the Scholastic Achievement Test. As if they were ashamed to include the word *achievement* in the name of the test, in 1941, the College Board changed it to the Scholastic Aptitude Test; the word *aptitude* suggests it evaluates the student's ability, i.e., the student's potential. In 1990, the name was changed again; this time to the more modest sounding Scholastic Assessment Test. In 1994, the name was changed to simply SAT (with the letters not standing for anything). The test has been modified and improved over the years. The last modification was in 2005. The new SAT (known as the SAT Reasoning Test) was first offered on March 12, 2005, with possible scores from 600 to 2400 combining test results from three 800-point sections (math, critical reading, and writing), along with other subsections scored separately.

Designed in the 1950s, the ACT test consists of four sections (math, English, reading, and science) and an optional essay part; scores on the ACT test range from 1 to 36. Some states have used the ACT to assess the performance of schools, and require all high school students to take the ACT, regardless of whether they are college bound. According to ACT, Inc., Colorado and Illinois incorporated the ACT as part of their mandatory testing program in 2001. Michigan has required the ACT since 2007, and Wyoming and Kentucky have required all high school juniors to take the ACT since 2008.

In contrast to the SAT, the ACT test contains an additional skill area — science. It's hard to understand why science has not been included in the SAT, which is administered by the College Board, if some colleges and universities, preferring the ACT test, believe that the level of students' knowledge in science is an important factor determining their ability to study at a college/university. The ACT test appeared as a new educational market product, and its developers demonstrated excellent marketing skills. However, the existence of two similar tests with absolutely different score scales creates additional difficulties putting order in the educational jungle.

Tests are very useful. However, machine-scored tests, which limit the feedback from students and variation of responses, don't take into account a student's possible nervousness and a need sometimes to clarify certain questions; thus they are not 100% reliable estimates of a student's knowledge. Much could be done to make the computerized tests more effective.

As indicated earlier, to apply to college or university, high school juniors should take the SAT or ACT tests, and their score is an important factor in determining which colleges and universities might accept them. Many guides have been published that teach how to prepare oneself for these tests. They contain examples from previous tests and so-called math and grammar refreshers, which in a concise form present the material needed for students to get a good score. Formally, this is the level of knowledge students ought to be receiving at school. That is why the term *refresher* is used. However, being well aware that most American schools do not provide such knowledge, the guide's authors offer "tools" to help students learn how to think logically and figure things out better and faster, especially in regard to math and verbal problems. Apparently, after 12 years of studying, many of those who want to continue their education face the fact that their schools have not prepared them well, and it is difficult to learn how to think logically in just a few months if one has not done it in 12 years. Moreover, some of the materials are absolutely new to many students because their schools' curricula ignored these topics. For example, *Gruber's Complete SAT*

Guide (Gary R. Gruber, Sourcebooks, Inc., Naperville, Illinois, 2008) contains an excellent description of English grammar, concentrating on frequently-used constructions. This part of the guide could serve as an English language textbook for many schools. Unfortunately, students attending, for example, schools in Maryland, have no textbook on the English language at all, and they are unfamiliar even with many of the terms used to discuss grammar. Try complaining that students can hardly be expected to write brilliant essays without the school providing the basics of English grammar. Chances are, the English department is headed by someone whose qualifications are unrelated — a lawyer, in one case I know. We cannot expect progress in schools that lack high level professionals, in appropriate positions, and in schools where bureaucratic habits and indifference take the place of devotion to the chosen profession.

Chapter 7. Climbing To the Top

> "It is not the mountain we conquer but ourselves." - Sir Edmund Hillary

Decision makers regarding school curricula and textbooks include elected officials, distributed across federal, state, and local levels, state bureaucrats, school boards, textbook committees, parents, and individual classroom teachers. The federal government is barred from establishing national curriculum standards, since there exists no such law. Education standards and goals proposed by the federal government are not legally enforceable. In reality, what students are learning at school relative to these standards is determined by states and school districts.

In response to the call for higher standards, the content of classes was forced to become more rigorous so that students in public schools could score higher and compete with children attending private school. These private school students receive college preparatory classes as part of the normal curriculum so they tend to fare better on standardized tests and the ACT/SAT tests in general. States worked hard to create curricula, tests and purchase textbooks that complemented content standards, and teaching colleges tried to train teachers how to develop lesson plans that taught important subjects without "teaching to the test." Still these efforts haven't brought the expected results.

CURRICULA AND EDUCATION STANDARDS

When a captain plots a course for sailing at sea there are different tools that he uses to piece together the navigation route. Learning methods, teaching methods, and curriculum design are all important parts of the route that students must take to reach their final destination — a good education. In *A Nation At Risk* many schools' curricula were criticized for offering easy courses that didn't challenge students and most at fault were the classes offered at the high school level. It was found that high schools that performed the lowest often offered what they referred to as a "curricular smorgasbord". This *smorgasbord* was made up of classes with important sounding names that in reality didn't offer meaningful, comprehensive, or useful instruction in the fundamentals. The smorgasbord classes contributed nothing to a formal education or preparing students for college. These classes were, of course, popular with students but did nothing to improve math, science, reading, and writing comprehension and, as a result, more and more high schools and colleges have been forced to offer remedial classes in the basics.

Preparation of curricula is linked directly with the established education standards, educational requirements to students of various grades. A curriculum, the aggregate of courses of study given in a school, can be also defined as a presentation of educational requirements to students. As indicated earlier, in 1768, Benjamin Rush outlined the curriculum suitable to American democracy. A college-oriented high school curriculum was recommended in 1892 by the Committee on Secondary Social Studies, often called the Committee of Ten, appointed at the meeting of the National Educational Association. However, specific features of the US education system, distinguishing it from the education systems of many other countries, allow many recommendations, including the mentioned curricula, to remain only recommendations, and states are not obliged to follow them.

American students benefit from the regular evaluation of their level of knowledge, based on which they are placed in different groups. They benefit from this procedure because relatively uniform groups allow students to learn more. In a case of uniform groups, the level of material isn't boring for advanced students and, vise versa, it isn't difficult for weak students, as it would happen if students of the same grade with different ability and/or level of knowledge are placed in the same classroom.

In the United States, students (mostly in high schools) can choose courses they prefer to attend. This corresponds to the merit of freedom the country was based on. Generally, high school students choose among a broad variety of classes. Curricula vary widely in quality and rigorousness. Usually, the following basic courses are required to receive a high school diploma: mathematics (usually three years minimum, including algebra, geometry, algebra II, and/or pre-calculus/trigonometry); English (four years); social studies (usually three years, including history, government, and economics courses, always including American history); science (usually three years minimum, including biology, chemistry, physics); physical education (at least one year).

Information for Reflection

Since ancient times human beings have tried to understand natural phenomena, and the study of "physics" began when people began studying their surroundings. Physics is considered a body of knowledge concerning the laws of nature and the universe which are widely used in practice. Webster's Dictionary defines physics as "the science that deals with matter, energy, motion, and force." The Oxford Dictionary of Current English defines physics as "the group of sciences dealing with matter and energy (e.g., heat, light, sound) but excluding chemistry and biology." As happens with many scientific definitions, the above are not perfect; but they indicate the wide and important areas embraced by physics. Special physical theories form separate scientific disciplines (astronomy, mechanics, optics, electricity and magnetism, thermodynamics, quantum mechanics, geophysics, etc.). They are based on the results of the 18th, 19th and early 20th century physics.

Should American students be familiar with basic physics? Should physics be considered as a basic subject? Unfortunately, in American schools it's embedded in a more general term, "science." There is only a one year short course of physics, which students can ignore, i.e., a student can graduate from high school without learning basic physics at all. Science is also taught in middle schools. However, this course is a hodge-podge of incoherent facts from anatomy, astronomy, geology, etc. Students cannot get any solid knowledge from such a course. Moreover, it is doubtful that a teacher knows so many different subjects well enough to teach them properly. Isn't it better to teach basic physical laws instead of general science course? Physics is in everything around us. We use physical concepts in almost everything we do. Physics is so important that it is considered to be the basis for other sciences. Living in a world dominated by the influence of science and technology, we cannot allow our young generation to ignore this subject.

Many states include in the core subjects a health course, in which students learn about anatomy, nutrition, first aid (in some states, sexuality and birth control are also included); anti-drug use programs are also usually a part of health courses. Foreign language (mostly French, German, and Spanish; Chinese, Latin, Greek, Russian, and Japanese are less common) and some form of art education are also a mandatory part of the curriculum in some schools. In addition, many high schools offer a wide variety of elective courses, although the availability of such courses depends upon each particular school's financial resources and desired curriculum emphases. Among them are: journalism, computers (word processing, programming); performing arts (drama, music, theater, band, chorus, orchestra, dance, television production); visual arts (drawing, painting, sculpture, photography, film); technology education (woodworking, metalworking, automobile repair, robotics); athletics (cross country, football, baseball, basketball, track and field, tennis, swimming, gymnastics, water polo, soccer, wrestling); and career-themed programs (radio production, video production; printing, graphics, and electronic media; accounting, financial planning, medical careers science; marketing, child development, electronics, cosmetology science, etc.).

Many high schools provide Honors, Advanced-level, Advanced Placement and International Baccalaureate courses. These are special courses for highly able and potentially high-achieving students. AP or IB courses are usually taken either as a replacement for a typical required course (e.g., taking AP US History as a replacement for standard US History), a continuation of a subject (e.g., taking AP Biology after completing Biology) or a completely new field of study (e.g., AP Statistics, or AP Computer Programming). Most post-secondary institutions take AP or IB exam results into consideration in the admissions process. As mentioned earlier, since AP and IB courses are intended to be the equivalent of the first year of college courses, some colleges and universities may count credits obtained at school that enables students to graduate early; but more prestigious universities don't give any credits and use the examinations results for placement purposes only.

The system of choice makes the US school educational system similar to the system of *credits* of colleges and universities. This creates certain difficulties in preparing the curriculum. The more courses included, the more experts are needed to prepare the detailed description of these courses. A curriculum without a detailed description of course components and indication of a textbook that covers this course is worthless. Too many courses offered in curricula require additional teachers able to teach these courses.

High School Course Bulletin 2006-2007 of the Montgomery County Public Schools (MCPS) of Maryland offers "several hundred interesting and rewarding courses that will help students for the demands of the postsecondary world of college and careers." Of course, this number cannot impress taking into account that by 1861 the Massachusetts secondary schools offered as many as 73 subjects. However, the middle of the 19th century was a period of knowledge explosion, discoveries in physics and biology, the industrial boom, a period of first steps in public education accompanied by various experiments. Many subjects taught at that time look obsolete now. The rise of information technology and computer science requires new school courses. Nevertheless, it's difficult to imagine that the schools have appropriate teachers to teach "several hundred" courses. In reality, some teachers are obliged to teach absolutely unrelated courses (e.g., physical education and social studies /history). Moreover, some courses exist only on paper; there are no teachers to teach or enough students willing to take them.

A reasonable question is: why are so many courses offered when it's known that American students lack necessary knowledge in the basic subjects — English, mathematics, and science? The response inevitably comes to mind — the existing local educational bureaucracy needs all this to demonstrate their "creative work." To keep their jobs, members of boards, superintendents and other administrators prepare rosy reports advertising their achievements. The MCPS Spring 2007 *Annual Report to the Community* "provides a glimpse of many amazing things going on inside ... 199 schools." It states in its Middle Schools section that "many MCPS students can compete with the brightest students from anywhere in the world." Unfortunately, the report doesn't say that MCPS students are not taught properly English grammar; they don't know even the meaning of Present, Past and Future Indefinite, Present, Past and Future Perfect, Gerund, Participle and many other grammar terms. The report doesn't say that high school teachers of mathematics are not satisfied with the level of knowledge in algebra obtained in the middle schools. Instead of adding elements of abstract algebra in the study of algebra in middle schools, which is empathized in the MCPS report, maybe it would be better to spend more time on traditional algebra, which develops abstract thinking and is the weakest place of students, so that universities are forced to teach it again. If a first year university student, taking the algebra course, presents the answer of the problem "Write ½ as a decimal" as 0.49999, this is a shame for schools the student attended and all educational bureaucracy of the corresponding state. This is an example from life showing that the pursuit for new courses, to impress higher authorities, at the expense of basic courses, usually hurts students.

The Department of Education restricts its participation in the educational process by formulating only guidelines of education policy. As we indicated earlier, curricula are the main concern of state departments of education and school districts. That is why they are different. That is why they include subjects which are sometimes more attractive to media rather than to students. Of course, this relates mostly to the so-called optional courses. As to the basic courses, it looks like there is a mutual agreement and understanding between educators concerning what material they should cover. However, the number of quarters the courses to be taught and the actual material still differ at schools of various states. Even in a case of the same courses of a curriculum, their realization is different; as a result, the students' level of knowledge is different. Many elective courses are questionable. Is it important for students to spend a quarter learning how to cook? Should art class, which requires a certain talent from participants, be taught? Maybe the time taken to teach these and similar classes would be better spent on mathematics and/or science?! Every extra item on a curriculum means extra money from the state budget and, as a result, higher taxes.

It's unlikely to find a private school that offers several hundred of different courses because the main concern of its administration is the quality of education (rather than quantity of courses) and costs. Public schools' educators are ready to spend lavishly public money. In league with politicians they try to persuade the public of the necessity of increasing funding to enhance the level of education. The relationship between educators of different states reminds the relationship between actors: everybody considers himself/herself great and better than others. To prove this, they compete with one another inventing new courses (e.g., cooking, sexual education) and don't care about the public reaction. Questionable courses continue to be a part of curricula at the expense of more important courses. Now more and more American schools offer special college-oriented courses for gifted students. The curricula for such courses and reasonable optional courses are a concern of these schools and corresponding school districts; everybody should agree with this. However, it's impossible to agree that the curricula of the basic subjects are in hands of states and/or districts.

Information for Reflection

The High School Course Bulletin *of the Montgomery County Public Schools of Maryland is more than 100 pages long. Mathematics courses fill three pages, English/English Language Arts take four pages, and science courses occupy five pages, whereas the Arts (dance, music, theater, visual arts) and Career-themed programs take six and thirty-three pages, respectively. The bulletin's contents look very impressive. Many college and art school courses have migrated to the bulletin; its Career-themed program section is prepared in tune with the federal educational directive that schooling must go hand in hand with practice. Educational bureaucracy knows how to make an impression.*

However, it's unclear how schools can find qualified teachers for very specific courses if there are still teacher shortages in high need subjects. The specific courses are useless if they are not taught properly. Moreover, copying special college courses with a certain simplification, taking into account the high school level of knowledge, is not effective. It's unlikely that such courses can gather many students. The bulletin contains such courses as carpentry, masonry, plumbing, cabinetmaking, cosmetology, introductory dramatics, stage design, ceramics/sculpture, painting, printing, professional restaurant management etc. If they are introduced to meet the requirements of the School-to-Work Opportunities Act, it's appropriate to ask whether they prepare "youth for high skills high wage carriers," whether these are the most important 21st century skills students need to acquire.

Can Americans allow themselves such luxury as financing the questionable or simply unnecessary courses, when they still have no progress in teaching the core subjects, while their property taxes are skyrocketing? Creating many courses does not mean to improve education. What is good for reporting purposes is not necessarily efficient in practice.

NECESSITY OF TEXTBOOK EXAMINATION

The educational goals embedded in curricula cannot be realized without appropriate textbooks. American textbooks look wonderful and such publishing companies as McGraw-Hill, Addison Wesley, Prentice Hall, McDougal Littell, Saxon Publishers, Seymour Publications, Holt, Rinehart and Winston, etc., deserve credits for that. The books have large fonts, so that it's easy to read them. The most important parts are emphasized, colored, and shaded, so that students can catch easier main ideas, formulations and procedures. The books contain many examples; their illustrations are informative. Students love how the books look. Maybe they shouldn't be so heavy; some students are bent under the weight of their backpacks. However, a book, especially a textbook, is judged not only by how it looks; its contents are the most important factor. To be maximally effective a textbook should be in tune with a curriculum. More precisely, its contents should correspond to the course specifications. The absence of the same curriculum and the detailed corresponding instructions even for the basic subjects results in several textbooks with slightly different contents that don't satisfy all schools. Unlike college textbooks, textbooks prepared for schools are not sold in an open marketplace. Their destiny is in hands of small groups that have made textbooks their business. Their distribution is close to a government procurement process, they are almost never reviewed by expert scholars. There exist only two small organizations (the Textbook League in California and American Textbook Council in New York) that review textbooks and other educational materials, and the decision whether to buy a textbook is limited to a relatively few state and local education officials. Two big states, Texas and California, account for a double digit percentage of the national textbook market, and publishers are oriented foremost towards satisfying the requirements of the education departments of these states. Not infrequently, the school districts produce additional learning materials. If a textbook contains too much "unnecessary" material or doesn't contain any needed material, students lose trust in such a book as a source of knowledge. It's ridiculous but it's a fact that in the world's richest country many schools are still unable to provide each student with all the necessary textbooks. True, some courses (e.g., science in middle school), creatures of local educators, are designed so badly, composed from elements of various scientific areas, that it's impossible to include such material logically in one book. But the lack of an English grammar textbook cannot be excused, and it isn't a surprise that many students don't use English grammar properly.

Information for Reflection

After World War II, the Soviet Union experienced shortages of food and necessary consumer goods; living conditions in the country were awful. However, at the beginning of a new school year, each student always received textbooks for every subject in accordance with the well-designed curriculum. Unfortunately, American students are not supplied with necessary textbooks, especially for such important subjects as English and Science.

Professional standards for teaching basic courses established by the corresponding professional organizations and the recommended textbooks should be discussed, modified, if necessary, and accepted to use in practice. The main problem of their practical realization is that there exist many educational organizations, supported by local school boards, which criticize one another and claim their leadership role. For example, the NCTM professional standards for teaching mathematics, supported by many math teachers and educators, were criticized in the report by *Mathematically Correct*, an organization founded in Southern California in 1995 by parents concerned about the weakness of mathematical programs available to students in California. This organization raised strong objections to the standards, curriculum materials and textbooks that focused on conceptual and skill development over rote memorization. The report was supported by Education Connection of Texas, a non-profit organization formed in 1998 for the purpose of providing information to the public about primary and secondary education, which conducts and publishes the research on textbooks, curricula, instructional practices and testing related to education. Stating that still "it is difficult for parents and educators to evaluate the merits of particular mathematics programs ... the sheer quantity of textbooks available leaves many parents, teachers, schools and districts wondering which books best address their needs" the report contains reviews of some of the major programs for grades 2, 5 and 7, and reviews of several mathematical textbooks. The proponents and opponents of the NCTM mathematical standards (professors of mathematics, board members, etc.) started the math war. Both sides used their rhetoric well. They spoke of higher-order thinking, conceptual understanding, the need of describing the most significant mathematical concepts and skills at each grade level and identifying important connections to other topics. Each side tried to prove eloquently that it knew better how to develop mathematical standards and curricula. Unfortunately, the Department of Education served the role of a passive arbiter pursuing the only goal — to stop the war. The words such as "a mile wide and an inch deep" used in this war concerning the math curriculum became popular and were applied by educators when criticizing other curricula. As mentioned earlier, in 2000, NCTM released the updated *Principles and Standards for School Mathematics*. However, the 2003 PISA report shows that the hot mathematical disputes didn't produce the expected results. The above mentioned example "Write ½ as a decimal" and the solution given by a first year university student show that the development of conceptual understanding is the most important part of educational process. Curricula and textbooks, especially for middle schools, must develop conceptual understanding which, at a certain degree, is undermined by computers packed with various programs that can solve immediately various problems. Instead of thinking and writing an obvious answer, the mentioned student used a low accuracy calculator and rewrote what was shown on its screen.

There is nothing wrong in hot discussions between NCTM and the opponents of the proposed mathematical standards. Concepts of teaching and learning were widely discussed in the past. The so-called progressive theories challenged the traditional ones, modern and conservative ideas were tested in practice. Battles over what to put in history, sociology and economics books have taken place for years in the states where state boards must adopt textbooks. The curriculum standards for these courses, reviewed every decade, serve as a template for textbook publishers. The conservative state board members want students to study the Judeo-Christian influences of the nation's Founding Fathers, the decline in value of the US dollar, including the abandonment of the gold standard and free-market economic theory, whereas its liberal members insist of including in the program such concepts as the separation of church and state and the secular nature of the American Revolution. Maybe it is better to include the views of both sides. Schools should educate rather than indoctrinate students. Healthy discussions are more useful than battles, and they are urgently needed for the basic subjects. It isn't excusable that the country with the best in the world scientific potential is unable to develop curricula, instructions, and textbooks that would allow its students to demonstrate that they are the best.

Information for Reflection

In his book Common Sense *(Glenn Beck, Mercury Radio Arts/Threshold Editions, New York, 2009, p.90) Glenn Beck states that "...we are losing the next generation to an education system that has fallen prey to political patronage and the Progressive agenda. History, reading, writing, and math are secondary to the incessant indoctrination of our kids to climate change, the evils of capitalism, and the benefit of big government. That works as a general anesthesia, numbing our children and rending them defenseless to the lessons and ideas that we work so hard to inoculate them from in our own homes. Given the importance of education in shaping the future of America, it's not surprising that it has been a main target of Progressive movement agenda."*

To be fair, the above statement is extreme and is not supported by facts. Progressivism as a political movement was a platform of the Progressive Party created by a split in the Republican Party in 1912. Education did not figure in its platform. Only in 1948 Henry Wallace, the Progressive Party candidate in the 1948 presidential election, promised to increase spending on education. Progressivism focused on a wide range of economic, political, social, and moral reforms. Some of them were useful and the members of this movement deserve credit for their implementation. As to the Progressive Party, it faded and many of its members returned to or joined ranks of both major political parties, Democrat and Republican. But the progressive movement and its ideas of social justice revived with a new strength in the last third of the 20th century and the label "progressive" passed on to Democrats who favor an increased government control and spending. The irony is that Progressive reformers' initial intention to eliminate corruption in government resulted in a larger government and an increased corruption. Glenn Beck is right when he goes against useless spending: "For too long we've believed the idea sold by politicians and bureaucrats that money is the answer to the problems with our education system. It's not — the answer is in standing against the Progressive policies that have led us to this destruction." But he is wrong in blaming Progressive reformers for the vices of the American education system. Although the term "progressivism" is vague, and schools indoctrinated in "climate change, the evils of capitalism, and the benefit of big government" can be considered as a part of the Progressive agenda, such schools are too few in number to consider them seriously. These schools might be under the influence of radical proponents of the so-called progressive education advocated by John Dewey (1859–1952), the most influential theorist of progressive ideas of education. Glenn Beck is right concerning such radical progressives who don't want learning to be from teachers to students, they want it to be based on the children's own experience and feelings...[and] want to develop a structure where children were 'equal participants' with their teachers in a classroom community."

Whether to enter the postsecondary world of college or university is up to the student. Students choose colleges or universities based on their desire to work in a certain field, to be experts in some area in the future.

Formally, the state is required to provide the opportunity for a sound basic education, but not more than the opportunity. Nevertheless, the United States government does strive to provide all the necessary resources for children to get an education that corresponds to the requirements of the 21st century, and it has the right to demand students to acquire at least the established nominal needed level of knowledge at every step of the education process. For that to happen, educators must formulate precisely the requirements for this level of knowledge, develop curricula with a detailed specification as to what should be taught and how, and choose appropriate textbooks for the basic courses of all middle and high school grade-levels. The absence of an appropriate textbook is not a problem. The intellectual potential of the country is huge, so that any book can be written in a short period of time. The real problem is that the nominal needed level of knowledge has not been established precisely for the whole country, and separate states and school districts interpret it differently trying to adjust it to their local conditions. Without a curriculum and detailed instructions for basic courses that meet the needed requirements and are accepted all across the country, the creation of such textbooks is impossible.

The national hesitation to involve the federal government in school practices and curricula makes the state governments responsible for any progress in education. It has been amply demonstrated that if we leave control of schools to the local and state level, we cannot ensure noticeable progress. Education at the elementary, junior- and high-school levels must meet requirements including the maintenance and improvement of nationwide education standards, guaranteeing of equal opportunities for education, and the provision of appropriate educational content.

The Department of Education should establish standards for curricula designed for use at elementary, middle and high schools and examine textbooks in consideration of their important role as the primary teaching materials. Although the authoring and compilation of textbooks is the purview of private-sector publishers, the appropriateness of textbooks, and their suitability for inclusion in school curricula, should be determined by government examination. Textbooks should be examined every four years for each school type/year level category. Without well-designed curricula and appropriate textbooks, progress is inconceivable.

Chapter 8. Teach the Teacher

> "Most teachers have little control over school policy or curriculum or choice of texts or special placement of students, but most have a great deal of autonomy inside the classroom. To a degree shared by only a few other occupations, such as police work, public education rests precariously on the skill and virtue of the people at the bottom of the institutional pyramid." - Tracy Kidder

In *A Nation at Risk* it was reported that many teachers didn't possess the necessary subject knowledge of teaching skills to be qualified to teach. But little if any impetus existed then or now to address the issue of subject knowledge and teaching skills. Instead, educators and other reformers have spent more time looking at the theories behind teaching in a classroom. Congress, of course, weighed in and came up with the Highly Qualified Teacher provision that was part of *No Child Left Behind*. But NCLB missed the mark and focused on getting as many teachers as possible certified as Highly Qualified Teachers under the NCLB system. Once again subject knowledge was ignored in favor of window dressing certifications that in the long run have done nothing to improve teacher performance, effectiveness, or subject knowledge.

Tied to teacher performance and training is the question of compensation. In most industries salaries, promotions, etc. are linked to performance and merit is what determines how someone moves up the ranks. For many years reformers have attempted to institute merit pay for teachers, but the powerful teachers' union has successfully lobbied Congress and fought this issue along with longer school days and school years. There are education administrators who struggle to implement evaluation systems for teachers so that poor ones can be remediated or removed and good ones can be rewarded and recognized for their work. Unfortunately, in many cases the hands of these administrators are tied by various bureaucratic rules and instructions, which interfere with a creative educational process and suppress initiative of good teachers.

TEACHERS' QUALIFICATION

The implementation of graduation tests, that reflects growing public support of a standards-based school reform, is accompanied by severe criticism coming from the American Federation of Teachers. Its head Sandra Feldman believes that the tests were set up too fast. "If you don't put a curriculum into place and don't prepare teachers and just give the kids a test, you will get a backlash," Feldman said. In other words, the AFT is defending teachers in advance against accusations that they did not prepare students to pass the tests. The AFT's head knows very well that state organized tests are in full correspondence with existing curricula, so that there is no need to "prepare teachers" if they are properly qualified. The problem is in the teachers' qualification, which is an important factor determining the level of education in the United States.

As mentioned earlier, Elwood Cubberly compared teachers with factory workers transforming raw material, the students, into finished products. This eloquent if over-simplified comparison is still valid. The professional role of the teacher is multifaceted. First of all, the teacher should possess knowledge in given fields and the ability to transfer the knowledge to students. The teacher is also a decision maker, mentor, and coach. The teacher is responsible for motivating, encouraging, and advising students. Teachers must love their career in order to provide a warm, encouraging professional environment to the students. A popular teacher becomes a model for his/her students.

In the past, parents and teachers alike used to strive to cultivate high virtues and morals in children. However, large-scale industrialization, social changes, and a high tempo of everyday life in the 20th century leave parents little time or energy for their children. As a result, education for the younger generation doesn't necessary mean making them better human beings; it's focused mostly on enabling them to get better jobs. Students are preoccupied with dreams of higher social status. Morals and values have gradually been ousted from education. The students tend to consider their teachers as their servants rather than their mentors, and the teaching profession doesn't enjoy due respect in society. The status of schoolteachers is lower than that of doctors, lawyers, engineers, etc.; even lower than that of successful salesmen or marketers, whose profession doesn't require any education. The saying, "He who can, does. He who cannot, teaches," from George Bernard Shaw (1856–1950) in his play *Man and Superman* (Brentano's, New York, 1905), is still used today. As a rule, high professionalism is the best recipe for winning respect and even admiration. The lack of well-educated teachers has contributed to the decline of respect for this profession and this, in turn, has decreased supply of teachers who are really qualified to teach.

Many parents hold teachers responsible for poor performance of their children. They tend to believe that their children are geniuses and the school simply doesn't teach them well. To the extent that there is some truth there, the main problem is that many American teachers have not received a good education themselves in the subjects they teach, and teaching standards in many states were low. In addition, the absence of rigorous standards and testing made the process of teachers' training ineffective.

The creation of public systems was accompanied with the formation of special teacher training schools supported by states. The first public school that offered one year of training opened in 1839 in Massachusetts. Practice teaching usually included a review of the so-called common subjects (arithmetic and grammar), advanced subjects (algebra, geometry, moral philosophy, and natural history), and basics of teaching. State laws and regulations determined the qualifications for teaching. Later teachers received degrees in four-year colleges, getting knowledge both in specialized fields and in educational methods. In addition, they were required to get licenses that were usually issued by a subdivision of the state department of education or related organizations. State certificate requirements became more rigorous, so that teachers needed to have a bachelor's degree. In 1940s, a master's degree was required for most secondary and many elementary school teachers. Unfortunately, because of shortage of such teachers this requirement wasn't realized completely.

Modern teacher educational programs at the undergraduate level include content courses such as English and history, method courses, and practice training. Content courses prepare for general teaching or for teaching in specialized fields. Method courses include instructional theory and related materials. Practice teaching familiarizes future teachers with how to translate curriculum standards into simple workable classroom structures, including giving good instructions, and making classrooms more active, practical, collaborative, democratic, and cognitive, while simultaneously meeting high standards across subject areas and throughout the grades. Graduate schools offer courses in specialized academic fields.

Teachers must not only graduate from college or a university, they need to earn a certificate to teach at a public school. Certification presents an additional filtering procedure that helps schools select proper teachers, but many state laws related to teachers' certification are arbitrary. Often teachers are licensed simply because they have accumulated college credits. Moreover, states frequently revise their teacher certification/licensure rules and requirements; and there are various types of teacher certificates. Here, each state is given an opportunity to demonstrate its creativity. For example, Florida has two types of certificates: the Professional Certificate and the Temporary Certificate. Both certificates require at least a bachelor's degree. The first one is valid for five school years and renewable; the temporary one is valid only for three school years. Holders of the professional certificate should demonstrate mastery of general knowledge and subject area knowledge for a requested subject, combined with the mastery of professional preparation and education competence. Holders of the temporary certificate should demonstrate only mastery of subject area knowledge or earn a 2.5 GPA for a requested subject. California has two types of temporary certificates called Preliminary Credentials (the Multiple Subject Teaching Credential and the Single Subject Teaching Credential) that allow an individual to teach at an elementary (with the Multiple Subject Teaching Credential), middle and high school level (with the Single Subject Teaching Credential). Their holders can teach five years. To continue teaching beyond that, the Professional Clear Multiple or Single Subject Credential is needed. Virginia and Maryland have their own rules. And so on.

States issue more so-called resident teaching certificates, limited certificates, conditional certificates or emergency certificates for temporary positions when there aren't enough certified teachers to go around; these bypass state licensing requirements. The names vary in different states but their goal is the same — to fill vacant teacher positions and to bring new teachers in public school systems.

The procedure for receiving teaching certificates also varies from state to state. Many states require individuals to take special teacher preparation program and pass special tests. In Maryland, holders of the Advanced Professional Certificate should have a master's degree or minimum of 36 semester hours of post bachelor's degree course work and a master's degree, or a minimum of 36 semester hours of post-baccalaureate course work (which must include 21 semester hours of graduate credit), or obtain National Board of Professional Teaching Standards certification and earn a minimum of 12 semester hours of approved graduate course work. In Virginia, SAT test scores may be used as a substitute for the PRAXIS I test. Certification subjects usually include elementary education; middle level English, general science, mathematics, social science and integrated curriculum; secondary level English, social science, mathematics, journalism, speech, biology, chemistry, earth-space science, physics, computer science, special foreign languages, physical education, health, art, music and some others.

Most tests consist of multiple-choice questions and a written assignment. They cover scientific, mathematical, and technological areas, historical and social scientific awareness, communication and research skills, written analysis and expression to evaluate a candidate's knowledge and skills in the liberal arts and sciences, in teaching theory and practice, and in the content area of the candidate's field of certification.

The variety of testing requirements is so great as to give the appearance that state departments of education are simply trying to prove how "hard" they are working. The renewal of the certificates is accompanied by similar tangled requirements as to "precisely" what courses and how many additional hours should be taken (only state departments know how all this is determined). Certification for teachers certified in other states is also rather complicated and varies from state to state.

Should English, mathematics or physics be taught differently in California than in Texas or Maryland? Do Californians speak different English than, for example, Texans? Do mathematical expressions have different meanings in California than in Florida? Why should the requirements for teaching identical subjects and the corresponding testing procedures vary from state to state? It's difficult to understand why individuals who chose the profession of teacher and graduated from universities obtaining a degree in a certain field should pass additional tests to teach courses related to this field. Such severe testing, at least judging by the certification requirements, should have provided schools with excellent teachers. However, as we know, this has not happened. What is the point of such a complicated procedure if it doesn't bring the expected results? It isn't clear why persons with a PhD should need to be "certified." Schools need such professionals; but many people consider this procedure a form of humiliation, since formally they can teach at any university without any certification.

The state process of teacher certification or licensing is useful and necessary. However, it all depends on the standards established. Moreover, certificates should be given automatically to individuals with a PhD and a master's degree in the fields they are going to teach.

The complicated procedures concerning teaching certificates don't favor the recruitment and retention of a highly qualified teaching force. An ageing teacher population and rising ranks of students has increased the demand for teachers at a time when aspiring teachers find that this profession can be unduly stressful, is under-appreciated, and brings salaries that are low by comparison with those in other professions with comparable qualifications.

Maintaining the Status Quo

The quality of teaching is often considered the most critical component of education. Some states have established programs that reward outstanding teachers by providing salary increases, bonuses, and promotions. But others argue that schools don't objectively identify the best teachers, and the National Education Association is against such programs because they create conflicts between teachers. If earlier the schoolteachers' job wasn't protected and they could be fired, now public school teachers attain tenure after three–five years of work on one-year contracts. On the one hand, the future life stability makes this profession more attractive. On the other hand, tenure makes teachers less interested in improving their professional level. The renewal certificate procedure can help to evaluate a teacher's level and to stimulate its improvement, if necessary. However, the existing renewal procedures require mostly not more than attending some additional professional courses, so that in reality they don't present any danger to the teachers' permanent status.

The role of large teacher unions in maintaining the status quo in the lack of professional development of teachers has meant that many teachers may be certified but are not trained to teach their subject matter. To address this weakness and bring new blood into the ranks, programs were developed that encourage experts in subject matter, dedicated people who wanted to make a difference, or successful executives and entrepreneurs, to bypass the traditional certifications and become teachers. Some of the organizations, such as Certification of Teacher Excellence, the National Council on Teacher Quality, National Center for Alternative Certification, Teach for America, Troops-to-Teachers, and The New Teacher Project, contributed to these programs.

As much as finding solutions to teacher qualification and compensation is difficult, finding talented, successful administrators willing to tackle the dizzying array of responsibilities, public relations issues, budget shortfalls, public dissatisfaction, and low student performance is impossible. Despite protests to the contrary, more money needs to be spent on schools and the funds need to be allocated differently than in the past. Paying to keep and recruit excellent teachers and leaders won't be easy, but neither category will dig the country out of the current disaster if we continue to short-change talented people.

Bureaucracy in Classrooms

What is remarkable about bureaucrats is their creativity. However, as a rule, they are creative in a specific field. Bureaucrats don't invent new machines, devices, tools or scientific methods. They invent documents — numerous, mostly useless instructions and regulations. Educational bureaucracy is the most sophisticated and inventive, and it has an amazing instinct and ability of survival. Every governmental effort to improve education resulted in increasing ranks of educational bureaucracy devouring all additional financial resources injected in the education system.

Nobody denies the necessity of rules and regulations. Without them society cannot function. However, too many rules leave no room for people act productively. A huge staff of educational departments of states, districts, counties and other related organizations have invented an enormous number of rules and instructions applying to all possible and impossible situations.

The numerous educational instructions penetrate into schools like bacteria and infect teachers. Under the weight of various instructions, the teachers forget their main responsibility — transfer their knowledge to students and judge fairly their achievements. Some of them simply stop thinking because almost all their actions are predetermined by the existing rules and regulations.

Even judges in courts have certain freedoms when they make judgments. But not teachers. Instructions require teachers to "record grades for individual tasks/assessments with the highest degree of precision." Unfortunately, this rigorous rule doesn't specify what "the highest degree of precision" is. Some schools resolve the highest precision problem by indicating that any grade resulting in a decimal fraction of 0.5 or higher should be rounded to the next higher number. According to the rules of Maryland, "when using points or percentages, a teacher assigns a grade no lower than 50% to the task/assessment." A student can return the task/assessment with only one sentence and get 50% because the fact of returning with "something" demonstrates that a student tried. Only if a teacher decides that the student did not attempt to meet the basic requirements of the task/assessment, the teacher may assign a zero. The instructions determine that "work turned in after the due date and by the deadline may be lowered no more than one letter grade or 10% of the grade." Although in this case teachers are given a small gap, the indication of a lower grade means that any delay must be punished regardless the reason for this delay. Students who miss work in class due to an absence are permitted to make up the work in accordance with a special schedule for make-up assignments. There exist instructions indicating how many grades a student should receive per three-, six- or nine-week period and the range of grades depending upon the material. Often, such instructions, accompanied with the grading scale, are given to students and their parents to sign. It is not clear why their signatures are needed — as if students have other alternatives to choose.

A grading policy is designed to guide the teacher in the assessment of student performance. Although every educator understands that no numerical system is an absolute indicator of such performance, educational bureaucrats continue to excel in instructing teachers how to grade, in imposing more and more grading rules and instructions. Any deviation from the regulations must be approved in writing by high-ranking bureaucrats prior to implementation. In most school systems, 90% is an A and 60% is a passing grade. But in Fairfax County Public Schools, Virginia, the twelfth largest school system in the nation, students should score 94% to earn an A and 64% to pass. After a year of intense pressure from parents who have argued that this grading policy hurts students' chances for college admission or scholarships, the Fairfax County School Board decided to abandon a strict grading policy and to move toward a more commonly used grading scale. In the past, School Board members have defended the tough grading system as an asset to a school system that sets a high bar for success. However, the adoption of a more standard language does not necessary mean lowering standards. Teachers give points; they and only they determine who deserves an A or another grade.

Students are graded on quizzes, writing assignments and tests, homework, class participation and class work, which may include group work. Strict grading instructions in the existing grading systems transfer teachers into robots. A student told me about a young teacher who responded, "Tell me what I did wrong," when at the end of a quarter the student with an 89.4% asked what he should do to get an A. If a new generation of teachers acts in this way, Americans can abandon a hope in the future improvement of their education system.

Mechanical manipulation, without thought, with points cannot serve as a reliable estimate of a student's achievements. Learning is a dynamic process. Different students accumulate knowledge differently. Usually, students from rural areas with a slow flowing and quiet life think more slowly than students from the areas around big cities where life flows faster. At the beginning these students may have difficulties with understanding the material. The widespread procedure of adding points wouldn't allow them to get an A. However, history gives examples of such "slow thinking" students who were able to make significant contributions in various areas of science and technology. Their initial slowness is the way to penetrate deeply in the subject. I had a university student who got a C and a B for two tests. Although I always allowed students to retake the previous tests before the final one, which was comprehensive, this student didn't retake any test. But the final test, which contained two rather difficult optional problems, the student did without any mistake and was the only one who solved correctly all optional problems. How can I give this student a total B (based on the existing mechanical procedure of summation and even applying weighting coefficients) if she demonstrated the best knowledge of the subject? Schoolteachers are judges in the classroom. They have enough time to know each student and his/her abilities. Teachers must have more freedom in evaluating students' achievements. The school administration should allow students to retake previous tests at the end of every quarter to demonstrate their final level of knowledge and, what is most important, teachers should encourage students to do that — not for reporting purposes but because they are responsible for preparing the new highly-educated generation. Unfortunately, many teachers not only refuse students to retake tests but they don't return their assignments in time, so that students receive their final grades without fully understanding whether they got what they deserved. These teachers allow retakes only if for reporting purposes higher grades are needed. Such teachers act as sophisticated bureaucrats since they violate the existing rules to the advantage of themselves and the whole bureaucratic system, rather than that of the students.

Points are given for properly prepared homework; but many teachers check them selectively, without looking thoroughly, and not regularly. Points are given for class participation, although this process is controlled by teachers who choose the students to answer questions. Grading quizzes, tests, and assignments with points looks reasonable for the subjects belonging to so-called exact sciences — mathematics, physics, chemistry, etc. A correct or incorrect answer can be determined easily and any controversy can be resolved quickly. However, educational bureaucracy offers the same "rigorous" rules for all subjects, even for those where a teacher's subjective judgment determines the students' grades. The course of English language, which is one of the basic subjects, educational bureaucrats supply with additional instructions and forms "how to write" related to the grading. Figure 8.1 shows one of such forms. It is not clear whether this form is prepared for teachers to make no evaluation mistakes or for students to write well. Losing time on filling these forms teachers spend less time on reading attentively students' work. Such forms do no good even to negligent and/or not knowledgeable enough teachers who in hurry may encircle a wrong score in the first column. For example, a ninth grade teacher of Montgomery County, Maryland, evaluated a student's introductory statement related to the play *Antigone* by Sophocles, which he took from a research paper, as "flawed," and as a result (in accordance with Figure 8.1), the student erroneously received a low grade and the school administration dealt with the complaint. (Never mind the question of why a play by Sophocles was included in an English language course, which by definition should cover English grammar and literature of English-speaking countries.)

However, in Maryland and many other states, English grammar is not taught. Students graduate from high school without knowledge of sentence structure and grammatical terminology. Do bureaucrats ask themselves whether it is possible to have a deep understanding of English books or articles without knowing English grammar? Every cultured person should know his language's grammar, or at least be familiar with the terminology. It is impossible to construct sentences and express thoughts properly, and of course write persuasive essays, without knowing grammar. Instead of teaching grammar, bureaucrats make middle school students read Shakespeare's plays. Maybe they think that archaic English is easier to understand? Essays are the main target of the English course. There exists several pages of instructions how to write them, which repeat the same: essay prompt, introductory paragraph, lead, thesis statement, body paragraph 1, topic sentence, example 1, explanation of example, etc. All this can be presented in several phrases and written on a blackboard. But by creating forms, bureaucrats seem to emphasize the importance of the amount of instructions produced.

How to make notes is an important topic that was included recently in the English language course (the task "Note Cards") in some Maryland public schools. Unfortunately, neither school nor university students like to make notes. They prefer to have a written text before them while they are taught. The quality of education suffers from that. Some teachers and university professors simply read the textbooks before the students. In the example, the task was well-designed and placed on a website, where students could fill in the spaces allocated for notes. However, bureaucrats overexert even with this useful topic. The instructions required four or more quotes with bullets for each paragraph. But not all the paragraphs contained enough information for four notes and "smart" students wrote almost the same thing over and over to meet the requirement. Those who made good notes with three instead of four bullets were penalized for not following the instructions and lost one point for each missing bullet. Teachers were counting bullets to fill the evaluation form rather than attentively reading the notes.

Classroom bureaucracy pays more attention to the form rather than the contents of works. It kills students' initiative and their creativity, and punishes any insignificant misses. A student didn't underline a title, and a point is lost. A student wrote an extra sentence, and several points are lost. A student wrote an additional paragraph to get a high A, but as a result he got a B. It looks like, in contrast to technical robots which become smarter with the development of artificial intellect programs, bureaucrats lose their ability to use their own, not artificial, intellect to properly evaluate students' achievements.

When various meticulous instructions only blur the whole picture, it is easier to express our opinion (and in many situations we act in this way) by words: excellent, good, satisfactory, and unsatisfactory or excellent, good, fair, and poor. Their codes can be, for example, 5, 4, 3, and 2; or 4, 3, 2, and 1; or A, B, C, and D. The simpler the evaluation system, the less chance one has of making crude mistakes. It is known that, for complex processes with multiple interconnected factors which are difficult to analyze, simplistic models work better than more complicated ones. The more professional teachers are, the more we should trust their judgment and not overload them with bureaucratic instructions. Free from burdensome grading instructions, the teachers are able to evaluate students' achievements better. Of course, all teachers must provide their students with a written grading policy. But it should be very simple and understandable. Moreover, it should describe globally all types of assessments without unnecessary details how each test will be evaluated. The grading policy shouldn't address such areas as class attendance, class participation, class notes or working with others. It must relate directly to a student's progress, a student's achievement, to the level of knowledge a student reaches during the grading period.

While there are many excellent teachers who sincerely care about their students and who are willing to change things to benefit the students, there are also many who fall into the system and refuse to do anything useful, to adjust to the needs of students and meet new requirements. These teachers adore bureaucracy, which helps them to survive, and they are a real brake on progress in education. Unfortunately, the current public school system is unresponsive and is answerable virtually to no one. Skillful bureaucrats block any sober proposals to improve the process. Tons of papers are spent on unnecessary instructions. The money saved by sweeping out of classrooms thoughtless grading forms and related instructions can be spent to provide each student with an English grammar textbook, which is more important than all this bureaucratic nonsense.

Total Points _____ /50

Score	Criteria for Success
5	This response demonstrates consistent mastery, although it may have minor errors. This response • effectively states and develops a claim, provides strong insights, and uses well-chosen detail to achieve its purpose. • is well organized, focused, and coherent. • uses language and vocabulary purposefully. • varies sentence structure skillfully. • is generally free of errors in grammar, usage, and mechanics.
4	This response demonstrates adequate mastery with occasional lapses in quality. This response • states and develops a claim, exhibits sound thinking, and uses appropriate supporting detail. • is generally organized, focused, and coherent. • generally uses language and vocabulary effectively. • demonstrates some variety in sentence structure. • may have some errors in grammar, usage, or mechanics.
3	This response demonstrates partial mastery, but it has one or more flaws. This response • states and develops a claim but needs more consistent thinking and supporting detail. • sometimes lacks organization, focus, and coherence. • generally uses language coherently, but some word choices are vague or inappropriate. • has little variety in sentence structure or has some sentence errors. • may contain a number of errors in grammar, usage, or mechanics.
2	This response demonstrates little mastery and is marred by one or more weaknesses. This response • has a vague or limited claim, weak thinking, and inappropriate or insufficient supporting detail. • is poorly organized, lacking focus and coherence. • uses limited language and vocabulary or incorrect word choice. • demonstrates simplistic or incorrect sentence structure. • contains errors in grammar, usage, or mechanics that sometimes hamper meaning.
1	This response demonstrates a lack of mastery and serious flaws. This response • does not state or develop a claim and provides little, if any, supporting detail. • is disorganized, rambling, or incoherent. • has numerous errors in vocabulary and use of language. • has serious flaws in sentence structure. • contains numerous errors in grammar, usage, or mechanics that consistently hamper meaning.
0	No response or a response that is completely irrelevant will receive a score of zero.

Comments:

Figure 8.1 English language evaluation form

Information for Reflection

Usually, families of high school students receive many letters from educational organizations specializing in tutoring and preparing for the SAT and ACT. Among them are multimillion-dollar giants like Kaplan and the Princeton Review. These organizations promise the best teachers, small group classes and/or private tutoring, and online programs. Various small group 15–20 hour tutoring programs cost $600–$1000, online programs cost $500–$600, private tutorial programs on hourly base cost $150/hour, and combination of classroom and personalized private instructions range from $1000 to $2000. These companies have qualified teachers who are paid better than in public schools and have better working conditions. The fact that companies involved in the tutoring business make a substantial profit shows the weaknesses of the existing system of public education; many high school graduates need additional training to be prepared *to continue education in colleges and universities. If the American education system had provided students with knowledge adequate to the ACT and SAT requirements, most students would have not needed any additional training. If high schools had had standardized tests that included the components of the ACT and SAT, there would have been no need for the ACT and SAT.*

Let us assume that in 2011 high school students demonstrated tangible progress. It would mean that fewer students would need help from companies in the tutoring business. Their profits would fall, and some of their employees would be forced to seek a job in public schools. The public education system would acquire new qualified teachers, who would help to increase student achievement and academic performance in 2012. This, in turn, would decrease the number of students needing additional training, and so on. The right step can bring highly promising results. But, as a proverb says, "The first step is the hardest."

Chapter 9. A Parent's Job is Never Done

"What a child doesn't receive he can seldom later give." - P.D. James

Children's success is dependent upon the interest and active participation of their parents, more than any other factor other than poverty.

When we examine the issues inherent in public education reform, there are many stakeholders that play a part in a school's success or failure, including the students themselves, teachers, parents, educational administrators, politicians and trade unions. But none have as much influence over a child's performance as parents do. Their active participation (or the lack thereof) can mean the difference between failure and success, and yet whenever the debate about reform is held, parents are the one stakeholder whose voice is either ignored or remains silent, although the *Educate America Act* of 1994 contains, as the national educational goal, parental involvement and participation in promoting social, emotional, and academic growth of children. Experts can at least agree on this aspect of a student's performance and as Jeanne Allen, president of the Center for Education Reform in Washington, D.C. has said, "Meaningful parental involvement does in fact have an effect on a child's success in school. Parents who are connected to schools and meaningful parent groups do help their kids achieve."

THE APPLE DOESN'T FALL FAR FROM THE TREE

It's natural that most parents worry about their children's academic progress, which, as they believe, predetermines the youngsters' success in the future. Joseph Kennedy's maxim "We want winners, we don't want losers around here" is valid for almost every American family.

Children's relationship with their parents is paramount because parents are their children's ultimate role model. Parents play a big role in setting a good example and emphasizing the importance of schoolwork and doing well; children are natural mimics and are bound to repeat or duplicate the actions of their parents. If a child feels that their parent values education then they will too. The parents' job is to instill their values and good moral judgment, so that their children want to do well — and not through cheating. Parents set the tone for home life and can convey that their child's success makes them proud and that learning is of paramount importance.

In the last twenty years, parents have been spending fewer hours with their children doing homework, visiting the school, and meeting with teachers. Parental noninvolvement has become one of the most difficult hurdles to overcome because it is not always a lack of interest or concern that causes a parent to disengage. There are other circumstances and conditions at work that make it either difficult or impossible for parents to dedicate enough time to their children. Teachers, parent teacher organizations, and school principals agree that getting parents more involved nowadays is hard because more women work outside the home, many parents have to work either long hours or more than one job to make ends meet; and parents are struggling to make ends meet. Stress, lack of time, and the day to day hassles of work mean that few parents have the time to volunteer at the school, much less help with homework.

But schools have made good use of the Internet, email, and other information technologies to help teachers and principals stay in contact with busy parents. Now, in addition to report cards half way through the quarter and at the end, parents can get information on their child's grades and progress daily from school websites and online Blackboard platforms. These same Blackboard platforms make it possible for students to communicate with their teachers; parents can see scores for tests and quizzes and view how homework has been graded, etc. This allows parents to react immediately to warning signals.

By staying on top of their children's schoolwork and knowing how they are doing on tests, parents can stay abreast of the children's progress. Of course, the family's background significantly influences a child's success in school. Having highly educated parents is not just a model for success; the parents can also be a reliable source of knowledge. High-income families can afford to hire tutors to help their children do better in school.

The provisions of NCLB force schools to pay more attention to the needs of students who have historically lagged behind on test scores and provide tutoring for such students. Schools failing to meet yearly progress established by the NCLB law face various remedial actions. Among them are tutoring programs, so that parents may make use of state approved tutorial services to help their children if they fell behind or didn't reach the right grade level.

The NCLB law requires that districts allocate at least one percent of their Title I grant to programs involving parents. A special section of Title I dealing with parent involvement in education states that every district and every individual school that is funded by Title I should have a written parent involvement policy, which must be developed with parental input and distributed to all the parents of children participating in the mentioned programs. The law requires each school district to assist parents in understanding the state's standards and local academic assessments, and to provide materials and training to help parents work with their children to improve their achievements. But is it a useful investment of taxpayers' money?

Nobody helps parents in Finland, South Korea and many other countries with significantly higher educational achievements than the United States, and nobody helped parents in the former Soviet Union to work with their children.

Of course, parental involvement in their children's education depends on the community and family culture, respect for book learning and other factors (for example, in some countries students who are unable to pass college entrance exams end up in the army, which is a good incentive for parents to do their best to help their children to succeed at school). However, it's hard to believe that American parents don't understand the importance of education.

Here is a case in point. One of my students surprised me when she refused to correct mistakes in her test paper, which she finished very fast (meaning she had time to correct what was wrong), and left. The next day I asked her the reason, and she explained that she was a single mother living in a poor (i.e., unsafe) neighborhood and she wanted to take her son off the streets as soon as possible and help him with his homework. Parents who care for their children don't need lecturing.

It is better to spend federal money to train teachers rather than parents. When bureaucrats in Washington make decisions related to education, they throw money in the air and say "we did a great job."

PARENTS' VOICES MUST BE HEARD

Every state has its code of regulations; each board of education has rules and procedures concerning complaints from the public. Parents' complaints range from relatively simple and narrowly local (e.g., related to grading, the quality of teaching, teachers' ethics in a concrete school) to very important (e.g., discrimination on the basis of gender; sexual abuse or sexual harassment of a student; expulsion; identification, evaluation, or educational placement of a student with a disability; distribution of nonschool materials to a student), which raise issues far beyond a separate school system. Usually, there are special forms that must be filed and the complaint will travel a long road from school to the office of the superintendent, then to the board of education — first to the local board and then to the state board. Of course, the trip can be short if the problem is resolved at the office of the superintendent, or not very long, if parents are satisfied with the decision of the local district board. However, usually parents should prepare themselves for a lengthy fight. Any bureaucratic system resists change and doesn't like to punish its members. The state boards usually don't substitute their judgment for the local boards unless the decision is blatantly arbitrary, unreasonable, or illegal. Most appeals are rejected with this formulation. In turn, the laws don't allow the local boards to interfere in many school principals' decisions, which are considered local affairs. Usually, many reasonable complaints don't bring any positive results rather than bring money in lawyers' pockets. Surprisingly, the state government hires to a law firm to respond a complaint reaching the state board, although a complainer never even thought to bring his/her case to the court. Educational bureaucracy spends lavishly taxpayers' money to defend the system. Maybe the procedure similar to the Hippocratic Oath taken by physicians that includes the promise "to abstain from doing harm" should be established for educational bureaucrats?

Individual complaints have less chance for success than complaints from a group of individuals. A growing public dissatisfaction with the public school education in the country makes more effective the activity of parent groups that try to influence decision-making at school. The so-called school-level Parent Teacher Associations (PTAs) serve as a kind of forum where parents, teachers, administrators, and other concerned adults discuss ways to promote quality education, and encourage community involvement. They are technically associated with the state PTA and the National PTA, an advocacy association that has nearly six million members. Independent parent groups not associated with PTAs are known generally as parent-teacher organizations (PTOs).

Potentially, all these groups can directly and efficiently influence the schools. Unfortunately, they have no real power to do that. Bureaucrats resist change. School administration is afraid of doing anything without the approval of the district board. Principals have difficulties firing teachers and usually prefer to leave them in place. Finally, parents have reason to worry about possible retaliation from the teachers they criticize; their children may receive lower grades. Local PTAs and PTOs must provide forums for discussing school policy issues and should not confine themselves to fundraising. Parents should be represented on committees (e.g., school curriculum, education, policy) and participate in the evaluation of school policies and programs.

Formally, the boards of education state their commitment to promote the involvement of all parents in forwarding the school system's goals and to encourage collaboration with parents and the community as participants in school governance. Unfortunately, the lack of policy direction and official mechanisms defining appropriate participant roles, the culture of traditional authorities in education (teachers in classrooms, principal in school, processes and bureaucracy in almost all levels of administration) still hinder constructive parent participation in important school related decision making.

Speaking about decision making, it is impossible not to mention the School Choice movement which wants parents, instead of the government, to be allowed to choose which school their children attend. The Friedman Foundation plays a critical and unique role in the school choice movement, since Nobel laureate Milton Friedman was the first who proposed school vouchers in 1955.

According to the *No Child Left Behind Act*, if a school that receives special federal funding for economically disadvantaged students has not met performance goals for two consecutive years, parents have the right to transfer their children to another school in the same district. Federal funds are provided to cover costs of such a transfer, and the school district provides transportation to the new school as long as the original school remains in need of improvement. The provisions of NCLB allow parents a choice of public schools within the district if their children attend a "persistently dangerous" school. However, according the Department of Education report, "less that one percent of the 3.9 million eligible students used the public school choice option during the 2003–2004 school year." By 2005–2006, this number increased only insignificantly. There are many reasons for the low participation rate. Among them are late parent notification, resistance of the better schools to take additional students, etc.

While school choice can be useful for low-income students living in poor areas with high levels of crimes, where parents are unable to do anything inside local schools, this idea would be expensive and unrealistic idea to implement on a nationwide scale. Transportation problems, administrative difficulties with the admission process (checking whether new students' level meets the school's requirements; admission limits, rules concerning local students and students from other areas, etc.), which can create an additional layer of bureaucracy, possible related legal problems — all this would only complicate the situation without resolving the main problem: what to teach and how to teach.

Chapter 10. Public Versus Private

> "The ink of the scholar is more sacred than the blood of the martyr." - Mohammed

No study of public schools would be complete without examining also how private schools educate their students. As mentioned before, the early days of the United States, education was private and usually left for the elite. Now, according to the National Center for Education Statistics, there are 33,740 private schools in the United States, serving 6 million K–12 students. Private schools account for over 25% of the nation's schools and enroll about 11% or 6.1 million of all students.

Cost, along with academic reputation, are the top two factors that people consider first when deciding private versus public. The obvious difference is that public schools are free and private schools can be prohibitively expensive, even if their academic reputation may make private schools far more appealing.

Private schools are not administered by local, state or federal governments. As a result, they retain the right to select their students and are funded in whole or in part by charging tuition. Students have to pay for their schooling, although many private schools offer full or partial scholarships to qualified students who show financial need. Private schools do not use tax dollars and this removes many state requirements that public schools have to meet. Whereas in public schools most of the subjects offered and much of what students learn is mandated by the state, private schools have significantly more freedom in the courses they offer and the curriculum standards they use. As long as parents agree with the intellectual, philosophical or religious basis underlying the curricula, the schools' independence from government interference is seen as a great advantage. Private schools also have the freedom to expel low performing or disruptive students, whereas public schools are forced to accept any student. Private schools tend to have higher academic standards and are often specifically college preparatory. Unlike public schools in a government-controlled education system, which must use state standardized tests to measure learning achievements of students, private schools can choose whether to use these or their own tests. It is also important to mention that while it is against the law for public schools to espouse and provide specific religious instruction, many private schools are built on the belief that religion should be a part of each child's education.

Private schools can be divided in the following categories: day schools, boarding schools, single-gender schools, and special needs schools.

In boarding schools, some or all students live with their fellow students and possibly teachers during the school term. (The word *boarding* is used in the sense of *bed and board*, i.e., food and lodging.) Boarding schools include many college-preparatory schools, military schools, art schools, religious schools, and single-sex schools.

Religious schools make up the majority of private schools. About 81% of private school students attend religiously-affiliated schools, which place equal emphasis on spiritual and intellectual growth and are usually associated with a particular faith. Usually, a student doesn't have to be a member of the related faith to attend the school, but as a rule he/she should attend regular religious instruction and prayer in addition to his/her secular classes. Some such schools teach religious education in parallel with the usual academic courses. For example, the Epstein School in Atlanta, Georgia, teaches conservative Judaism. Others use the denomination as more of a general label to describe their broad orientation, while still maintaining a fine distinction between academics and religion. "Parochial school" is a term which is most often used to denote Roman Catholic schools, but it can refer to other defined groups. Protestants, Jews, Muslims and the Orthodox Christians all have private schools at the K–12 level.

Because the Constitution specifically states that Church and State must be kept separate, it is not appropriate to use tax-payer money for schools that provide religious instruction. But there are many parents who want their children to receive a parochial education. If the school has high academic standards and a reputation for getting students into college, a parochial school might be the ticket. However, in most parochial schools the overall quality of education still tends to be lower than in secular private schools.

In addition to religiously-oriented private schools, the United States has many nonsectarian private schools. (The term *nonsectarian* is narrowly used to describe secular private educational institutions not affiliated with or restricted to a particular religious denomination.) For these schools, academic excellence is the most important goal. Most nonsectarian private schools are relatively young. Although 8% were founded before 1904, about three quarters of them date back only to the mid-1950s, and about 40% were established in the past 20 years. Nonsectarian regular schools are located in all regions of the country, but they are more heavily concentrated in the South.

College-preparatory schools focus strongly on providing a solid precollege curriculum. Military schools, which are an excellent gateway to get military jobs in the future, place equal emphasis on academics and discipline. Nowadays, they are an alternative to ordinary schooling. Arts schools allow students to pursue advanced study in subjects such as dance, writing, theater, music, and/or visual art.

Special needs schools aim to improve the lives of their students by providing services tailored to very specific needs of individual students. They have prescriptive programs for emotionally disturbed, socially maladjusted, or learning disabled children. Some of such schools provide diagnostic services, psychological services, speech/language/occupational therapy for children with mental retardation, autism, speech delay, attention deficit, etc.

Private schools include the so-called independent and proprietary schools. Independent schools are private nonprofit schools governed by elected boards of trustees. Any surplus funds in a current year are reinvested automatically to be used in the next year. About 1,500 private schools are independent. Proprietary schools, a relatively new type of private schools, are run, similar to businesses, for profit. Their policy is determined by owners.

Although private schools often avoid some state regulations, in the name of educational quality most comply with regulations relating to the educational content of classes. Religious private schools often simply add religious instruction to the courses provided by local public schools. Some schools have academic standards which are probably higher than those of many colleges and universities. They have good libraries and highly qualified teachers. Others have lower standards and/or different programs and emphases. Many religious schools still insist students wear a uniform. However, most private schools simply maintain a dress code, i.e., the students must wear certain kinds of clothes at certain times of the day.

Annual tuition at K–12 schools range from nothing at tuition-free schools to more than $40,000 at some boarding schools. Tuition varies depending on many factors, including the location of the school. High tuition, schools claim, is used to pay higher salaries for the best teachers and also used to provide enriched learning environments, including a low student to teacher ratio, small class sizes, and services such as libraries, science laboratories and computers. According to the National Center for Education Statistics, average tuition for private K–12 schools is about $8,300. It is less (around $5,800) at Catholic and other religious schools (around $5,750) and more (around $13,000) at non-sectarian schools.

What are the reasons for parents to send children to a private school? Compared to other societies where birth-derived status and prestige are important, American culture believes that individuals should be rewarded and recognized based on their personal achievement. This belief is a driving force for people to compete for success. Differences in prestige seem less significant than differences in wealth and power. But nobody can deny the fact that the wealthy and the powerful have high prestige. Although the symbols of prestige have become available to an increasing number of Americans, these symbols are mainly of a material nature — cars, houses, respectable jobs, etc., and are associated mostly with wealth.

Is a private school a symbol of prestige? The analysis of schools attended by children of the wealthy people answers this question. In December 2006, the US Census Bureau released data on the social and economic characteristics of students enrolled in the nation's schools in October 2005. It turns out that of the eight million youngsters in grades K–12 who come from families with annual incomes of $100,000 or more, 80% (6.4 million) attend public schools and only 20% (1.6 million) attend private schools. Parents and students consider multiple factors when selecting a school. For most parents, the most important thing to consider is the school's tuition rates, as well as the other expected expenses. Some parents choose a private school based on their desire to give their children a specific peer group, whether that is based on discipline, cultural or religious background, or philosophical beliefs. There are some parents, however, who believe that the school's prestige and reputation is the most important thing to consider when selecting schools. The main reason why some parents place prime importance on prestige and reputation when selecting schools is that a prestigious school promises more career opportunities in the future.

For many parents, the money they'll spend on their children's education in a reputable school is a smart investment because they believe that a degree from a prestigious school will translate to more and better employment opportunities for their children after graduation. In this sense, the high tuition is considered as a worthy investment because the academic degree will ensure better careers for their kids. It is well known that many companies in the professional world prefer, and they have a reason to do that, applicants who hold degrees from reputable universities, medical and law schools, and graduate schools. The reason is that a prestigious school provides its students with higher quality of education, and providing high quality education is still indisputably one of criteria through which academic institutions earn a good reputation. Reputable schools have highly competent and knowledgeable teachers, which means that the students get solid knowledge. College admissions officers usually have a pretty good idea of a school's academic standards if the school has previously submitted applicants. There's nothing wrong with making prestige and reputation the primary considerations when choosing a school, as long as parents ensure that the money they spend will bring results. Moreover, to attend a private school can be an important psychological factor that motivates young people to work hard to justify their parents' belief in them.

Private high school teachers usually have a first degree in their subject. Many also have a master's degree. Teachers in nonsectarian schools usually are more highly educated, less likely to be state-certified, and better paid than private school teachers in general. More teachers in nonsectarian regular schools had received advanced degrees: three in seven held masters or doctoral degrees. Their teaching experience (59% had more than 10 years experience) is similar to that of private school teachers overall. Over one-third (38%) of teachers in nonsectarian regular schools don't hold state teaching certificates, compared to 29% of private school teachers overall.

One of the reasons many parents consider private high school is because most private high schools are fairly small. Less than one-quarter of private schools have enrollments of more than 300 students. Only 6% of nonsectarian private schools have more than 300 students, and 53% -have fewer than 50 students. That's much smaller than the typical public high school, which usually has more than 1,000 students. Teacher to student ratios are typically 1:8 for nonsectarian schools and larger (up to 1:15) for private schools in general. Class sizes in nonsectarian regular schools tend to be somewhat smaller than in private schools: only one quarter of nonsectarian regular schools have 20 or more students per class, and 35% have fewer than 15 students per class. Small class sizes and low student to teacher ratios are important because they mean that your child will get the personal attention he/she needs and craves. These two factors are often at the center of debates about what constitutes a quality education. If a school is burdened with too many students, then it defeats the purpose of being private, which is to provide the best possible education. Too many students either in the class or in the school means that teachers and staff spend more time doing crowd control rather than teaching. It's simple: the smaller the class, the more individual attention a student gets from the teacher. Most public schools have classes numbering 25 students or more.

One of the biggest issues facing schools is crime and violence. Crime used to be a primarily inner city or big city problem, but the shootings at Columbine and at Virginia Tech changed earlier perceptions of school safety forever. Managing dangerous, rude, or threatening students from a public school is never easy unless a student has an adult criminal record. A school can't refuse to enroll anyone, with good reason, so instead schools have to fight crime in their hallways. For many parents, small private schools with the selective admission process look safer than public schools.

Rich libraries and media centers are important components of just about every private high school, large or small. Private schools also have first-rate athletic facilities. Many schools offer tennis, racquet sports, basketball, football, swimming, lacrosse, field hockey, soccer, and some of them even horseback riding, hockey, and also dozens of other sports. Extracurricular activities are a major part of private high school programs as well. Choirs, orchestras, bands and drama clubs can be found in most schools.

In contrast to many public schools, where the kids who want to learn and who are smart are branded as nerds and become the objects of social ridicule, in private schools it's cool to be smart. The smarter a student is, the more the school will do to stretch his/her intellect to its limits. That's one of the things private schools do rather well.

Although in many private schools teachers' salary can be less than their public school counterparts (there is no need to prove that in private schools accountability and profit are the necessary components of their functioning) many teachers prefer private schools since, they feel, they have more control over school curriculum, the choice of textbooks, and class content. Teachers accept a position in a private school for less money simply because they feel that the teaching environment is friendlier. Teachers who want to be creative, who want to teach their subject, who want to light the fires of enthusiasm for learning among students, who want to get satisfaction from their job — those teachers choose private schools, because these schools do not follow state-mandated curricula to the letter and are flexible in the choice of texts and of teaching methodologies. Private schools create a climate for serious teaching because of their simple management structure, small class sizes, and ideal teaching conditions. Being an independent entity, a private school is not part of a large bureaucratic structure like a school district. There is no need to go up or down through layers of bureaucracy to deal with issues. Private schools are autonomous units of manageable size, and all problems are resolved fast within their structure. Small class sizes allow teachers to teach effectively, to give students the needed individual attention. Small schools allow teachers to know all their students as well as others throughout the school community. As a result, many private schools present communities organized around common goals and values. Private schools have much greater control over the discipline of their students than public schools, and it is often easier for private schools to remove disruptive students from classes and even to expel if they don't adhere to the school's policies or standards. Private schools are allowed to expel students and choose not to allow certain students admittance. In fact, many private schools are difficult to get into. As mentioned, public schools allow all students, regardless of religious creed, academic abilities or any other factor.

Private schools set their own admission requirements. Many private schools require admission testing. In most cases, private schools are selective on who they admit to their schools. Because the admission process is selective, the students that attend a private school are more likely to be homogenous than those at a public school. The graduation requirements generally meet or exceed state requirements. Emphasis in most college prep schools is on the Advanced Placement and the International Baccalaureate Program programs. Only some public schools have such programs. Nonsectarian regular schools relied more heavily on academic records for admission than did other schools. Among high schoolers at these schools, graduation and college application rates are high (98% and 90%, respectively). Some schools are very difficult to get into. The list of boarding schools (see *www.boardingschoolreview.com*) which accept less than 25% of their applicant pool includes such names as Phillips Andover, Phillips Exeter, Hotchkiss, St. Paul's, Lawrenceville and Milton Academy. In many instances what they offer far exceeds anything many colleges can offer. But this is accompanied by high tuition costs. For example, the acceptance rate at Phillips Andover (Massachusetts) coeducational nonsectarian boarding high school, which has about 1100 students, 220 number of faculty and charges $39,100 for boarders and $30,500 for day students, is only 20%. The acceptance rate at Phillips Exeter (New Hampshire) coeducational nonsectarian boarding high school, which has 10450 students, 200 number of faculty and charges $36,500 for boarders and $28,200 for day students, is 21%. Similar percentage rates are at the smaller boarding high schools Hotchkins (Lakeville, Connecticut; coeducational nonsectarian, 570 students, 105 faculty, tuition $36,225 for boarders, $30,900 for day students) and St. Paul's (Concord, New Hampshire; coeducational Episcopal, 527 students, 100 faculty, tuition $41,300). The above-mentioned schools offer their students financial aid. About 42% of Phillip Andover and Phillip Exeter and 34% of the Hotchkins and St. Paul's students, respectively, receive financial aid. With an acceptance rate of 24%, Milton Academy (Milton, Massachusetts; coeducational nonsectarian, 680 students, 139 faculty) charges higher tuition than the above schools — $48,275 for boarders, $31,175 for day students.

Of course, not many families can afford such luxury sending their kids in the mentioned schools. Is it necessary? There are excellent private schools and there are excellent public schools. There are public schools with the AP and IB programs. There are public schools which have produced outstanding scientists, Nobel laureates, and prominent politicians. As we indicated many times, the school name and class size are not decisive factors that determine students' achievements. By improving the public education system state mandated curricula — cutting bureaucracy, developing well thought-out curricula and textbooks, implementing well-developed tests, attracting qualified teachers — the quality of public education can be brought close to the quality of education at the best private schools.

Chapter 11. Charting the Way for Charter Schools

"The most valuable of all education is the ability to make yourself do the thing you have to do, when it has to be done, whether you like it or not." - Aldous Huxley

What makes a good school? First of all, the school's climate; students should feel that the school is *theirs*. The principal is a key figure who sets the tone for the school. The school should have high expectations for all students: acceleration classes, program for gifted students, services for students with special needs, various types of activities. A safe and healthy environment — the physical safety of students in the classroom, cafeteria, restrooms, at recess and when they arrive at and depart from school — is necessary. Sanitary conditions are also important. After-school activities (sports, clubs or other extracurricular programs) are significant. Library resources and computer equipment are also an essential indicator of a good school.

The so-called charter school, elementary and secondary, presents a special type of public schools. Such a school receives public money but operates with freedom from many of the regulations that apply to traditional public schools in exchange for some type of accountability for producing certain results, which set forth in each school's charter. NCLB reserved money to establish charter schools to compete with traditional public schools. This is an experiment that gets funding from the federal government, the state, and locally; but a charter school can also raise money from foundations, corporations, etc., because of its nonprofit status. Charter schools are released from many bureaucratic restrictions. They might not have to hire certified teachers, do not have to deal with the teachers unions, and are free to design their own curricula, spending money on salaries and computers, whatever they think will help teachers teach. And more importantly, they can decide for themselves what solutions to try and what to do if they don't work.

Charter schools are one of the fastest reforms in the country. The first charter school opened its doors in St. Paul, Minnesota in 1992 and now, a decade and a half later, nearly 4,600 charter schools (see *www.edreform.com*) are serving over 1.4 million children across 40 states and the District of Columbia. Some charter schools are founded by teachers, parents, or activists who are unsatisfied with existing traditional public schools. Charters schools not affiliated with local school districts are often established by non-profit groups, universities, and some government entities. Additionally, school districts sometimes permit corporations to open chains of for-profit charter schools.

As mentioned earlier, charter schools are given more latitude in creating a curriculum; the administrators can hire just about anyone they want as teachers and pay them whatever they want. The goal is to give charter school administration enough flexibility to create a learning environment close to the existing one in private schools, the environment that best serves the individual needs of students. Charters schools are a response to failing public schools and deficiencies in the traditional public school system. They are part of the public education system and are not allowed to charge tuition. The charter establishing each such school is a performance contract specifying the school's goals, program, students served, methods of assessment, and ways to measure success.

Charter schools operate on three basic principles: choice, accountability, and freedom. Charter schools provide enhanced parental choice, in the spirit of the *No Child Left Behind Act*, and give parents an opportunity to choose the school most suitable for their child's educational wellbeing. In turn, teachers of these schools have an opportunity to create the best working and learning environment for their students and themselves. Charter schools are judged on how well they meet the student achievement goals established by their charter contract. Charter schools must also show that they can perform according to rigorous fiscal and managerial standards. If a charter school cannot perform up to the established standards, it will be closed. With the freedom and choice of having access to a quality education, charters set higher education standards and must meet them to stay in business. While charter schools must adhere to the same major laws and regulations as all other public schools, they are exempt from many statutory and regulatory requirements. Instead of constantly walking through bureaucratic procedures established by the state and local boards of education, charter school leaders can focus on setting and reaching high academic standards for their students.

Some charter schools look just like many other public schools and their programs focus on the basics — reading, writing and the traditional school subjects. But they attempt to provide a better and more efficient general education than nearby public schools. Some charter schools provide a curriculum that specializes in a certain field (e.g. arts, mathematics, music, etc.) Other schools have special programs oriented to children who will go to college. Parents and teachers, who prefer charter schools over traditional public schools, are guided by the same reasons as in the case of private schools. Smaller school and classes, less bureaucracy — these are main features that allow teachers and students to work more efficiently and, as a result, students produce better results and teachers are more satisfied with their job.

Charter schools are started when community members (parents, educators, civic groups, business leaders, service organization, etc.), who see an educational need and decide to actively address it, submit an application to open and operate a charter school. Every charter school is required by law to have a board of directors that is ultimately responsible for the school's activity. The board oversees the operations of the school and makes sure it is financially sound and follows the law. The board, which often includes parents of children attending the charter school, also helps to create the vision for how the school should operate. The charter application should be approved by the charter school's sponsor responsible for the school's success in the future. Sponsors are ultimately responsible for the operational and educational integrity of each charter school they sponsor and for closing any one that fails to function properly. Depending on the state charter school law, sponsors are local school boards, state boards of education, state universities, state departments of education, or a separate entity created by law that has the sole duty to sponsor and oversee charter schools in the state. The content of the state charter law plays a significant role in the relative success or failure of the charter schools that operate within that state. The best charter laws do not limit the number of charter schools that can operate throughout the state but allow many different types of groups to apply to open schools. The best charter laws exempt charter schools from most of the school district's laws and regulations, allowing a charter school to be its own legal entity and give parents the most options. In addition to hiring the same certified teachers as traditional public schools, charter schools can hire qualified individuals that often have significant professional experience in their subject area. It is easier to fire a teacher from a charter school than from a traditional public school.

Statistics shows that charter schools do a better job of educating poor kids, and in Washington charter schools are beating out traditional schools by a long shot. On December 15, 2008, *The Washington Post* ran an article by Dan Keating and Theola Labbé-DeBose entitled, "Charter Schools Make Gains on Tests." The reporters point out that in the District of Columbia charter schools have changed the face of public education. The article say, "With freedom to experiment, the independent, nonprofit charters have emphasized strategies known to help poor children learn — longer school days, summer and Saturday classes, parent involvement and a cohesive, disciplined culture among staff members and students." The tests scores at many of these charter schools are beating out other public schools. At the middle school level the charter schools scores were 19 points higher in reading and 20 points in math. Free to set their own rules about attendance, and to expel students, there is a culture of student accountability and pride at the charter schools that is in sharp contrast to the traditional public schools.

Similar examples can be found across the country, and if these schools are better funded, better run, do a better job with disadvantaged children why can the same things occur at traditional public schools?

To run efficiently a charter school needs have control of its own finances. This lets a charter school buy property, enter into contracts, and have control over staffing. Charter schools, as public schools, are entitled to receive the same amount of funds as all other conventional public schools. They are funded according to enrollment (also called average daily attendance) and receive funding from the district and the state according to the number of students attending. The ways and amounts at which charter schools are funded compared to their district counterparts differ dramatically in an individual state and even in individual communities within a state. According to data of the Center for Education Reform, on average, charter schools are funded at 61% of their district counterparts, averaging $6,585 per student compared to $10,771 per student at conventional district public schools. Additional funds can be received from federal education grants. However, these money are distributed either directly by the US Department of Education through its own application process or through state education agencies, which usually award only already established and recognized charter schools.

Now almost every state allows the formation of charter schools, which with the same or a smaller budget per student as other schools in the district at that level (elementary, middle or high school) should demonstrate higher student achievements than traditional public schools. Conversion schools begin with established capital, namely the school and its facilities. A few states provide capital funding to start-up schools, and some start-up schools are able to take over available unused district space, but most must rely on other independent means. Many charter schools convert spaces such as rented retail facilities, former churches, lofts and warehouses into classrooms and related workplaces. There are some federal grants specifically for start-up/facility costs. Recent federal legislation provides funding to help charters with start-up costs. After the start-up, it is easier for a charter school to acquire loans and move to more suitable or permanent facilities. State legislation and loan agencies are beginning to tackle this problem by providing start-up funding and providing charter schools with the information needed to obtain favorable loans. Usually, help with private funds or alternative credit comes from the school founders, volunteers, parents and local professionals. Typically, charter schools engage local businesses and other organizations to help provide resources and services to the school.

One of the weighty arguments in favor of charter schools is that these schools are based upon accountability: if a school does not meet its contractual obligations, or fails to meet goals, it will be shut down. However, who is accountable for the school's unsatisfactory operation, for money spent in vain. If a company becomes bankrupt, its shareholders become victims of mismanagement and, in some cases, fraud. If a charter school fails, the taxpayers are victims. The fact that the government can stop financing and close a charter school cannot be considered as an advantage of charter schools. This is the right way to punish any failed public school.

Do charter schools cost taxpayers less than traditional public schools? The answer is "Yes" if it is based on the above-indicated funding per student data. However, these data ignore *facilities* and other start-up and capital costs. The average funds per student at charter schools are about twice less than the average tuition of nonsectarian private schools, which, excluding the average profit of these organizations, can serve a better indicator of the cost of educational public structures created similar to private ones. As a rule, the increase of load and capacity decreases costs. It is difficult to imagine that by creating a wide network of charter schools we can decrease already mounting educational costs. And if it may be possible because charter schools cut significantly bureaucratic operations and corresponding apparatus, the best way to improve public education is to dismantle the existing educational bureaucratic structure.

The experiments with charter schools and other experimental initiatives of the boards of educations are usually supported by state politicians and various educational research organizations. Both sides benefit from such initiatives. On the one hand, the initiative demonstrates the "creativity and hard work" of the board of education and may generate additional federal money; politicians will use it in their purposes as supporters of a high quality education. On the other hand, the educational organizations see in the initiative an opportunity to get funding needed for their existence. Do students benefit from these experiments? Since charter schools have smaller classes than usual public schools, it's logical to expect better results from students of these schools. Although some research results show no evidence that charter schools are efficient, most of them indicate higher achievement levels of charter school students. Some results in support of charter schools produced by well-known universities look fuzzy. For example, Harvard (now Stanford) University professor and economist Caroline Hoxby released a study called *A Straightforward Comparison of Charter Schools and Regular Public Schools in the United States*, which compared fourth grade students in charter schools with fourth graders in the public schools. She stated that compared to students in the nearest regular public school, charter students are four percent more likely to be proficient in reading and two percent more likely to be proficient in math, on their state's exam; compared to students in the nearest regular public school with a similar racial composition, charter students are five percent more likely to be proficient in reading and three percent more likely to be proficient in math. It is unlikely that these results can be statistically reliable to make any conclusions. Nevertheless, scientific argumentation in favor of charter schools allows politicians to declare themselves supporters of small size classes. However, as we indicated earlier, the class size isn't a decisive factor influencing a student's performance. Flirting with charter schools cannot solve the existing educational problems. The above-mentioned study, as many others, diverts substantial financial resources (federal and state) allocated for education from much better utilization than feeding various educational organizations to provide fuzzy research and in many cases — with almost obvious results.

Chapter 12. System Approach to Educational Problems

> "Let us think of education as the means of developing our greatest abilities, because in each of us there is a private hope and dream which, fulfilled, can be translated into benefit for everyone and greater strength for our nation." - John F. Kennedy

It is more than 50 years since the USSR launched Sputnik and triggered America's efforts to improve its public education system. But after 50 years, still there are no encouraging results. Maybe it is time to stop experimenting and to examine seriously the educational achievements of other countries and to learn from their experience.

In Russia, the Bolsheviks came to power promoting the idea of mass literacy. With 45% literacy in 1917, Russia caught up with the United States to become a fully literate society by 1930. Soviet leaders always considered education to be an extremely important indicator of progress.

Similar to the that of the U.S., the Soviet educational system was organized into three levels: elementary schools (grades 1st through 4th, and later 3d), secondary schools (grades 5th through 7th, and later 4th through 8th) that gave the so-called *incomplete secondary education*, and secondary schools (grades 8th and later 9th through 10th or, in some republics, 11th) that gave the so-called *complete secondary education*.

Uniting 15 separate republics and well over 100 significant ethnic divisions, the USSR Ministry of Education planned the curriculum of all schools so that central administrators knew what was being taught in every part of the country. The Academy of Pedagogical Sciences and its associated research institutes were responsible for the overall coordination of educational research and development. Ministries of Education of the union republics and local educational agencies had a minor say in curriculum decisions, which dealt with local issues.

It should come as no surprise that the highly centralized Soviet system of public education with its emphasis on mathematics and the hard sciences spurred Soviet economic and technological progress. But students of South Korea are also successful in science and mathematics, although these subjects were not a traditional strength of East Asians. And the success came at the end of the 20th century.

The South Korea government doesn't spend an extraordinary amount of money on education (about 4.5% of its GNP). Middle school class size averages 40–50 students, almost twice the average class size in most developed countries. It looks like American politicians and educators who fight for small classes and increased federal investment in education aren't familiar with this data. There is one important factor that explains South Korea's educational success. All its elementary and secondary schools follow the same national curriculum and use the same textbooks.

Some pundits see the secret of the Korean success in the efficacy of East Asian Confucian culture (strong family structure, hard work, and high valuation of education). But if this is the case, then why didn't these features work in the 1960s or 1970s?

The educational success of Finland, whose culture has nothing in common with Confucian culture, demonstrates that cultural specifics cannot be considered as a decisive factor. Finland's 15-year-old students earned some of the highest scores in the world. They are way ahead of their American counterparts in math, science and reading. Some educators try to explain the reason in a certain uniformity of Finnish society (the people are far more homogeneous in terms of ethnicity as well as income and education; there are no poor and no wealthy schools; each school educates children at the same per pupil rate). But clearly more important, Finland considers education as a national priority. The Finnish parliament sets the broad educational agenda, outlines the general principles of educational policies, and frames educational legislation. The government, Ministry of Education, and National Board of Education (NBA) are responsible for the implementation of policy at the central administrative level. The NBA is in charge of the development of educational objectives, content, and methods used in education and training, as well as evaluation of education. It is also the board's responsibility to prepare and adapt the core curriculum for the schools. The country has a national education policy and national testing. The government established a single straightforward curriculum for all schools and guaranteed well-trained teachers respect and freedom to teach. The teachers make all decisions about how their class will be run, how the education material will be presented and what books are to be used as long as they adhere to the core national curriculum. Teaching is a prestigious career in Finland. Teachers are highly valued and teaching standards are high; a master's degree is a requirement.

The above examples of quite different countries, which over 30–50 years created efficient education systems, cannot but suggest an idea as to what factors contribute to success. Educational scholars of Harvard, Yale, Stanford and other respectable universities focus mostly on local, purely educational classroom problems instead of looking at wider issues. They need to examine the educational structure of nations demonstrating substantial educational achievement.

It doesn't require special knowledge to notice that in all three chosen countries the government determines and controls a national education policy, national testing, and a national curriculum.

Of course, blind imitation never gives the best solution; a country's specifics (its size, social and governmental structures, etc.) cannot be ignored. But it is also inadmissible to close eyes on the success of others and to refuse learning from their experience.

EDUCATION AND NATIONAL GOALS

The United States invests in each student significantly more than other countries. Americans should be smart investors, and this requires specific knowledge and a specific approach. Most of the research related to educational problems are produced by educators, narrow experts in this field. They consider various approaches that can improve the teaching process, analyze students' performance, discuss curricula, etc. However, when they try to discuss the educational structure, the analysis does look more as a political statement rather than a scientific consideration. Usually, the term *model* is used when a certain experiment is implemented in several schools.

Being bound by the states and the local districts educational programs, the educational reform became, to a certain extent, a series of experiments with some programs in separate states; the results of the successful programs were spread among other states. For example, in 1991, about 3,500 schools tested one of seven whole-school reform models developed by a privately funded nonprofit organization New American Schools (NAS). The NAS initiative ended with cautious optimism. The education reform based on such experiments couldn't produce the desired results. The real education reform requires a drastic rebuilding of the American education system rather than patching holes in the existing school system.

The above-mentioned term *model* is widely used in such areas as system analysis, operations research and control. However, these areas of applied mathematics require appropriate knowledge and, what is more important, a specific approach to problems under consideration. Experts in education were unable to make well-reasoned judgments concerning the drastic improvement of the existing education system, since this problem requires a system approach and, hence, different kinds of experts.

The history of RAND corporation (its name comes from a contraction of the term *research and development*) shows that scientists equipped with the system approach methodology are able to resolve complex problems in various fields not being necessarily experts in these areas. Its scientists demonstrated that civilians were able to make valuable recommendations related to a vast spectrum of military problems, to provide independent objective analysis and effective solutions of many urgent domestic social and economic problems; its scientists were also involved in projects related to specific educational problems.

We will apply the system approach to the system of public education only on the qualitative level, i.e., we will try to make judgments without the quantitative analysis, without any calculations. Any attempt to improve the existing system (in our case, the system of public education) starts with establishing the goals to be achieved. It's logical to assume that the Goals 2000 have not been accomplished partially because of their fuzzy formulation. The goals of the *No Child Left Behind Act* are, to a certain degree, more modest and more concrete:

1. By 2013–2014, all students will reach high standards, at a minimum attaining proficiency or better in reading/language arts, mathematics and science.

2. All limited English proficient students will become proficient in English and reach high academic standards, at a minimum attaining proficiency or better in reading/language arts and mathematics.

3. By 2005–2006, all students will be taught by highly qualified teachers.

4. All students will be educated in learning environments that are safe, drug-free, and conducive to learning.

5. All students will graduate from high school.

The *No Child Left Behind* law faced opposition from many fronts. It emerged from different directions: from some members of Congress, from states governments, as well as individual school districts and organizations. In 2004, fourteen states requested the federal government to revise a number of regulations that had been developed to enforce the law. In November 2007, Hillary Clinton mentioned in her speech at an elementary school in Iowa that the United States should end *No Child Left Behind* "because it is just not working." Some criticism was reasonable while many critical remarks were politically motivated. The Vice President of American Federation of Teachers Adam Urbanski believes that "NCLB attaches high stakes to standardized tests, narrows the curriculum, labels schools unfairly, siphons away much-needed funds from impoverished districts and schools, and allows privateers to prey on public-school children. ... And when it comes to NCLB, the cure seems worse than the disease."

Opponents of NCLB criticized almost any aspect of the law, even its obviously positive parts. Even such objectives of the NCLB law as the improvement of the security in schools and the reduction or elimination of the impact of illegal drugs (Part A of Title IV of the NCLB law titled *Safe and Drug-Free Schools and Communities Act*), which everybody should agree upon, nevertheless, found critics. The provisions of the law dealing with school security and drugs were included because of a continuing public concern that many schools are unsafe. As indicated in the 2004 US Departments of Education and Justice report *Indicators of School Crime and Safety*, in 2002, students between twelve and eighteen years of age were victims of approximately 1.8 million nonfatal crimes at school; this includes 88,100 serious crimes including rape, sexual assault, robbery, and aggravated assault. The same report indicates that teachers were the victims of approximately 234,000 total nonfatal crimes at schools including 90,000 violent crimes. Despite of these alarming facts, a 2007 report by the American Civil Liberties Union titled "Criminalizing Schools: The Overpolicing of New York City Schools" claims that too much police hurts the learning process.

The report of the Center for the Study of Testing at Boston College indicated that in Texas, the dropout rate increased after the implementation of rigorous testing programs and it was suggested that schools were "pushing large number of kids out" in order to raise average scores. The assertion of some critics that NCLB narrows curricula and instructions to focus on test preparation rather than academic learning is illogical since, if the curriculum and tests are developed properly, inconsistencies won't exist. The statement that education is gradually transferred to the marketplace because of the voucher system as well as the criticism presented by progressives, who are against traditional methods used in schools, are not worthy of serious consideration. They are not supported by any arguments deserving attention.

Many critics of *No Child Left Behind* argue strongly against the unrealistic goals of NCLB and many aspects of the law, especially, such as federal financial aid policy, how academic progress is measured, and the penalty policy for insufficient performance. The law states that by the 2013–2014 school year all children must reach "world class standards." It is obvious that allowing each state to determine what to teach and how to test creates uneven standards and inability to compare results among the states. As a result, it is almost impossible to reach definite conclusions on the effect of the NCLB law unless a national curriculum and testing are mandated by the federal government. Since there are variations between the states regarding teacher certification requirements, the term "highly qualified" becomes unmeasurable.

The NCLB legislation pays special attention to teaching mathematics in elementary and middle schools. As former Secretary of Education Margaret Spellings said, "it's about planning the seeds of higher-order thinking for later in life." The mandatory testing in grades three through eight in the areas of reading and math forced many schools to increase the time spent on teaching these subjects and, as a result, to decrease the time spent on other subjects (e.g., social studies, art, and music). However, the goals established by NCLB (annual improvement rate for forth and eighth-graders should be, respectively, 3.9 and 7.5 faster than the rate of increase between 1996 and 2003) are unrealistic and cannot be reached without a thought-out national curriculum. The countries with the highest scores on international tests have a national curriculum, and the students at each grade level use a rigor-ous well-designed curriculum.

The components of the NCLB performance evaluation were not thought out thoroughly, as well as their influence on the yearly progress tabulation that determines whether a school is a success or a failure. For example, the reported graduation rate, which is significantly lower for African-American, Hispanic and Native American students, has little effect on the high schools progress evaluation, although studies show that nearly one third of all public high school students fail to graduate in the traditional four years. Of course, it is absurd to demand that immigrant children who have been in US schools for little more than a year to meet the standards.

Many educators and education organizations criticize the main method based on the so-called adequate yearly progress (APY) measurement system, which they characterize as too inflexible, too arbitrary and too punitive. Some of them wish to reduce the emphasis on testing and to evaluate student achievement by multiple estimates. But former Republican Secretaries of Education Rod Paige and William Bennett strongly support national standards for testing and curriculum, at least in English language, mathematics, and science.

While opponents of the *No Child Left Behind Act* try to challenge almost every aspect of the law, its proponents defend it by using the most favorable statistical data. According to the reports of the National Center for Education Statistics, public school enrollment increased between 1985 and 2006. In the upper grades (9-12), the net result of changes in enrollment over the same period was a 21% increase. Public and private elementary enrollment is projected to continue increasing, with an overall increase of 5% between 2006 and 2015. Secondary enrollment is expected to decrease between 2007 and 2013, before starting to increase again. The projected number of high school graduates (diploma recipients only) in 2006–2007 was 3,232 million, including 2,912 million public high school graduates. The dropout rate among 16- to 24 -year-olds has declined over the past 20 years. In 2003–2004, the averaged freshman graduation rate (a measure of the percentage of the incoming freshman class who will graduate 4 years later) was 74.3% for public schools. The average freshman graduation rate in 2003–2004 was higher than in 1993–1994 (73.1%), but about the same as the rate in 1983–1984 (74.5%). About 3.2 million elementary and secondary school teachers taught in public schools in 2006-2007. The number of public elementary and secondary school teachers rose by 19% between 1996 and 2006. During that period, the number of public school teachers has risen faster than the number of students. The average salary for public school teachers was $49,568 in 2004–2005 (in 2005–2006 dollars). After an adjustment for inflation, teachers' salaries were 7% higher in 2004–2005 than they were in 1970–1971. About 55% of the teaching force had at least 10 years of full-time teaching experience and almost all teachers held at least a bachelor's degree. Trends in reading achievement show improvements for the country's 9- and 13-year-old students between 1971 and 2004 (*Digest of Education Statistics*, 2006, table 110). Seventeen-year-olds scored about the same in 2004 as in 1971. In mathematics, average proficiency for 9- and 13-year-olds improved between 1973 and 2004 (*Digest of Education Statistics*, 2006, table 121). The average score at age 17 in 2004 wasn't measurably different from the average score in 1973 or 1999. Between 1996 and 2005, the national average 4th-grade science score increased from 147 to 151; there was no measurable change in the 8th-grade score; and the 12th-grade score decreased from 150 to 147 (*Digest of Education Statistics*, 2006, table 128). Significant gaps continue to exist between racial/ethnic groups.

The above-given statistics enables us to evaluate the efficiency of the public primary and secondary education system. Without deciphering "high standards," the most important Goals 1 and 2 of NCLB sound as many items of Goals 2000; they must be formulated more precisely. Moreover, if the standards are determined by states, they become the state goals rather than the national goals and, in reality, reflect the states' current achievement. Absence of the precisely formulated national educational goals allowed the states to cheat the central government.

Figure 12.1 presents a simplified structure of the public system of education described in Chapter 4. The ED represents here the central federal government; the symbols SBE, DBE and S denote state, local district systems of education, and schools, respectively. This type of structures belongs to the so-called active structures, in which subsystems can function independently from the center.

As indicated in the previous chapters, in the United States education is primarily a state and local responsibility. The history of American education shows that states and communities, as well as various public and private organizations, established schools and colleges, developed curricula, and determined requirements for enrollment and graduation. The structure of education finance in America reflects this predominant state and local role. Of an estimated $1 trillion being spent nationwide on education at all levels for school year 2007-2008, nearly 89% comes from state, local, and private sources. This is especially true at the elementary and secondary level, where just over 91% of the funds come from non-federal sources. Without national goals established by the federal government, state, and local education systems would function satisfying the needs of their communities, and formally their goals should reflect the communities' requirements.

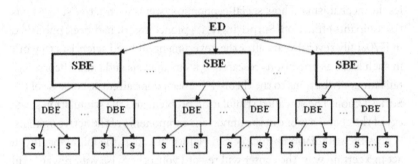

Figure 12.1 Structure of Education System

Now the involvement of the federal government in education differs from its activity many years ago. Although the primary function of the US Department of Education is still in gathering information that can help the state public systems of education, it engaged also in federal funding programs and monitoring funds related to these programs. By formulating national goals and supplying states with money to accomplish these goals, the federal government significantly increased its involvement in education. As we indicated earlier, the federal government has no jurisdictional control over the educational institutions. Since the US Constitution doesn't mention education, public education has always been controlled by the individual states. If earlier, when the federal involvement in education was insignificant, the state authority over education was taken for granted, now the expanding role of the federal government in public education has become a subject of heated debates. On the one hand, some senators and members of Congress think that the US government is overstepping its constitutional bounds. On the other hand, many public officials believe that local and state control of schools was and still is the brake on educational reforms.

The state education system can be considered as an independent centralized system since its functioning is determined by the state laws and controlled by the state departments of education. The system of independent subsystems becomes an active interconnected system when the center influences their behavior by formulating its goals and offering incentives to subsystems which contribute to achieve these goals.

The active systems theory (developed in the former Soviet Union) studies the mechanisms of how social-economic systems with active subsystems (participants) function. Surprisingly, its pioneer work had been published in 1970, only several years after the government allowed scientists to work in such areas as operations research, system analysis and game theory. Significant contributions to the theory have been done after the collapse of the Soviet Union. The so-called stimulation problem and the stimulation strategy of the center are one of the important components of the active systems. A possible stimulation principle can be formulated as the following: if you act in a certain way, the center will reward you; otherwise your reward will be zero. To be awarded, separate subsystems, acting in their own interests, can try to deceive the center providing inaccurate information about their functioning. The optimal stimulating strategy should make it disadvantageous for the subsystems to generate misinformation. The stimulating strategy of the center is the pivot of resolving the conflict between the interests of the center and the local subsystems.

The current public education system is an active system, in which the center (federal government; the Department of Education) tries to implement the national education policy by providing financial aid to state education systems (subsystems of the whole education system). It's obvious that states should be interested in accepting the educational goals formulated by the federal government since in this case the incentives of the center would be maximal.

The federal government efforts to improve education failed because of its inability to formulate properly the national education goals and functional requirements for state education systems as part of the stimulating strategy. Goals expressed in words are likely to remain empty words if no indicators of performance are attached to these goals. The efficiency of the whole system, as well as its separate subsystems, is characterized by the so-called performance criteria. Even if the goals of its subsystems coincide with the goal of the center and the performance criteria of the subsystems are of the same type as the performance criteria of the center, the optimal functioning of the whole system is possible only if the center operates with reliable information related to the functioning of its subsystems. Applying the above to the US system of public education, we can state that the US education system can function effectively only if the state and local systems of public education pursue goals formulated at the federal level, and only if the US Department of Education induces the state and local departments of education to evaluate their efficiency and degree of progress identically, and provide the ED with reliable information.

ACHIEVING GOALS

It's reasonable to believe that Goals 1 and 2 will be achieved if US students' scores in the basic subjects are above a certain level (as compared to students in the other leading industrial countries, for example, based on the TIMSS, PIRLS and PISA tests). The contents of the tests matters and so does how the tests are prepared. There is no need for the federal government to mislead everyone by offering easy tests. A national standard test (a national set of tests in the basic subjects approved by the US Department of Education) should be prepared by the ED, or the Department should appoint respectable educational organizations to do that. Since the deadline for achieving NCLB's Goal 1 has been shifted to 2013–2014, the decision should be made whether a national standard test should immediately correspond to the 2013–2014 requirements or this should be done in several steps. Usually, the higher the bar is set, the more intensive the effort needed to pass it; and those who cannot jump that high should be evaluated on the basis of their improvement.

However, instead of establishing a national test, the *No Child Left Behind Act* says: "The purpose ... is to ensure that all children have a fair, equal, and significant opportunity to obtain a high-quality education and reach, at a minimum, proficiency on challenging State academic achievement standards and state academic assessments."

This means that pursuing the goals established by the federal government, the states are allowed to develop and adopt independent standards for public school students and use their own standard tests to measure student performance, i.e., to develop their own performance criteria to evaluate student achievement. Such an education system cannot be considered optimal.

Since the state bureaucracy determines the level a student must reach to be considered "proficient," by lowering standards many states were able to claim themselves to be high-performing under the mandates of the *No Child Left Behind Act*. To evaluate whether the states manipulated tests, the test data they submitted was compared with the scores of students in the federally funded National Assessment of Educational Progress (NAEP) test (see Chapter 5). This test, given to a sample of students in every state, is called *The Nation's Report Card*. The state tests measure a student's performance against the state content standards, which must outline what all students should know and be able to do. But while the NAEP standards were designed to establish what students ought to know, the state standards usually reflect what good students actually do know in each state. Mediocre education standards set by many states to "satisfy" the vaguely formulated requirements of the federal government mislead the public about student performance. These states regularly inflate student achievement. The states that try to mislead the government, as well as their own residents, set not only low standards and give weak tests; they also switch tests from year to year to prevent unflattering comparisons over time.

As a result, students who perform well on state tests do poorly on the Scholastic Assessment Test, and the deceptive tactics become obvious. As Jay Mathews wrote in *The Washington Post* (September 3, 2006; page A01), "Many states, including Maryland and Virginia, are reporting student proficiency rates so much higher than what the most respected national measure has found that several influential education experts are calling for a move toward a national testing system.... Maryland recently reported that 82% of fourth-graders scored proficient or better in reading on the state's test. The latest results from the Nation's Report Card, the nationally representative assessment of what America's students know and can do in various subject areas, show 32% of Maryland fourth-graders at or above proficiency in reading. Virginia announced last week that 86% of fourth-graders reached that level on its reading test, but the NAEP data show 37% at or above proficiency."

In their article *Why We Need a National School Test* (The Washington Post, September 21, 2006), former US Education Secretaries Rod Paige and William J. Bennett pointed out that "most states have deployed mediocre standards, and there is increasing evidence that some are playing games with their tests and accounting systems," i.e., they indicated what can be predicted from the analysis of the active systems with a structure similar to the one shown in Figure 12.1.

The most important part of the Obama administration approach to education reform (its five pillars of education reform: early childhood, standards and testing, teacher quality, innovation, and higher education) is the desire to develop national standards to replace the currently existing fifty sets of state standards. President Obama announced that he will seek to raise academic standards across the country by requiring states to certify that their benchmarks for reading and mathematics put students on track for college or a career. A state can show that its benchmarks meet the expected level two ways: by adopting standards developed through a consortium of states or by certifying, in a process to be developed with universities, that their existing standards are high enough. The first option incorporates an initiative governors and state schools chiefs launched in 2009 to draft new benchmarks for math and English language arts (see the proposal at *www. corestandards.org*). The Obama administration supported the effort and offered a $350 million grant competition to encourage states or groups of states to adopt common high-quality standards and develop tests based on them. Moreover, to put pressure on states to develop high academic standards, under the government proposal, $14.5 billion in annual education aid for students from poor families would be tied to states' action on standards. This is a step in the right direction. However, it is a timid and indecisive approach. Instead of using money to bribe states to certify their standards, the federal government should develop national standards and curricula for the basic subjects and persuade states (if necessary, by using stimulus funds) to accept them.

It would be a mistake if readers conclude that the author wants the federal government to impose full control over the public school curricula and the subjects that should be taught. Such a policy would contradict the US democratic system. We mean only a partial involvement of the federal government related to the global problem — the development of basic skills among the young generation. The point of discussion is only strict government control over the basic subjects. If the central government concentrated its attention only on three or four subjects, would that mean that America's freedoms are in danger? Would it mean that Americans are dogmatic and against any educational innovation? Not at all. A lot of room remains for various other subjects that can be determined on a local level. Assertions by some so-called educators that a tax-supported compulsory education system is the complete model of the totalitarian state, that compulsory education usurps parental control over children and hinders the growth of the power of reasoning and independent thought among children, cannot be taken seriously. Absolute freedom is impossible, and the amount and kind of freedom that is essential for American society is determined in the Constitution. Each person's education is an investment in his/her human capital which allows him/her to contribute to society in a productive way. Education should be considered as a public service, and if it invests in education, the government has a right to demand desired results.

The influence of politicians on proficiency standards is one of the main factors impeding the setting up of a national test. Some policymakers are tempted to keep standards low so that schools will look successful; others seek to set them high to stimulate schools to improve. The political obstacles of a national test are formidable mostly because of a long tradition of local control over public education. Some republicans still believe that the Republican Party, the party of states' rights and a small federal government, shouldn't support any initiative that would increase the power and size of the federal government; so education issues should be left to the states. There are even politicians who are against the public system of education. The rhetoric of such persons brings only harm to education reform. But they are in a minority, and as Diane Ravitch, who was an assistant US Education Secretary under President George H.W. Bush, said, "The more discontented the public is with confusing and dumbed-down standards, the more politically feasible it will be to create national standards of achievement." Chester E. Finn Jr., president of the Fordham Foundation, an organization supporting research, publications, and projects in education reform, a former Reagan administration official and one of the architects of the NAEP standards in 1990, believes that creating a national test will be difficult; but nevertheless, it can be accomplished. "There's an assumption around that national standards are political suicide even if they make educational sense," Finn said. "We need to bust through that... I think it's a manageable hurdle, especially with presidential leadership."

Until the public understands that educational progress can be achieved only if students of all states are tested identically in the basic subjects, until the public demands the politicians not to refer to the US Constitution of 1776 as a weapon to oppose a national standard test, and until the public demands trade unions not to interfere in the educational process, education reform will not bring any tangible positive results.

The problem of introducing a national test is linked with the necessity of creating identical basic subjects curricula in all US public schools. Only under this condition, a national standard test can be an effective and fair measure of student achievement. How can we expect close results from students of different states on a national standard test if their curricula are different and they use different textbooks? We cannot demand that students answer questions on material which isn't covered by their curricula. To be fair, a national standard test should include only questions on material covered by all curricula. Absent a standardized national curriculum, such a test would have to be too simple and would not reflect the real level of students' knowledge.

As mentioned earlier, some critics of NCLB assert that it reduces effective instruction and student learning because it may cause states to lower achievement goals and motivate teachers "to teach to the test," i.e., to teach a narrow subset of skills that will increase test performance rather than to focus on a deeper understanding. This is possible only when different schools follow different curricula, more precisely, only in the case of unsatisfactory curricula. If you test a child on basic math and reading skills, and you are "teaching to the test," you are teaching math and reading. If the curricula (and the textbooks selected) cover the material properly, then tests will match the material covered in the textbooks, and teachers would have no other motives than to teach the material from the textbooks. The best existing books should be chosen and made obligatory in all public schools. If necessary, new books will have to be commissioned. For students of different level classes, a different level of material should be taught. Exams should be oriented upon the lowest admissible level of knowledge. The recommended textbooks should correspond to the developed curricula for the core subjects that the public schools all over the country are supposed to follow.

Information for Reflection

Does the term 'teach to the test' make sense? Any well-designed test covers the material that meets the curriculum requirements, the material that can be found in a corresponding textbook and was discussed in a classroom. If the national test is well designed, then 'teach to the test' means to teach well, to provide students with knowledge they need.

Now many high schools offer SAT or ACT Preparation courses. Instead of spending money on private companies specializing in tutoring and preparing for the SAT and/or ACT, students have an opportunity to prepare to the SAT/ ACT in school. These tests are specific, and it is useful for students to learn their composition and develop a certain strategy how to perform. But the SAT/ACT preparation is needed mostly because many schools have different curricula and don't give their students knowledge necessary to get a high test score. The same applies to other college preparation courses.

A national standard test should be introduced in all public schools altogether with curricula and recommended textbooks for the basic subjects. Any half-measures cannot bring the desired results. The United States has a huge scholarly potential to develop the necessary standards and implement them in practice. Once a year the tests should be prepared by the US Department of Education and sent to the state and district boards of education, which should be responsible for carrying out the tests and processing the results. Possible modifications of the curricula and recommended textbooks could be discussed, for example, every five years. Identical final exams all over the country would provide a reliable statistical data for analysis and decision making. This statistical material would allow the central government to make proper decisions concerning financial aid, various initiatives and recommendations that would improve the level of education of various groups of the population and decrease dropouts. Systematic testing would provide all departments of education with data that sheds light on which schools are not teaching basic skills effectively, so that interventions can be made to reduce the achievement gap.

The implementation of a national standard test will silence those critics of tests who stated that teaching for tests created deceptive information about the students' real level of knowledge. A well-designed test oriented on a well-written textbook is an excellent measure of student performance. Without any doubt, the initial test results can be disappointing for the states with low educational requirements; this is one of the reasons they opposed a national standard test. Nevertheless, these test results will serve as indicators for future improvement. Making the US Department of Education responsible for the basics of curriculum and annual tests will save money of the states and districts, and they would be able to reduce their staff performing these functions.

There is no need for the central government to micromanage education in the country. This is the obligation of the states and districts. But the central government must establish — and it is its direct responsibility — the national goals, check whether they are achieved and measure (evaluate) the progress in achieving these goals. It would require a small group in the US Department of Education which, working with various existing educational organizations, would handle textbooks recommendations, basic curriculum issues, as well as annual tests in the basic subjects.

Basics mean something that is fundamental, an essential ingredient. The knowledge of the basic subjects is an important element of students' knowledge needed in their everyday life and that would allow them to advance further in various fields. Nobody is forced to take the so-called gifted and talented courses, advance level or advanced placement courses. A national standard test should be oriented toward on-level courses which every student must complete successfully. However, lowering standards and requirements for districts with a poor population is not a good practice. Graduates with fuzzy diplomas are unable to compete with others in the job market. Sometimes they don't understand the reason and consider their rejection or firing as an act of discrimination. Giving diplomas to minorities without giving them the necessary knowledge creates difficulties for employers, who can be sued for alleged discrimination.

There is a lot of room for states to develop curricula for non-basic courses, for example, gifted and talented courses, advance level or advanced placement courses, and to encourage students to take these courses. State education systems can also develop optional courses, test their efficacy, and share the experience of teaching them.

Some educators say that the skills young people will need to perform the jobs of the 21st century are different from what students needed 20 years ago, and schools need to do a better job of helping students acquire those skills. Critics of NCLB use this argument to assert that in its current form NCLB forces schools to narrow their curriculum by focusing on math and reading and the approaches to those subjects, rather than encouraging schools to prepare students to succeed in the 21st century global economy. Their criticism is accompanied by pompous phases such as: the education is the foundation of American democracy; American schools and teachers help young people develop the 21st century skills they will need to be productive citizens and tomorrow's leaders; the career impact of a quality education begins long before a student enters college or a technical institution; quality K–12 education is indispensable for later life. This is empty bombast. Without any doubt, the contents of the core subjects should be reconsidered from time to time. But it is irresponsible to deny the need to focus on math and English.

Moreover, it's unlikely that these "21st century courses" can be mastered and used in practice anyway without good skills in English and math. For example, critical thinking, problem-solving skills, computer and technology skills, communication and self-direction skills are considered 21st century skills. Is it possible to develop them without a solid knowledge of English and/or math?

Furthermore, not only subjects oriented to the new technological era should be taught. Former House Speaker and former educator Newt Gingrich indicates this in his book *Winning the Future (A 21th Century Contract with America)* (Regnery Publishing Inc., Washington, DC, 2005), reminding us that moral qualities should be developed in students, the qualities and values that 18th- and 19th-century educators were focused on. He believes the Department of Education should establish a program office in "patriotic education" and writes: "Our children — not just immigrants — need a patriotic education which today is denied them by an entrenched education bureaucracy."

Linda Darling-Hammond, professor of education at Stanford University and a creator of the Stanford Educational Leadership Institute, who believes that standardized tests produce more harm than good, wrote (in the *San Francisco Chronicle*. October 14, 2007): "And a key problem for the United States is that most of our tests aren't measuring the kinds of 21st century skills we need students to acquire and that are at the core of curriculum and assessment in high-achieving countries." Her opinion is similar to the views of the Partnership for 21st Century Skills, the organization that includes many member organizations (among them: Microsoft, Apple, AT&T, Cisco Systems, Intel Foundation, SAP, Texas Instruments, McGraw-Hill Education, Education Teaching Service) and characterizes itself as "a catalyst to position 21st century skills at the center of the US K–12 education by building collaborate partnerships among education, business, community and government leaders"; it provides "an online, one-stop-shop for 21ˢᵗ century skills-related information" and, based on polling, advocates 21ˢᵗ century skills.

No polling is needed to prove that parents would agree students need more than just the basics of reading, writing and math; that schools need to incorporate a broader range of skills. Moreover, many schools require students to get a technology credit. In the Maryland Public School system, the technology credit means choosing from the following courses: computer programming, website development, software application management, foundations of technology, communication systems technology, food trends and technology, and others. However, if students can earn the credit by taking the course "food trends and technology," in fact "cooking," instead of taking more challenging and serious courses, it is reasonable to ask where to place the blame if students have not taken courses needed in the 21ˢᵗ century. NCLB or the state education systems? The subjects that are considered to correspond to "21ˢᵗ century skills" should be at least discussed at the federal level.

As indicated earlier, the United States possesses a huge intellectual potential to prepare a national standard test and curriculum that would establish a well-reasoned and properly calculated level that students must reach to move successfully forward. We can expect that, initially, many schools will not show good results. They shouldn't be punished; they need several years to adjust to the new curricula and textbooks. But the federal government must be sure that the educational process in these schools corresponds to the new requirements.

The above discussion relates to the most important goals, #1 and 2. Goals 3–5 are secondary because their realization influences the realization of the prime goals. The time to achieve Goal 3 has already expired. The federal government, through the Title I program, sends billions of dollars a year to states to ensure that students from low-income families get extra services and support.

The *No Child Left Behind Act* required teachers of all core subject areas to be highly qualified by the end of the 2005–2006 school year.

According to the federal government, a highly qualified teacher is one who has at least a bachelor's degree and a full state's certification and can demonstrate mastery in the subject area he or she teaches. There is a big difference between the qualifications of teachers in the highest-poverty and highest-minority schools and those serving in schools with few minority and low-income students. A report released by the federal government found that no state had achieved this goal. Acknowledging this fact, the Secretary of Education issued a new goal of 100% compliance by the end of the 2006–2007 school year. This time has expired as well without tangible results being attained. Goal 4, the easiest one, has been reached in many schools. More attention should be paid to the neediest schools, i.e., to the high-poverty and high-minority schools. Goal 5 has not been achieved. A high level of graduation (ideally 100%) depends not only on schools but on parents as well. Despite the compulsory education law, dropouts remain an old, unresolved problem, especially among poor and minority students.

All problems related to the secondary goals must be resolved by the states, within their education systems. Some states do their best to achieve these goals. For example, in an attempt to accomplish Goal 3, North Carolina established a variety of teacher programs that repay college loans for new graduates who agree to work in the neediest schools, that pay teachers extra for taking on more responsibilities and increasing student achievement, and that allow to retired teachers to be rehired so that they can combine a salary with retirement benefits. The federal government helps as well to achieve this goal by partially supporting such organizations as Teach For America (whose mission is to eliminate educational inequality by creating teams of outstanding recent college graduates of various academic majors and career interests, who commit two years to teach in urban and rural public schools in the lowest-income communities).

Teach for America is an implementation of recommendations of the 1983 *Nation at Risk* report. According to the National Council on Teacher Quality, by 2002, forty-five states had initiated alternative teacher education programs. The federal government has allocated several billion dollars each year under Title II of the *Elementary and Secondary Education Act* for such programs. In 2007, President George W. Bush proposed increasing investment in the Teacher Incentive Fund to nearly $200 million the next year to reward teachers who teach in low-income schools and who help their students achieve great results.

The federal government can make another significant contribution in achieving Goal 5. The main reason for the high dropout rate is that many young people do not feel the need of education for their own future and the society. School is a turn-off, and they find everything about it unpleasant.

There are many straightforward ways to associate the idea of "school" with positive feelings.

As just one simple example, the beginning of a new school year is a major event in children's life. In many countries, it is traditional to celebrate this date, emphasizing the importance of education for a new generation. But in the United States, each state chooses it own date for starting a new academic year. Even separate counties of the same state allow themselves to choose different dates. This event may be mentioned in local TV news, but no more than that. Usually, the leading newspapers omit the event altogether. In the United States, the beginning of a new school year is routine and insignificant. To generate enthusiasm and excitement, this should be a national rather than a local event. The beginning of the new school year in the United States should be considered a special holiday event. Would the protectors of states' rights accuse the federal government of expanding its power if the beginning of a new school year was declared a special day in the country's life?

TRUST BUT VERIFY

Americans spend more on education than almost any other country. According to the 2006 report of the National Center for Education Statistics, federal on-budget support for education showed substantial growth between fiscal years 1965 and 2006. (On-budget support excludes education funds that are generated by federal subsidies, such as Federal Family Education Loans and Federal Direct Student Loans.) Especially large increases occurred between 1965 and 1975. After a period of relative stability between 1975 and 1980, federal funding for education declined approximately 16% between 1980 and 1985, after adjustment for inflation. From 1985 to 2006, federal on-budget funding for education generally increased, showing a rise of 146%, after adjustment for inflation. In 2005–2006, expenditures for public and private education, from pre-primary through graduate school, were estimated at about $922 billion, including $558 billion for elementary and secondary schools (*Digest of Education Statistics*, 2006, table 26). The amount spent on elementary and secondary education represented approximately 4% of the Gross Domestic Product (GDP) for the year, and it exceeded non-military discretionary spending of the federal government (all of the money spent on the activities of the federal government other than entitlements, the military and interest on the debt) during the year. For the school year ended in 2007, expenditures totaled approximately $599 billion, which represented 4.5% of GDP for the year. The state share of revenues for public elementary and secondary schools grew through most of the 1980s, but the trend reversed after 1987. Between 1987 and 1994, the local share of school funding rose while the proportion from state governments decreased. Between 1994 and 2001, the state share rose to 49.7%, the highest share since 1987, but decreased every school year afterward until 2004, when the state share was 47.1%. Between 1994 and 2004, the federal share of revenues rose to 9.1% and the local share decreased to 43.9%. Total revenues increased 78% between 1994 and 2004. During this time period, federal revenues increased 129%, state revenues rose 85%, and local revenues increased 63% (*Digest of Education Statistics*, 2006, table 158).

Would such an increase in federal involvement in education, which has now risen to the rank of a major national problem, mean interference in states' rights? It is help rather than interference. President Ronald Reagan, famous for his use of quips and quotes, used the old Russian saying, "Doveryai no proveryai," that is, "trust but verify." Applying this proverb to the US education system, the federal government must establish strict control for the money it spends on education. However, the existing system of funding educational programs influenced significantly by politics is not effective. That is why a huge money injection in education hasn't brought the expected results. In the context of "education reform" the term "accountability" is used rather to justify mismanagement, the careless and wasteful way of handling financial resources, than to demonstrate real educational achievement.

As indicated many times, the US education system has predominantly a local character. State and local taxes are the source of funding state education systems. Historically, the federal government serves as a kind of "emergency response system," a means of providing additional support to states for education when critical national needs arise. Formally, the money is given based on a well-reasoned request. Accountability means that the money should be spent properly, i.e., their allocation should bring the expected results. If, for example, a state needs money to renovate or build new schools, install new computers or information networks, or increase school security, the federal government can easily check whether the money was spent on such projects. In 2005, the Arkansas Department of Education was awarded by the ED a $3 million grant for the construction of a data system that will enable it to manage individual student data, analyze it, and use it more effectively to support decision making at the state, district, school, classroom and parent levels, in order to eliminate achievement gaps and improve the learning of all students. In 2007, the Arizona Department of Education obtained a nearly $6 million education grant to strengthen the state system to collect information on individual student academic progress and other important data (annual achievement results, attendance rates, and graduation data along with demographic information) that will improve the decision making process at the state, district, and local levels. Similar grants were given to many other states. Such programs were funded by the federal government and can be funded in the future because they are concrete, narrow targeted and easily verified.

However, government support is not limited by funding the construction of the new schools and/or the modern technological equipment for the existing schools; it is significantly wider. Without additional specification, the term *accountability* loses its sense when applied to the above-considered Goals 1 and 2. Since these goals weren't formulated in a more precise form, states have a lot of room for their own interpretation. If the states' education standards that interpret the main Goals 1 and 2 are different and there are no national standards, accountability is nothing more than a political slogan. There is no assurance that federal money will be used properly to improve the educational process rather than to feed the educational bureaucracy.

Information for Reflection

Accountability is "a policy of holding schools and teachers accountable for students' academic progress by linking such progress with funding for salaries, maintenance, etc." (Webster's Encyclopedic Unabridged Dictionary of English Language, Random House, New Jersey, 1966.)

Before reaching schools, federal money travels a long distance with multiple stops along the way, where a part of it settles, so that the sums of money that left Washington may be quite different from the amounts that arrived at schools. The educational bureaucracy eats up a significant chunk of initial amounts. The federal government may help states to build new and renovate old schools, to supply schools with computers and software related to education; it may allocate money to award good teachers and support poor parents to increase the options for educating their children. Federal money shouldn't help states to fund dubious research projects — on how to improve education. The answer is clear without any research: schools need well-designed curricula, textbooks and good teachers. To receive federal help states should present their education budget including administration costs. To stop feeding the educational bureaucracy, federal help should be given only to states allocating only a small percentage of the budget to administration costs.

Investors always try to choose well-managed companies with a solid balance sheet. Why should the federal government act in a different way? Let us consider the boards of education, or their equivalents, of various states. On average, they consist of 9–10 members with voting rights. However, Florida is able to control education policy using only an 8-member board. California and Texas have the eleven member boards, whereas Ohio and Tennessee seem to need no fewer than 19 or 18 members, respectively, to cope with the educational problems. The boards of New Mexico, New Jersey and Maryland have 14, 13 and 12 members. The boards of South and North Carolina consist of 17 and 11 members, respectively; it's unclear why South Carolina would need a board fifty percent larger than that of North Carolina. Wisconsin doesn't have a state board of education for K–12 education at all. The Wisconsin Department of Public Instruction (DPI), headed by the elected State Superintendent of Public Instruction, is the state agency responsible for K–12 education. This shows that the state education structures can be simplified. Let's try another proverb: "Too many cooks spoil the broth."

If wastefulness starts from the top of the educational pyramid, it's not difficult to imagine what is going on its lower levels. A fashionable word *accountability* brought to life new divisions or subdivisions (accountability or assessment & accountability) handling test development, testing administration policy, models for classroom assessment, categorical assessment, adequate yearly progress, statewide achievement, longitudinal analysis, accountability report, etc. Bureaucrats try very hard to prove their importance; they use new terms (e.g., longitudinal analysis) to persuade the public how difficult their work is and that only individuals with special skills can do it.

Information for Reflection

Usually, bureaucracy is defined as a formal, hierarchical organization with many levels in which tasks, responsibilities, and authority are delegated among individuals, offices, or departments, held together by a central administration. Today we also think of bureaucracies as inefficient, slow and generally bad. Since the power of a bureaucrat is determined by the number of subordinates, i.e., how many people report to him/her, it is natural that a bureaucrat is motivated to increase the staff, so that bureaucracy has a tendency to grow. The poor performance of American public schools is a direct result of the way the school systems are managed. The study group of Chicago business leaders found that the ratio of administrators to students in the Chicago Public Schools was one to 143, while in Chicago's Catholic Schools the ratio was one to 6,250. ("Educational Choice: A Catalyst for Reform. A Report of the Task Force on Education of the City Club of Chicago," 1989). The study confirms that any additional funds injected in the education system typically bloat bureaucracy and rarely reach the classroom. Almost any federal involvement in education and the corresponding educational acts are accompanied by increasing local educational bureaucracy (formally, to supervise the fulfillment of federal directives). The accountability problem can be resolved only by decreasing significantly the local educational bureaucracy. The establishment of a national standard test, curricula for the basic subjects, and related textbooks can help to resolve this problem.

Two smart politicians offer different approaches to reach the same goals (improve the US education system while cutting the tax burden caused by spending on education) according to their political views. In his book *Winning the Future*, Newt Gingrich writes: "We should set a goal eliminating fifty percent of the education bureaucracy outside the classroom...and dedicate the savings to financing the improvement in math and science education.... The more we spent on education, the smaller the share we have spent on inspiring and rewarding those doing the education." Chuck Schumer in his book *Positively American* claims that the goal to cut property taxes by fifty percent within ten years could be achieved if districts would agree to freeze property taxes that go to education. Newt Gingrich offers a simpler and faster solution — eliminate fifty percent of the education bureaucracy. Schumer wants the federal government to supply states with boundless money for education so that there will be no need to increase state and local taxes. Gingrich believes that cutting the education bureaucracy outside the classroom and moving the right teachers into the classroom will bring the same results without government interference in state and local education matters. However, there is an obvious flaw in their reasoning. Chuck Schumer is right when he asserts that without a national standard test, i.e., without increased government control over education, progress cannot be achieved. He understands the importance of accountability to prevent local interests and preferences from swallowing federal funding without tangible results. However, he ignores the fact that it is the education bureaucracy that devours most of these funds. Newt Gingrich is right when he blames the education bureaucracy for the inefficiency of the education system. But he believes that states must resolve this problem themselves without interference by the federal government. If the politicians of both parties looked for common ground rather than accusing one another of sabotaging education reform, logic would persuade them that a national standard test and curricula don't mean intrusion in states' affairs; before investing in a state education system, the federal government has the right to ask the state to prove that its education system isn't overstaffed. A national standard test and curricula provided at the federal level would allow states to shrink their curriculum and testing departments, creating savings that will essentially come on top of federal funding. Moreover, eliminating some of the educational personnel not directly involved in teaching would relieve the education budget and maybe even reduce local taxes.

Positioning themselves as pro-education, politicians, motivated by various factors, mostly support testing. Nevertheless, a greater push comes from a much less noticeable source — the testing companies. Publishers enjoy close relationships with state authorities who choose instructional materials and tests. States and districts spend huge sums on testing and standards, money that goes to companies, which also publish school texts. According to the Association of American Publishers, the market for tests has been growing much faster than the market for textbooks and instruction materials and promises to become much larger. A national standard test and curricula provided by the federal government will decrease significantly states spending on testing and standards, i.e., allow states to diminish their education budget or to use the released money to improve education.

The educational bureaucracy works closely with various educational organizations, which take money not only from the federal government but also from the state and local departments of education. In the U.S., more than a thousand education service agencies offer research, innovative approaches, new methods of teaching and/or training, critical analysis and other services. On its way to classrooms, education money dissolves in these organizations, so that classrooms, i.e., students and teachers, receive only a small part of the money initially allocated for education.

For example, Wisconsin, like many other states, received more than two million dollars in federal funding to improve mathematics and science achievement in classrooms. It was indicated that "the mathematics and science partnership grant program is based on *research* that has shown a direct relationship between teachers' knowledge and skills and student achievement." A question inevitably arises: what kind of research was involved? There is no need to prove the obvious. As to federal funding through grants, the money comes mostly to the state's colleges and universities. Some grants focus on teacher training. Teachers should attend lectures, but there is no guarantee that the lectures will make them better qualified. It's also unclear why the state's colleges and universities that receive funding from the state cannot organize such lectures without using federal money. Moreover, similar courses usually exist already; students and teachers take them and there is no need to develop new courses. If a state is interested in increasing the qualification level of school teachers, a real partnership between schools and universities can be created inside the state, and school teachers would be able to attend university courses without spending additional financial resources.

But for the state educational bureaucracy, NCLB presents a new opportunity to dip into the government pocket and extract money for fancy and unnecessary projects. For instance, the South Carolina Department of Education uses federal funding on such projects as the development of "new and innovative assessment tools to measure the progress of students with limited English proficiency," "online decision-making tools to assist educators in selecting valid testing accommodations for individual English language learners and students with disabilities on large-scale assessments." The Alabama Department of Education spends federal money funding "the research, planning, implementation, and promotional activities directly related to the development or expansion of a career academy."

Among recent government grant award recipients are the Nevada Department of Education, the Minnesota Department of Children, Families & Learning, the University of Minnesota's National Center on Educational Outcomes, and the University of Minnesota's Center for Advanced Research on Language Acquisition, the Assessing Limited English Proficient and Assessing Special Education Students, Center for the Study of Assessment Validity and Evaluation at the University of Maryland, consultants from the University of Oregon, Michigan State University, and the University of Nebraska, as well as the District of Columbia, the State of North Carolina, the State of Maryland, the City of Austin, Texas, the American Association for the Advancement of Science, and a law firm specializing in educational law issues.

Have federal grants to such respected universities as Harvard, Yale, and Stanford resulted in something useful to improve education in the country? It's up to the readers to judge the importance of the ED-awarded projects.

However, their limited usefulness in enhancing students' knowledge is obvious.

Leaders of educational organizations demonstrate an extraordinary creativity in getting money from various sources to support their activity. They react almost immediately to any event in the education arena. For example, in 2006, the Department of Defense (DOD) requested about $10 million for a new National Defense Education Program that would provide scholarships and fellowships to undergraduate and graduate students entering critical fields of science, mathematics, engineering, and languages in return for a commitment to national service after completion of their studies. The Association of American Universities (AAU) strongly supported this initiative as a positive step toward addressing US science and engineering workforce needs. AAU recommended to expand this initiative in 2007 and also suggested the need of a comprehensive, multi-agency national defense education initiative to encourage more US students to study in critical fields of knowledge. It's known that the defense and aerospace industries are having trouble attracting and retaining scientists and engineers and that about thirteen thousand of DOD laboratory scientists will be eligible to retire in the next decade without sufficient numbers of security-clearable US students graduating to replace them. Based on this information, the National Aerospace Development Center (NADC), a nonprofit organization that "promotes the use of aerospace at the primary, intermediate and secondary education levels as a thematic tool for motivating students to learn and excel across the curriculum, particularly in science, technology, engineering and math" offered an education project, the so-called Aerospace Challenge for Educators initiative, designed "to promote aerospace in the K–12 classroom by training and supporting educators in the use of aerospace as a thematic tool for inspiring students to become greater learners, particularly in the areas of math and science" and asked members of the American Institute of Aeronautics and Astronautics (AIAA) to volunteer in developing online training sessions on various aerospace topics and to prepare short learning segments on aerospace topics that teachers can take online. Although the importance of this initiative is questionable, since even an elementary presentation of the aerospace basics requires knowledge of mathematics not covered by the high school curricula, we cannot help admiring the NADC's creativity. The above example also shows that the discussion of the 21st century skills is still under way. Charter education opened doors for new types of grants, for projects analyzing advantages and disadvantages of charter schools, testing and student achievement at these schools. Again, money is spent on research rather than on students and teachers.

Effective educational accountability is impossible without the accountability requirements applied not only to state and local education systems but to the US Department of Education as well. Only projects that reach students in classrooms, rather than feed educators outside the classrooms and in the educational bureaucracy, should be funded.

Senator Tom Coburn's extensive 2010 report on federal education "help" shows that billions in the education budget were spent on "School House Pork." For example, Las Vegas school district received a $25,000 earmark in 2005 for a mariachi music program. Several education earmarks funded local and national halls of fame. The National Baseball Hall of Fame got $450,000 in 2005, the Rock and Roll Hall of Fame got $200,000 in 2002 and the National Aviation Hall of Fame got $400,000 in 2001, then another $200,000 earmark in 2005. Through seven earmarks, more than $5 million went to the Andre Agassi College Prep Academy.

Accountability policies linked closely with the stimulating strategy in the mentioned earlier active systems, the strategy which is the main factor determining the efficient functioning of the whole system. Regrettably, during the last two decades, the design of a proper accountability policy has become the focus of public debates about education but a satisfactory solution has not been found yet.

Deficiency of the Existing Educational Structure

The pyramid structure of the US education system given in Figure 12.1 assumes that instructions (commands) from the center (the federal government) follow down to the structure elements (state departments of education, local departments of educations, school principals) and influence the education process in schools. However, as shown in the previous chapters, this isn't how the US education system works. Since according to a rigorous interpretation of the US Constitution the federal government has no authority in education, states are not obliged to implement any federal education policy. Even when it comes to the *No Child Left Behind Act*, participation in NCLB is technically optional. Does it mean that the structure in Figure 12.1 is wrong? Not at all. The federal government directives are accompanied with financial resources to enable states to realize these directives. Formally, states don't need to comply with NCLB as long as they don't accept federal funding for their schools. However, if states decide to accept federal funds, they are obliged to use them according to the federal government education policy.

Such an interpretation of the *No Child Left Behind Act* leaves no grounds for the critics of NCLB who believe that NCLB federalizes education and sets a precedent for the erosion of state and local control. The experience with NCLB shows that states understand the need to improve education and readily accept government funding to do that. It means that the pyramid structure in Figure 12.1 reflects in general features the real picture of the US education system. But unfortunately, the pyramid also inherits the negativities of any centralized system: information delays, distortion, and sluggishness in decision making.

The main reason for a low efficiency of many centralized systems is its dependence upon the quality of the information obtained by the center from the local subsystems, i.e., from the system feedback channels. The feedback principle is widely used in automatic systems to increase their performance. A feedback loop is formed by measuring a physical quantity in the output, such as position, temperature, size, or speed, and comparing it with a pre-established standard; based on this comparison action is taken to maintain the measured quantity within the limits of the acceptable standard.

The feedback principle has been used for centuries. Norbert Wiener, an outstanding American mathematician and the father of cybernetics, emphasized the universal character of the feedback principle. He noticed that the feedback principle is also a key feature of life forms from the simplest plants to the most complex animals, which change their actions in response to their environment; the feedback principle helps them to adjust to the environment. The suggestion that closed functional circuits are of importance in the living organisms dates from the time of Hippocrates.

The feedback principle lies at the heart of the education process. On the one hand, test or quiz results enable a student to see where his/her knowledge is weak, and thus to know where more work is needed; at the same time, the results help a teacher to improve the methodology of teaching. Properly applied, the feedback principle can also help students take control of their own learning, i.e., become "self-regulated" learners. Experts in control theory know that well-design feedback systems have very high performance. However, badly-designed feedback channels (with the so-called transportation delay and/or noise) can significantly decrease the system performance and make it even worse than in the system without feedback, the so-called open-loop system. In our life, we have analogous examples. The decision making process is based on the feedback principle. We succeed because of our ability to create particular kinds of feedback loops that distill and simplify data and provide us with valuable information. But our inability to create good feedback loops can bring negative results.

Here we apply the feedback principle to evaluate the US education system. First of all, without a pre-established standard, feedback is useless. Americans cannot expect real positive results from NCLB if various states establish various standards. There would have been no need to increase central control of education if all states had established and followed the same standards, which could be linked with a national test, curricula and textbooks for the basic subjects. Then the role of the federal government would be minimal. However, this is an ideal situation Americans should strive to reach. In reality, to achieve the national goal — in accordance with the 2000 Goals and NCLB, the country should make more efficient the existing system of education. As we discussed earlier, the establishment of a national standard test and curricula for the basic subjects will allow the US Department of Education to evaluate more precisely the level of education in various states based on more reliable information concerning student achievement. This will diminish significantly erroneous information related to the low and arbitrary established state standards and reporting focused on getting government funding rather than on improving education. As indicated above, a badly-designed feedback system (the situation we have now, which is the reason why a lot of federal money is spent on useless projects) brings negative rather than positive results. The current high level of information technology and an extensive government funding of state and local education information systems allow the ED to create a reliable feedback, an information network that will supply it with reliable data concerning student accomplishment. Based on this information the Department will be able to make more reasoned and responsible decisions in helping the states to reach the national educational goal. The educational structure with pre-established nationally standards (a national test and curricula) for the basic subjects, i.e., with the pre-established standards for state and local education systems, which function independently without government interference, represents a decomposed system consisting of independent subsystems. The government role for such a decomposed system will be reduced to supervising a national test, gathering and evaluating information related to student progress in achieving the national goal and making decisions concerning additional financial resources for states to achieve this goal. Such a model would strike a reasonable balance between the federal and state involvement in education. A state unwilling to participate in the national education reform will not receive any federal support. It makes the state government responsible for the progress in education and its citizens will judge the state's education policy. They are the main factor influencing possible future changes in the state's education system. If a state accepts federal funding, it must follow the national goals incarnated in a national test and curricula. In this case, the state would face two auditors: its citizens and the federal government. The federal government will evaluate accountability on the federal level, i.e., how effective its funds were spent, whether they brought the expected results; the state's citizens will evaluate accountability on the local level, i.e., whether their state and local taxes are used properly to improve education.

Finally, as mentioned earlier, the accountability requirement should be applied as well to government spending on education. It is unacceptable to fund projects with a political rather than real educational implication. In addition, the federal government has an obligation to interpret properly the obtained yearly statistical data. The statistical material, if it isn't presented extremely rigorously (to satisfy this requirement in the social sphere is very difficult), can be interpreted differently and leaves a lot of room for possible manipulation. The federal administration can use this data for its own political purposes trying to demonstrate the success of its education policy. For example, the publication "The Condition of Education 1990" of the US Department of Education stated that "American schools continue to provide a high quality — in many ways vastly more sophisticated — education to the type of student they traditionally served, while greatly expanding their service to larger number of students previously excluded from the system." The report creates an impression that the situation with education is not bad. In 2005, the Department of Education indicated the improving student achievement in reading and math based on the NAEP results. However, only achievements were widely advertised. They related mostly to nine-year-old students: "More progress was made by nine-year-olds in reading in the last five years than in the previous 28 years combined." A very modest statement describes a wider picture: "Forty-three states and the District of Columbia either improved academically or held steady in all categories (fourth- and eighth-grade reading and fourth- and eighth-grade math)." Fuzzy statistics gives a lot of room for maneuvering to various arguing sides. The one fact cannot be denied. The high school completion rates under the current education system prove nothing about the quality of higher education. Diplomas obtained in weak schools have no value because the level of graduates is very low. Without a well-designed national test, Americans will continue dealing with fuzzy statistical data, from which sophisticated demagogues can draw any conclusions they like. In his nomination acceptance speech President Richard Nixon admitting that the government isn't always honest with people (a mistake he repeated himself) said, "Let us begin by committing ourselves to the truth, to see it like it is and to tell it like it is, to find the truth, to speak the truth and live with the truth." To achieve real success in education it is better to face the truth, whatever it is. This is the only way to improve education in the country in the shortest period of time.

Discussing briefly the main features of the active system models, we emphasized that the stimulation problem and the stimulation strategy are the pivot in resolving the conflict between the center and the local subsystems. Applying the approach of the active systems theory to the educational problem, we can conclude that one of the reasons for the lack of success of NCLB, in addition to the mentioned earlier imprecisely formulated educational goals on the federal and state levels, is the insufficiently thought-out stimulation strategy of the federal government. Historically, first the states were asked to develop education standards, then testing that could evaluate whether students' achievement meets these standards. Later the accountability issue, the obligation to demonstrate and take responsibility for performance in light of agreed expectations, as an important factor to stimulate the education progress, was raised. It looks like from the beginning the approach to improving the public education system has lacked a reliable scientific base. Unfortunately, experts able to analyze and build large scale systems were not participants of NCLB. If the educational bureaucracy and politicians continue to dominate in the decision-making process related to the government education policy, there is no chance of future success. There is a provision in the NCLB law that says that it will remain unchanged until Congress acts in some way on reauthorization. Despite a severe criticism of

NCLB and the rush to make changes in the existing law, it is better not to hurry and first to bring proper persons who are able and not afraid of making radical changes rather than putting patches on the existing NCLB Act.

CHAPTER 13. IMPROVING THE SYSTEM OF HIGHER EDUCATION

> "A whole ship was my Yale College and my Harvard." - Herman
> Melville

ACCREDITATION AND QUALITY OF EDUCATION

The previous chapters relate to elementary and secondary public education. For our children, this education is a start in life. But it's only a start, and it is a necessary condition to succeed and make a certain contribution to society. The rising demands of global economy, an increased competition among industrial nations and fast advancing India and China require the US to educate more students to higher levels than ever before. But the education system is not keeping pace with these growing demands. Of 20 children born in 1983, six did not graduate from high school on time in 2001. Of the 14 who did, 10 started college in 2001, but only five earned a bachelor's degree by spring 2007. To meet requirements of the 21st century American children should continue their education at colleges and universities. Without higher education, they will not be able to realize completely their potential. That is why in this chapter we include information concerning higher education. Public colleges and universities should be available for all school graduates. Sharply increasing tuition fees of public institutions of higher education became a serious obstacle to building an educated workforce that would guarantee the US continuing dominance in science and technology.

As if public, i.e., available to all population, institutions of higher education stopped being public, stopped performing their main functions — to serve the public. Federal and state tax dollars flow to colleges and universities, and the cost of education has risen faster than inflation, while the productivity of their employees has actually fallen 12.5% from 1976 to 2000. Here an attempt is made to explain reasons for the increasing cost of education. The accountability problem discussed earlier concerning elementary and secondary public education relates also to public higher education, and we will touch on it below.

Higher education in the United States means graduation from degree-granted institutions, mostly, from colleges or universities. If at the beginning of the 20th century, American colleges were isolated and scientifically weak, now their number is big enough and the scientific level of many of them is very high. Usually, colleges are smaller and offer only undergraduate degrees, while universities also offer graduate degrees. Community colleges, called also two-year colleges, are community-based institutions with close links to high schools and employers that provide two-year associate degree programs or vocational certificate programs; their graduates receive the associate of arts (A.A.) or associate of science (A.S.) degrees, or certificates, respectively. In most states, community colleges are operated either by a division of the state university or by local special districts subject to guidance from a state agency. Technical and vocational colleges offer short-term programs (not exceeding two years) that train students in a specific vocation or technology. Associate degree programs may be *terminal* programs, which lead into specific careers upon graduation, or *transfer* programs, which correspond to the first two years of a bachelor's degree program. Usually, graduates of community colleges can move easily into the third year of a bachelor's degree program at the local state four-year college or university. Some community colleges have automatic enrollment agreements with a local four-year college, where the community college provides the first two years of study and the four-year college provides the remaining years of study, sometimes all on one campus. The bachelor's degree typically takes four years to complete, though some students take slightly less time to finish, and others may take longer. Four-year colleges and universities offer bachelor's degree programs (the bachelor of arts (B.A.) or bachelor of science (B.S.) degree), with a small number also offering associate degree programs.

The above-indicated colleges, as well as universities, can be public or private. In 1955, 44% of students attending universities went to private rather than state universities. By 1999, that number had declined to 23.5%. Public colleges and universities are founded and subsidized by state governments to provide low-cost education to residents of these states. As a rule, state (public) universities are large, with enrollments of 20,000 or more students, and generally admit a wider range of students than private universities. State university tuition fees are generally lower than those of private universities. In-state residents (those who live and pay taxes in that particular state) pay significantly lower tuition than out-of-state residents.

The bachelor's degree program in the United States is highly flexible. Students can usually choose from a wide variety of courses and create their own unique program of study. The degree is awarded after a student completes a specified number of credits. A unique feature of the US higher education system is its adherence to the liberal arts and sciences philosophy, i.e., it's based on the concept that students should receive a wide academic education that develops the student's verbal, written, and reasoning skills. Students are required to take some courses in humanities, social sciences, in mathematics and, possibly, the sciences. Choosing the so-called *major* subject in which to specialize, students take about 25 to 50% of their classes in the major area. Some students enroll in *double majors* or *minor* in another field of study. Even those who don't follow a liberal arts program and instead plan to major in a specialized subject like engineering are usually required to take some classes in the humanities and social sciences to complement their studies. Similarly, a student who wants to complete a major, for example, in history is required to take some classes in mathematics.

Graduate schools of universities offer two types of graduate degrees — the master's degree, which can be a master of arts (M.A.), master of science (M.S.), master of business administration (MBA), or other, less common, such as master of education (M.Ed.), and master of fine arts (MFA), and the doctoral degree, which can be a doctor of philosophy (Ph.D.) or others (e.g., doctor of arts, doctor of education, doctor of medicine, or doctor of jurisprudence). At least one year beyond the bachelor's degree is necessary for a master's degree, while a doctor's degree usually requires a minimum of three or four years beyond the bachelor's degree.

Higher education institutions differ in their quality and academic reputation; usually, the most prestigious schools are private, rather than public.

Admissions criteria involve the grades earned in high school courses taken, the students' GPA, school ranking, and standardized test scores (the SAT or ACT tests). Most colleges also consider more subjective factors such as a commitment to extracurricular activities, community service, and an interview. Many states have two separate state university systems. Professors of the more prestigious universities are involved in conducting advanced research in addition to teaching (some of them have special research centers), while the less prestigious universities are focused only on teaching. The best ten-twenty American universities (Princeton, Harvard, Columbia, Stanford, Yale, etc.) are mostly private. Most public and private institutions fall into this middle range; their academic reputations vary widely, as well as the reputation of departments within each of these schools.

The quality of colleges and universities and their degrees are maintained through an external review, an informal private process known as accreditation, over which the Department of Education has no direct public jurisdictional control. Accrediting agencies set certain standards in areas such as faculty, curriculum, administration, and student services, which colleges and universities should meet, and establish policies and procedures for accreditation. In turn, they may go through a recognition process in which their standards, policies, and procedures are evaluated. The accrediting agencies that are recognized by the US Department of Education as reliable authorities regarding the quality of the programs and schools they accredit are listed on its website. Some accrediting agencies are recognized by a private organization — the Council on Higher Education Accreditation (CHEA). The absence in the United States of a centralized system of accreditation created a favorable climate for illegal institutions to operate (especially, through the Internet) and grant degrees in exchange for money, often without requiring students to show proof of knowledge of the course material or complete a necessary coursework or testing. Such "schools" print diplomas, which are difficult to distinguish from legitimate diplomas of higher education, so that it's important first to check accreditation of a college or university and be sure that they are legitimate.

According to the data of the National Center for Education Statistics, college enrollment rose from 13.8 million in fall 1990 to 17.5 million in fall 2005. In 2005, 11.0 million students attended four-year schools and 6.5 million attended two-year schools. Between 1990 and 2005, full-time enrollment increased 38%. Graduate school enrollment was steady at about 1.3

million in the early 1980s, but rose 38% between 1990 and 2005. Between 1994–1995 and 2004–2005, the number of people earning associate's degrees increased 29%, bachelor's degrees 24%, master's degrees 45%, first-professional degrees 15%, and doctor's degrees 18%. In 2004–2005, the following number of degrees was given by colleges and universities: 697,000 associate's degrees; 1,439,000 bachelor's degrees; 575,000 master's degrees; 87,000 first-professional degrees; and 53,000 doctor's degrees. Although the number of master's degrees and higher is quite impressive, their quality depends on the quality of the institution the degree was awarded. Unfortunately, to resolve their financial problems, even high-level universities organize evening classes with significantly lower requirements and not only on their campuses but also in different cities hiring temporary local faculty members. The value of such diplomas is lower than the diplomas earned by attending classes taught by permanent faculty members, and employers pay attention to this factor.

REASONS FOR THE INCREASING COST OF EDUCATION

The familiar everybody words *academic freedoms* assume non-interference of state governments in academic affairs of institutions of higher education, their autonomy and independence. Although states were always reliable donors of state colleges and universities, for many years their independence in decision making, as well as academic freedoms inside the campuses, were considered as standing to reason. However, the time when institutions were governed locally by faculty and ceremonially by boards became a thing of the past. Throughout the last fifty years the relationship between state government and the institutions of higher education became more strained; regulations limited institutional rights to govern themselves. The main reason for these changes was the accountability problem and the growing cost of education. The states' increasing control over higher education matters coincides with explosion of higher education in the 1960s. During the last fifty years, states created various coordinating and governing boards that exist in the 21st century. In the 1980s, as if responding to the increased government involvement in education, states reevaluated its higher education system in terms of quality, accountability and efficiency; states broadened responsibilities of the boards — up to firm control of the institutions rather than working as advocates for them. A certain coordination between faculty interests, campus interests and state-level concerns was established.

In a 1998 report released by the American Association of State Colleges and Universities, the national job market was predicted to grow by 18.6 million positions between 1996 and 2006. Service industries were predicted to outpace the growth of goods-producing industries. For the early 21st century, the report forecasts an urgent need of jobs in such areas as business and health care rather than in manufacturing and production. These changes and the continuing boom in the information technology and communications require an appropriate shift in the educational programs of institutions of higher education. Not all colleges and universities wish to adjust their programs to the new requirements of time. The pressure coming from coordinating and governing boards is damped by the trade union organizations and the academic rules established earlier, so that the expected changes slow down, similarly to the changes in primary and secondary education.

By creating governing and coordinating boards state governments tried to build a rational system (regarding educational programs and educational costs) of higher education. However, the desire of the governing boards to set guidelines for higher education meets resistance of institutions, which want the governing boards to be mostly advocates for funding. The relationship between states and state institutions of higher education more and more reminds the relationship between the federal government and states in the area of K-12 public education. The state's leaders lack of logic when they stand against federal involvement in education and insist on their right to evaluate how effectively the federal money on education were spent; but when it relates to the state money on higher education, they don't trust their institutions of higher education and want to control the educational costs. The mixture of money and politics doesn't favor a healthy educational climate and hinders the educational progress.

Currently, state governments fund higher education using mostly the so-called incremental funding system, i.e., the next year funding is based on the previous year budget. However, state funding isn't the only source of financing. To balance their budget, institutions of higher education use private sources and endowments. According to the National Center for Education Statistics, the public higher education revenue attributed to state government funds increased by 125% from 1980 to 1996. Revenue attributed to private sources increased 363% from 1980 to 1996, and endowment (donation) income increased by 236%. In the 2003–2004 academic year, public colleges received 24% of their revenue from states, 16% from tuition and fees, and 13% from federal grants and contracts. A large percentage of school funding comes from alumni. According to the Council for Aid to Education's annual survey, nearly half of the $25.6 billion raised nationally in 2005 came directly from individuals, with alumni accounting for 28%; gifts from foundations accounted for 27%; corporate giving made up 17%. In the 2006–2007 school year, private donations to higher education rose 6.3% to $29.75 billion, according to the annual Voluntary Support of Education survey. The already wealthy, mostly private schools, with leading faculty researchers and the most sophisticated fundraising operations, had the most success attracting new donations. The practice called *matching grants for donations* is a matching grants scheme established by the government to fund universities when they receive donations. In order to obtain donations, the universities must establish plans to solicit donations from corporations and individuals, plans to encourage individual departments and staff to solicit donations and may provide acknowledgement and recognition of generosity of donors. Colleges and universities face increasing demands from the public and in Congress to spend more of their endowments, particularly to keep tuition rises in check.

Despite increased higher educational funding, tuition and fees grew with a significantly higher rate (more than 3 times) than funding, i.e., states increasingly relied upon tuition and fees to provide necessary funding for their higher education institutions. According to the National Center for Education Statistics, states increased resident undergraduate tuition and required fees by 19% between the years of 1997 and 2001. Annual undergraduate tuition varies widely from state to state. Tuition for applicants from outside the state is higher and usually comparable to private college or university prices, which are typically much higher, although they vary widely depending on the reputation of the institution. Depending upon the type of institution and program, annual graduate program tuition can vary from $15,000 to as high as $40,000. Moreover, these prices don't include living expenses (rent, room/board, etc.), cost of textbooks or additional fees that institutions add on such as *activities fees* or health insurance. Room and board fees can range from $6,000 to $12,000 per academic year. Textbooks cost on average about $900 a year. College costs continue rising. Only for two years, from 2002 to 2004, tuition rates at public colleges and universities increased by over 14% (largely due to decreasing state funding) compared to the 6% increase at private institutions. In 2004, tuition at the nation's public universities rose an average of 10.5%, the second-largest increase in more than a decade. In 2005, the increase was the highest, about 13%. For the 2005–2006 academic year, average annual undergraduate charges for tuition, room, and board were $12,108 at public four-year colleges and $27,317 at private four-year colleges (*Digest of Education Statistics, 2006, table* 40). In the past four years, average tuition and fees have increased by about 24%. In 2010, four-year public universities nationwide have increased their tuition and fees by almost 8%. On average, for residents of the state a year's tuition is about $7,605 at a public four-year college or university and $2,713 at a community college. Most families cannot afford to send their children to college without being burdened with loans. The vast majority of students lacks the financial resources to pay tuition up front and must rely mostly on student loans. While college attendance has grown over the past two decades, state and federal aid was unable to keep pace with the rising cost of higher education. As a result, students should rely on loans to pay for a bachelor's degree, and they start their post-collegiate lives with significant debt. In 2004, two-thirds of all four-year college graduates left school with student debt. To make higher education more affordable, the federal government passed the legislation to reduce student loan interest rates for low- and middle-income students. It provides also an additional grant aid to low-income students. About 71% of all full-time undergraduate students at public colleges received some form of financial aid in 2003–2004. Full-time students obtained aid through a variety of programs: 62% received some sort of federal aid, 23% received state aid, 31% received institutional aid, and 23% received aid from other sources (*Digest of Education Statistics, 2006*, table 326). For all full-time undergraduates, the average student aid package from all sources (including grants, loans, work-study, and other) totaled $9,899 in 2003–2004 (*Digest of Education Statistics, 2006*, table 324).

In 2005-2006, the average salary of full-time instructional faculty on 9-month contracts in degree-granting four-year and two-year public colleges was $67, 952 and $55,405, respectively. In fields with high-paying nonacademic alternatives (medicine, law, engineering, and business, among others) earnings exceed these averages, whereas in such fields as the humanities and education they are lower. Many faculty members of four-year colleges and universities have additional earnings from consulting, teaching additional courses, research, writing for publication, or other employ-ment. As indicated earlier, the average salary for public school teachers was $49,568 in 2004–2005 (in 2005–2006 dollars). Comparing the above sala-ries of school teachers and two-year college full-time teaching staff, their correlation looks reasonable. The qualification of two-year college teach-ing staff is assumed to be higher but the teaching load is a little bit less and working conditions are better than at schools. However, the salaries of four- and two-year colleges look incompatible.

Of course, market forces, the increased number of school graduates ap-plying at four-year colleges and universities, drive up tuition fees and sala-ries of instructional faculty. However, this is not the only reason and not the most important one of skyrocketing tuition fees in state colleges and universities. Many four-year colleges are focused only on teaching. As a rule, the qualification of their instructional staff is higher than their colleagues in two-year colleges. However, usually, the teaching load in such colleges is lower, so that it's logical to think that the relationship between the salaries of this type four -year colleges and two-year colleges should be similar to the relationship between the salaries of two-years colleges and schools. As to the colleges and universities with an extensive research, in our opinion, the widely spread system of establishing salary of the instructional staff is obsolete and unfair. The existing system isn't only the reason for rising tu-ition fees but it also doesn't award properly many hard working professors. Salaries of professors of high-quality universities, who are productively en-gaged in scholarly research, usually reflect more their high scientific poten-tial than their teaching skills. But their high salaries influence, to a certain extent, the salary range of less gifted professors, which is also high enough. The normal teaching load in such universities is significantly lower than in pure teaching colleges; on average a professor teaches five courses a year; each one-semester course consists of two or three lectures a week. As a re-sult, professors have a lot of free time, which is assumed to be spent on re-search. Various publications in journals increase a university's prestige and help to bring grants and contracts to the university. However, there is no an efficient mechanism that would encourage professors to write proposals and participate in research. This doesn't relate to real scientists devoted to their profession, who try to make a contribution in science and technology. However, they present only a part of faculty. Other, usually, are very active to reach a certain position and salary and then stop at what has been accomplished. Having a lot of free time, they use it on consulting, open their own companies and even do business that has nothing common with their profession. They don't bring money to the university, and the university pays them more than they deserve.

Scientists rarely generate ideas continually. During certain periods, mostly when becoming older, they stop bringing money to the university. Moreover, they are reluctant to prepare new courses that would attract more students than the old ones they have been teaching for many years. As a result, the university pays out their former rather than current services.

Usually, when a professor receives a grant or a contract, he gets additional money for up to three months in accordance with his basic salary. It's unclear why professors who write proposals have no right to set their salary for various projects. If a limit for a *teaching salary* were established and more freedom were given to professors in setting their *research salary*, both the university and its highly qualified and hard working professors would benefit from such rules. Those who are involved in research would get more money than they have under the existing system, and those who prefer only to teach would earn less.

Universities offer various graduate courses that attract students who want to deepen their knowledge in specific fields. Graduate courses are taught mostly by the most experienced professors. Time determines what scientific and technological areas are more attractive. Now, for example, students are more interested in business, computer science and communications than in mechanical engineering. As a result, professors of some department are without load; only several students sign to some courses. It looks like foreign students from India, China and other countries are familiar with this situation, because they apply to less popular departments to receive master's degrees under condition that the department would provide them with a part-time job to pay for their education. Chairmen of the departments have no choice. As a result, instead of bringing money to the university, some foreign students don't pay tuition but use the university money. They work as graders, teaching assistants, etc. It's unclear why taxpayers' money should be spent on educating foreign students and supporting unpopular departments. University administrators know about this but close their eyes. The artificially created job-positions, such as a "grader," are wasteful. A professor, especially one with a relatively low teaching load, can grade several tests during semester. However, if it's possible to get state funding without a rigorous audit of spending and if it's possible to raise tuition fees, then there is no need to worry. Academic freedom permits almost anything. Accountability of all chains of the education system, starting from the education staff, is the necessary condition to decrease the cost of education and make it available for all high school graduates.

Should Tenure Be Abolished?

The existence of tenure, a granted professor's permanent job contract, is one of the reasons for the above-indicated lessening productivity of some faculty members and the rising cost of higher education. A professor who achieves tenure is secure; his position is permanent until retirement. Moreover, even after reaching the retirement age he cannot be fired. Lifetime tenure, permanent employment, doesn't serve as a stimulus to work hard. Vice versa, it induces laziness, stifles initiatives and decreases job performance because tenured professors are accountable to no one. In small colleges and universities, a faculty member's eligibility for tenure is determined by teaching ability, publication record and a combination of departmental service (participation in various faculty committees) and student advising. In larger universities, research is often considered as important as, or even more important than, teaching. For such universities, the ability to develop research, scientific potential and creativity are very important factors. The problem with faculty is that once they have arrived at tenure there is no incentive for them to work hard: generally, their salaries rise modestly, and if greatly, it is only because they publish widely and are sought after by other institutions. If tenure for an associate professor still leaves him/her room for growth and a noticeable salary raise, then for a full professor there is no place further to grow within the institution.

The question whether the tenure system should be preserved or eliminated is being widely discussed. Proponents of the tenure system have, as they believe, a strong argument: tenure is the guarantor of academic freedom. Tenure is considered the key that is supposed to foster academic freedom on America's campuses. Academic freedom and tenure are two sides of the same coin. The current view of tenure was established in 1940 when the American Association of University Professors (AAUP) and the Association of American Colleges (AAC) agreed upon a restatement of principles set forth in the 1925 *Conference Statement on Academic Freedom and Tenure.* This restatement is known as the 1940 *Statement of Principles on Academic Freedom and Tenure.* (The governing bodies of the associations, meeting respectively in November 1989 and January 1990, adopted several changes in language in order to remove gender-specific references from the original text.) It contains: "Teachers are entitled to full freedom in research and in the publication of the results, subject to the adequate performance of their other academic duties; but research for pecuniary return should be based upon an understanding with the authorities of the institution...Teachers are entitled to freedom in the classroom in discussing their subject, but they should be careful not to introduce into their teaching controversial matter which has no relation to their subject... After the expiration of a probationary period, teachers or investigators should have permanent or continuous tenure, and their service should be terminated only for adequate cause, except in the case of retirement for age, or under extraordinary circumstances because of financial exigencies."

The concept of academic freedom, like most abstract terms, is fuzzy and admits ambiguous interpretation. Formally, it assures faculty the right to pursue any line of inquiry in the course of their teaching or research without being censored, penalized or fired by university administrators. Then it's not clear why academic freedom cannot flourish without tenure. The Statement of Principles states mostly *the rights* of tenured faculty members rather than their *responsibilities.* The granting of tenure gives a faculty member complete job security. A professor cannot be dismissed by a university unless the university

- can prove extreme financial need,
- abolishes the professor's department, or
- determines that the professor is guilty of serious delinquencies.

The contents of the last item sound vaguely and are difficult to apply in practice. Since now colleges and universities don't experience a shortage of students, an attempt to buy out a tenured faculty member, the institution wants to get rid of, is a more realistic approach than firing. To fire a tenured professor requires a legal battle and financial resources, which can be used to hire part-time instructors rather than being spent on lawyers. It's almost impossible to do something against tenured professors who demonstrate laziness because in reality there are no grounds for removing someone with a lifetime employment guarantee, because they are "untouchable." This doesn't allow departments to hire new talented professors.

Those who defend tenure assert that to get tenure requires time and tenure is a compensation for many years with low salaries, that tenured faculty members sacrifice material gain for job security and accept lower salaries in exchange for guaranteed employment. This assertion was reasonable in the past when salaries in colleges and universities were notably lower than in technological and consulting companies, business firms, medical institutions, etc. Nowadays, faculty salaries improved significantly and became comparable to those of other professionals. One more point in favor of tenure is that, by abolishing tenure, institutions risk losing highly qualified faculty who could prefer to find an absolutely secure job. Professors would be constantly looking for better deals at other institutions and wouldn't show any feeling of institutional loyalty. Of course, a stable highly professional faculty is a valuable asset of the institution, and tenure is a way to create it. Having a loyal and reliable faculty, the university doesn't need to seek constantly new professors. It is understood that tenure provides the faculty member with job security and the university with a loyal member to rely on. However, if a tenured professor sees a better opportunity, usually, he/she does not pass it up.

Proponents of tenure also state that abolition of faculty tenure would mean higher tuition since non-tenure salaries would be higher. This is absolutely false, since these days any open professorial position attracts dozens of applicants, so that it's not difficult to find a well-qualified individual to fill the position and save money. Moreover, universities use widely many part-time and non-tenure track faculty members in the professoriate who, by accepting these positions, show a certain satisfaction with their status.

Some educators believe that tenure should exist but the standards for granting tenure should be changed — they should be more rigorous, i.e., tenure rules should be enforced so that it would be possible to terminate a tenured faculty member who is unproductive. Opponents of tenure believe that more productive would be the system with a limited tenure, a granted professor's five-seven year job contract. After this period, a faculty committee and the governing board of the institution should evaluate the professor's performance and make the decision whether to renew the contract. Such system exists in many countries; it was also in the Soviet Union. Valuable faculty members shouldn't see any danger in this modification of tenure, while the university administration would have more freedom to get rid of non-productive and not diligent faculty members. Universities, whether or not they abolish tenure, must develop new personnel policies to adapt to the new requirements of the 21st century. Only a free-market employment structure can guarantee institutional flexibility and high quality public education.

THE IVY UNIVERSITIES — DREAMS AND REALITY

In the former Soviet Union, any student who had earned a gold medal (the highest grades for the final year at school) was accepted without exams at any university. The reason is obvious — the country needed a highly qualified workforce. There exists no such rule in the United States. Does it mean that America doesn't need highly educated scientists and engineers?

Usually, states invite their best students to state universities by offering scholarships or other incentives. However, the best private American universities not only refuse to follow that rule, but it looks like they ignore any fair rules of competition. Of course, the existing mess in the school grading system creates certain difficulties to choose the best students. However, if a university accepts a student with low grades and denies a student with GPA of 4.0 (which reflects grades for all years in high school), this indicates that something is wrong with the country's education policy. Moreover, if the university's doors are open to low level students at expense of students with significantly higher achievements, it is possible to suspect various violations of ethical norms and even bribery. Since private universities receive money from the federal government and states in the form of grants and/or contracts, there exist levers to improve the existing situation, described in detail below.

Many youngsters wear shirts with the word *Harvard*. They know that Harvard is the number one university and by wearing such shirts, they try to advertise their high intellectual ability, their smartness. Even sophisticated O'Reilly uses his Harvard education as a strong argument in some debates. Almost every ambitious student dreams to be in Harvard or in one of others the so-called Ivy League schools, the eight oldest private schools, which are viewed as some of the most prestigious universities. All of the Ivy League's institutions place near the top in the *US News & World Report* college and university rankings (the numbers indicate their rank as of 2010). They are Harvard University 1, Princeton University 1, Yale University 3,

University of Pennsylvania 4, Columbia University 8, Dartmouth College 11, Cornell University 15, and Brown University 16).

The "Ivy League" was coined in the early 1930s by a newspaper columnist to describe football competition at the ivy-covered Northeastern universities. Over the years, a number of other institutions (Stanford University 4, Massachusetts Institute of Technology 4, California Institute of Technology 4, Duke University 10, University of Chicago 8) have been associated with selective admissions status by being referred to as "Ivies" or Ivy-like schools. We'll use the term *Ivy* referring to the above-mentioned 13 schools.

The question is: Who is likely to be accepted? Here, to formulate a question is significantly easier than to answer it. Unfortunately, to have very high GPA, SAT and/or ACT scores and even, in addition, an excellent leadership record is not, using the rigorous language of mathematics, a sufficient condition to be accepted. Moreover, in some cases it is not even a necessary condition. Being private universities, the Ivies have the right to take anyone and to reject anyone without explaining the reason.

Each university's alumni, and "special" people, the wealthy and/or influential, seem to have a special pass for their children.

Then, since many college sports are extremely popular on both regional and national scales, and games bring in revenue and winning brings prestige, athletes are given preferential treatment. They are admitted with significantly lower grades and SAT/ACT scores than other students, often demonstrating poor academic performance, and those who graduate don't even use their college degree later. In their books *The Game of Life* (Princeton University Press, 2001) and *Reclaiming the Game* (Princeton University Press, 2003), William Bowen and James Shulman collected and analyzed data (admissions preferences, absolute numbers enrolled, and academic performance) related to athletic recruits from 30 elite colleges and universities across the country through the early 1990s. According to their studies, while originally Ivies athletes were mainly specialized in revenue-producing sports (football, basketball and ice hockey), now athletes across the full range of men's and most women's sports spend more time on sports than on studies. In very large numbers they select easier majors and the easier courses within them. Is it normal that the Ivies, with their primary commitment to academic excellence routinely select 10 to 25% of their student body solely on the basis of athletic ability?

Daniel Golden, author of *The Price of Admission* (Three Rivers Press, New York, 2007), sharply criticizes the admissions practices of colleges and universities for favoring students from wealthy families, children of alumni and athletes. He estimated those students make up a 30-40% of the student body at many top colleges and believes that such practices are inadmissible: "It's indisputable that students from rich families and private schools are over-represented at America's top universities....There's something about these admissions perks for the rich that violates our basic notions of what America stands for — fairness, equal opportunity, upward mobility, particularly in an era of growing social and economic inequality. The unfairness breeds cynicism among teenagers who represent America's future and learn even before they're old enough to vote that money talks louder than merit."

Trying to be politically correct, the Ivies pay special attention to economic and ethnic diversity on their campuses. They opened doors for students of low income families and minorities. Moreover, at Yale, Columbia and Harvard, if a student's family earns less than $60,000 a year, they will pay nothing for their education. At both schools, the percentage the student pays goes up incrementally (from zero to 10% of annual income) with family earnings of $60,000 to $120,000 a year. Dartmouth eliminated tuition for students from families with incomes under $75,000. In 2008, Brown University announced that it was eliminating tuition for families earning less than $60,000 a year and would substitute grants for loans in award packages to families making less than $100,000. The Massachusetts Institute of Technology committed to give a free ride to undergraduates from families making less than $75,000 a year. Princeton supplies grants for all students to pay for all demonstrated need. In Stanford, under the new program, parents with incomes of less than $100,000 will no longer pay tuition. Financial aid awards that include no loans and no parental contribution for most families with incomes of $60,000 or less are given also in other Ivies. This is a positive fact that extended opportunity to get an excellent education for talented low-income students. If the Ivies accept about 30-40% of their enrollment from wealthy and influential families, and about 8-12% in low-income students, and approximately the same percent of athletes and foreign students are admitted to the Ivy League schools, it becomes clear that the middle-class, which determines the strength of American society, is underrepresented in the elite universities. Thousands of students from middle-class families want to get into Ivies but the door is hardly open.

In 2008, the rates of admission were the following: Harvard University 7.9%; Princeton University 9.9%; Yale University 8.6%; Stanford University 9.5%; Massachusetts Institute of Technology 11.9%; California Institute of Technology 17.4%; University of Pennsylvania 16.9%; Columbia University 10%; University of Chicago 27.9%; Duke University 22.4%; Dartmouth College 13.5%; Cornell University 20.7%; Brown University 13.7%.

In 2009, the acceptance rate for the most of Ivies was lower: Harvard University 7.1%; Princeton University 9.79%; Yale University 7.5%; Stanford University 7.5%; Massachusetts Institute of Technology 10.2%; California Institute of Technology 17%; University of Pennsylvania 17.1%; Columbia University 9.82%; University of Chicago 26.8%; Duke University 17%; Dartmouth College 12%; Cornell University 19.1%; Brown University 10.8%.

It looks logical that the student's level of knowledge must be a decisive factor of acceptance. Moreover, the best way to choose students who meet the university requirements is to establish entering exams. Many universities in various countries used in the past and continue using this procedure of selection the best candidates. The standard in most international universities is extremely formulaic, generally based on a single set of examination results. In 1892, Stanford's applicants had to be accredited either by certificate or exam in 10 subjects. In 1905, Harvard College adopted the College Entrance Examination Board tests as the principal basis for admission, but later it decided to cancel this rigorous selection procedure. The reasons are obvious. The arrangement of testing is an additional load for the university staff. The test results as the base of admissions decision making may create difficulties for the administration to reject certain applicants. In 1920s, Harvard started asking applicants to write personal essays, demonstrating their aptitude for leadership, list their extracurricular activities, answer questions related to their personal life. An applicant's character was included in the evaluation procedure. The personal interview became a key component of admissions and the letter of reference became mandatory. The Ivy League schools justified their emphasis on character and personality by arguing that they were looking for leaders, for the students who would have the greatest success after college. "Above a reasonably good level of mental ability, above that indicated by a 550–600 level of SAT score," says the former dean of admissions at Harvard Wilbur Bender, "the only thing that matters in terms of future impact on or contribution to society is the degree of personal inner force an individual has."

Personal statements and essays have become a necessary part of the application package. They should demonstrate the student's writing ability and provide information about the student's personal background beyond the basic biographical information from the application and the student's academic and extracurricular credentials. But it is unlikely that they are a reliable source of information about the student's character. Even such high level universities as the Ivies have no experts to make reliable inferences based on this material. Some universities (e.g., Yale, Columbia) require an applicant to write an essay in which the applicant should explain why he/she prefers the chosen university. This requirement looks more like a justification of the money charged for considering the application than a request for informative input about the applicant's skills. Since students usually apply simultaneously to several universities, such requirements force them to be insincere. Harvard, Princeton and Stanford ask applicants to give short answers to simple questions (e.g., "tell us how you spent the last two summers"), which are more informative than, for example, "why Columbia?" or "why Yale?" However, since various organizations offer essay services as a part of admissions consulting services (see, e.g., *www.RoadtoCollege.com*), there is no guarantee that the student has prepared the above indicated materials independently.

There are other components of the application package that can influence the applicant's fate. Among them — letters of recommendation, which are written by school counselor and teachers. There is a simple reason why in most cases they are positive, especially if the student applies to the Ivies. Usually, students choose teachers who they feel will write a good recommendation letter. Besides, any decent person follows the rule: if you have nothing good to say about a person, it is better to say nothing at all, and simply decline to write a reference letter. Besides, the more students are accepted by the Ivies, the better it is for the secondary school because this increases its rank and prestige.

As if they suspect that letters of recommendation and essays may mislead them, many Ivies prefer to interview applicants in person to examine deeper their personal qualities. Usually, alumni are used as interviewers and their evaluation is taken into account by the admissions staff. Although admissions directors usually say that the interview is rarely the deciding factor, it serves as a screening event as an unfavorable evaluation often results in refusal of admission, whereas even a highly positive one can have a negligible effect. Many reviewers complain that the students they highly recommended were not accepted.

Of course, an interviewer's impact depends on the interviewer's personal qualities and achievements. Only a small percentage of Ivy graduates reach the heights they dreamed of when they applied to these schools. But usually they are too busy to volunteer as interviewers. Mostly, those who volunteer are proud to belong to the Ivy community and for some of them this activity is a way to demonstrate their "importance." While most reviewers are benevolent, these persons dominate during the interview and can prevent an intimidated student from demonstrating his/her qualities and, as a result, such interviewers frequently knock out talented applicants.

Stanford University doesn't interview its applicants. Instead of an interview, the students are asked to write something that would demonstrate the student's interest in expanding his/her intellectual horizons, intellectual curiosity, passion for new knowledge. The university believes that although the student's scholastic achievements and extracurricular accomplishments are important factors taking into account during the admissions decision making, his/her intellectual vitality is a dominant factor because it is what sets the student apart from so many of other peers. It is impossible to disagree with that. There is a low probability that such essays can be produced by "essay services" or other helpers. A student who submits an interesting essay with some ideas or facts, a creative piece which shows his/her spark — nonstandard thinking — this student deserves to be accepted even if his SAT/ACT scores and GPA are not impressive. It is known that many outstanding scientists weren't the best in the class and hadn't high scores in all subjects. That is why the intellectual vitality test is the best additional indicator, much better than any interview, about the applicant's potential and ability. On the subject of SAT scores, the former director of Stanford's office of undergraduate admission John Bunnell said, "I always viewed them the way a drunk uses a light post: more for support than illumination." During all university history, the primary criterion for Stanford's admission is still academic excellence, now with additional emphasis on the intellectual vitality; the most important credentials are the transcript and letters of recommendation. This is more persuasive than the assertion that leadership and character are the most important factors. Calling for an "Ellis Island for Yale" to make sure incoming students were of suitable "character, personality, promise and background ," *The Yale Daily News* as if ignored the fact that the rules for millions of immigrants passed through Ellis Island to start a new life in the United States were established and strictly controlled by the federal government. The Yale's admission rules based on such a vague term as *character* serve as a cover-up of the university's arbitrary actions.

All colleges and universities have developed methods to evaluate applicants in ways that make sense within their particular situations. Each admissions department establishes its acceptance policy, which it keeps usually in secret as if not to be caught for its violation. Different school curricula and scoring systems, the existing mess in American education system, all this creates difficulties for admissions departments to choose the best students. That is why the departments gather information about private and public schools to be familiar with the quality of education in various schools, so that the school range influences its student's evaluation. Rejecting the test standard used in most international universities, American universities rely instead on the student's SAT/ACT scores. Since these tests are the same for students of different level schools all over the country, it is natural to assume that their level is below the requirements of such high ranking universities as the Ivies, and students only with the top SAT/ACT scores should be admitted (in a case of absence of the intellectual vitality essay). However, this doesn't correspond to reality. Below we provide admission statistics concerning GPA, SAT and ACT scores obtained from various sources (Boston Globe; The Daily Princeton; Princeton in Brief, *www. princetonreview*; *www. forbes.com*; *USAtoday.com*; the Ivy's websites; *mychances. net*; *www.admissionsconsultants.com*; *www.about.com*; *collegeconfidential.com*; *www. collegedata.com*; etc.). Unfortunately, some data presented by different sources doesn't coincide, so that small errors are possible. (But we are dealing with statistics!) Although research has shown average high school GPA of first-time freshmen to be a better predictor of success in college than SAT/ACT scores, many schools prefer not to share their GPA admissions data. This creates an impression that in general all is possible: pay about hundred dollars for application and take the chance. The more applications, the more money the university gets. We weren't able to gather the same type of information for all universities. Together with the 2009 SAT/ACT scores, we provide the average GPA for just a few of the Ivies. With the high percentage of admitted "privileged" students, many Ivies prefer to conceal the GPA data. Nevertheless, it is important to examine the below data characterizing the level of admitted students in previous years when an applicant tries to figure out at what school to apply. The test scores are presented by using 25/75 percentile (the 25th percentile is the score that 25 percent scored at or below; the 75th percentile score is the one that 25% scored at or above).

Harvard University Admissions Data:

SAT Composite 2070/2350

SAT Critical Reading 690 / 780

SAT Math 690 / 780

SAT Writing 690 / 790

ACT Composite 31 / 35

ACT English 32 / 35

ACT Math 31 / 35

Princeton University Admissions Data:

GPA 3.88

SAT Composite 2090/2350

SAT Critical Reading 690 / 790

SAT Math 700 / 790

SAT Writing 690 / 780

ACT Composite 31 / 35

ACT English 32 / 35

ACT Math 31 / 35

Yale University Admissions Data:

SAT Composite 2100/2370

SAT Critical Reading 700 / 800

SAT Math 700 / 790

SAT Writing 700 / 780

ACT Composite 30 / 34

Stanford University Admission Data:

SAT Composite 2010/2300

SAT Critical Reading 660 / 760

SAT Math 680 / 780

SAT Writing 670 / 760

ACT Composite 30 / 34

ACT English 30 / 35

ACT Math 29 / 34

Massachusetts Institute of Technology Admissions Data:

SAT Composite 2030/2320

SAT Critical Reading 650 / 760

SAT Math 720 / 800

SAT Writing 660 / 760

ACT Composite 32 / 35

ACT English 31 / 35

ACT Math 33 / 35

California Institute of Technology Admissions Data:

SAT Composite 2160/2330

SAT Critical Reading 700 / 760

SAT Math 770 / 800

SAT Writing 690 / 770

ACT Composite 33 / 35

ACT English 33 / 35

ACT Math 34 / 36

University of Pennsylvania Admissions Data:

GPA 3.83

SAT Composite 2000/2280

SAT Critical Reading 650 / 740

SAT Math 680 / 780

SAT Writing 670 / 760

ACT Composite 30 / 33

ACT English 30 / 34

ACT Math 29 / 34

Columbia University Admissions Data:

GPA 3.9

SAT Composite 2050/2320

SAT Critical Reading 680 / 770

SAT Math 680 / 780

SAT Writing 690 / 770

ACT Composite 28 / 34

ACT English 28 / 34

ACT Math 28 / 34

University of Chicago Admissions Data:

SAT Composite 2040/ 2320

SAT Critical Reading 690 / 780

SAT Math 680 / 780

SAT Writing 670/760

ACT Composite 28 / 32

ACT English 28 / 34

ACT Math 27 / 33

Duke University Admissions Data:

SAT Composite 2060/2350

SAT Critical Reading 690 / 770

SAT Math 690 / 800

SAT Writing 680 / 780

ACT Composite 29 / 34

ACT English 30 / 34

ACT Math 29 / 35

Dartmouth College Admissions Data:

SAT Composite 2010-2330

SAT Critical Reading 660 / 770

SAT Math 680 / 780

SAT Writing 670 / 780

ACT Composite 29/ 34

Cornell University Admissions Data:

SAT Composite 1940/2230

SAT Critical Reading 630 / 730

SAT Math 670 / 770

SAT Writing 640 / 730

ACT Composite 29 / 33

ACT English 28 / 34

ACT Math 29 / 34

Brown University Admissions Data:

SAT Composite 1990/ 2300

SAT Critical Reading 650 / 760

SAT Math 670 / 770

SAT Writing 670 / 770

ACT Composite 29 / 34

ACT English 29 / 35

ACT Math 28 / 34

Analyzing the above data we can see that the best chances have applicants with GPA above 3.5, SAT and ACT scores above 2000 and 33, respectively.

The above statistics shows that the Ivies' doors are open practically for almost everyone. As a result, the universities receive a huge number of applications and add ample amount of money to their budget for processing them.

The student's file including the complete application, essays, recommendations, and other judgments is a subject of evaluation, which according to the admissions departments assertion is designed to be holistic. The phrase *holistic approach* covers up any actions, thoughtful and fair, negligent and arbitrary. It sounds scientifically, creates impression of hard work but in reality means nothing. Private universities, as any private businesses, have the right to act in accordance with their own best judgment and to serve their own interests.

In addition to the above mentioned multiple factors included in the holistic admissions decision making, there are other factors, which have nothing common with a student's achievements and skills, leadership qualities, commitment to public service, and excellent recommendations, etc., but which may decrease his/her chances to be accepted. By pursuing *geographic diversity* and *ethnic diversity*, i.e., trying to make a "uniform," from all states and ethnic groups, student representation, the Ivies establish certain quotas for different states and counties. As a result, only a limited number of talented students are accepted from a certain area. That is why it is not a surprise that last year Harvard rejected one in four applicants with a perfect SAT score 2400.

Here is a case which came to my attention in 2009 and which displays some of the admissions practices discussed. A student with a very high GPA and SAT/ACT scores, an outstanding leadership record, extensive extracurricular activity, and excellent recommendations, applied to Yale University under its early admissions program. In two weeks, she was called and asked for an interview. Her secondary school, a high ranking public school, considered this to be a good sign and many believed that that she would be admitted. The interviewer, a woman about 50 years old, dressed in Yale's colors, asked whether the student knew the university's colors and why she hadn't dressed properly. The surprised student responded that this would have looked like brown-nosing. The interviewer mentioned that Yale was mainly for the privileged and she actually said, "it is not for you." She recommended the student apply to a local college, which, as the student found out later had an 80% acceptance rate. The student adamantly defended her determination and qualification to get in Yale. Then the interviewer said that she disliked the student's school because it was "full of drugs." This information was false, and the student disagreed with her. In addition, the interviewer was rude and interrupted the student, each time reminding that she was the "boss."

It is wholly inappropriate for an interviewer to say at the beginning of the interview that the applicant should choose another university, or to discuss poverty and drug problems — problems that have nothing to do with the topic of interview. Only when Yale informed the student that she wasn't accepted, although significantly weaker applicants were at least deferred, it became clear that the interviewer's behavior predetermined the result. The parents called the interviewer, who now denied having recommended the student apply to the local college and telling her that Yale was not for her. The Dean of Undergraduate Admissions responded to the parent's letter, which contained the transcript of the interview: "There is no appeals process here — over the past forty years, Yale has never changed a decision of the admissions committee. We also do not supply detailed explanations of the decisions. The reason is that we could not possibly do so without being unfair to all the other outstanding candidates to whom we must deny admission every year." In turn, Yale's provost indicated that "the decisions of the Office of Admissions are final and cannot be appealed to other University officers and deans." Is it possible to believe that in forty years there hasn't been a single mistake due to absentmindedness or negligence of the staff? Of course not. We can only guess what the Dean would have responded if he had received the interview transcript the day after it occurred.

The student applied to several other Ivy League universities. The interviewer from Princeton, a middle-aged man, told her that the admissions department had informed him that the applicant's interests were close to his own when he was at Princeton. The discussion was focused on the student's ability to make judgments, argue and write eloquently. The interviewer praised the student and said that he would do all possible to get her in. Moreover, knowing that her mother had come to pick her up, the person approached the mother's car, introduced himself and told that the mother should be proud of having such a daughter.

Harvard's interviewer, a young man, about 30, who was also focused on the student's mental ability, her interests, etc., praised her and promised to write a very positive review. However, he mentioned that unfortunately this might not be enough since in the previous year none of the five students he interviewed was accepted.

Different universities and different attitude to applicants. But despite of the assurance of the interviewers that they would highly recommend this gifted student, and without any doubt they did that, the student was not accepted. One probable explanation is the regional limit for areas with many rich and influential families — in accordance with a dubious geographic diversity and ethnic diversity policy. Don't the established quotas and privileges for certain groups of students look like discrimination against many other applicants?

In his letter, the Princeton interviewer (who was hired by the White House under President Clinton and now again by the Obama administration) gave a different explanation: "I wrote a very positive letter to Princeton on your behalf, and I have a lot of confidence in what you can do.... but you were unlucky.... There is randomness in the process, and this year you did not get the good fortune your hard work likely merits."

It looks like he is right, as the following example shows. Two friends from the same high school applied to Columbia University: a student, one of the best in the school, with the highest possible scores and an outstanding leadership record, thus with high expectations of being accepted, and a student with very modest achievements (a low GPA, etc.) who simply decided to give it a try, with low expectations. The second student was interviewed whereas the first student wasn't, and only the second student was accepted.

It's known that healthy and fair competition brings benefits to society and guarantees its progress and prosperity. Scientific and technological progress needs the best and brightest young people. Unfortunately, the selection process used by the Ivies brings in not necessary the best and leaves a touch of bitterness among those rejected students who deserved to be accepted.

It's natural that students who do very well at school want to apply to the Ivies. These are wonderful schools with enormous financial resources, state-of-art-facilities, and a small faculty/student ratio. Moreover, the Ivies are considered a luxury brand and their graduates earn on average 20–30% more than the graduate from a moderately selective school. This is the main factor why parents would fight to get their kids into the Ivy League schools. Many parents also believe that Harvard, Yale, and Princeton would offer their children an almost exclusive path to membership in the American elite. In the past, the Ivy League has produced a number of prominent figures in American politics. Most recently, former president George W. Bush, former president Bill Clinton, his wife, Secretary of State Hillary Rodham Clinton, former presidential candidate John Kerry were graduates of Yale University. Former president George W. Bush attended also Harvard Business School. President Barack Obama attended both Columbia University and Harvard Law School. John F. Kennedy, Jr. attended Brown University. However, the previous statistics doesn't necessary guarantee that the same picture will be in the future. The vast majority of current senators got education attending universities in their own states. Now the level of American leading universities, private and public, is very close. Moreover, the level of knowledge corresponding to a bachelor's degree obtained in the leading American colleges is approximately the same; it's not high enough to be an expert in a certain field. Graduate schools open wider opportunities for those who are interested in obtaining deep knowledge and are eager to contribute in specific fields. Harvard, Yale, and Princeton, as well as other Ivies, are not uniformly excellent in all fields. A high school student interested in history can do very well at Yale, but one interested in philosophy might do better at Rutgers University or one interested in physiology might do better at University of California, Berkeley. Sergey Brin, the co-founder of Google, Inc., the world's largest Internet company, earned his undergraduate degree at the University of Maryland and then continued his education at Stanford University. This is one of many examples proving that a hardworking and intelligent person will do well regardless of where he/she went to school. (An additional information and advice can be found on the website *www. randtc.com*; see its Education page). Unfortunately, many students and their parents don't understand this.

Financial speculation around the Ivies has given birth to education counseling organizations, which "maximize each family's chances of academic success." Former university admissions officers use their experience to prove that admission papers prepared by experts rather than student knowledge can guarantee admission success.

In his article "Show Them the Money", (*The New York Times*, 11/17/2006) Michael Wolff writes, "My children's education is my greatest extravagance and, possibly, folly. By the time my son follows his two sisters, God willing, through college, I will have spent $1.7 million on tuition and other unavoidable add-ons (SAT tutors are one pricey add-on) for my kids' fancy schools. ... The colleges we've eagerly bribed on behalf of our genetic material are most likely not just another part of the market economy, but a bubble market in themselves — of greatest value to the closed circle of people who pay the money that gives them value." The author of this article doesn't exactly admit that he and other of that ilk are active participants in the existing educational market. By creating the so-called *shift in demand*, they support the ugly admission policy and related questionable services.

Although all above material may look less significant in comparison to the discussed global educational problems, nevertheless it completes a gloomy picture of a deep crisis on all levels of the American education system.

CHAPTER 14. MONEY MAKES THE WORLD GO AROUND

"Riches are for spending." - Francis Bacon

Education is a huge part of the US economy. It is rapidly becoming a $1 trillion industry, representing about 10% of the US Gross Domestic Product and is second in size only to the health care industry. Federal and state expenditures on education total $780 billion.

The industry, which comprises for-profit, nonprofit and public organizations, can be defined by five main categories:

1. Traditional Public Educational Institutions (preschools, schools, colleges and universities)

2. Schools/Service Providers (alternative/special education services, education management organizations, charter schools, private schools)

3. Education Service Providers (education consultants, education information and research, education investment services, education policy specialists, and technology services)

4. Supplemental Education Service Providers (learning centers, tutoring services, training and assessment services)

5. Products (educational products, publishing, and supplemental products)

Basic public education services (learning at schools, colleges and universities) are performed mostly by the a unionized workforce which lets low-performers obtain salary raises right along with those who really deserve it and make it difficult for educational organizations to fire employees not working well and/or not willing to improve their performance. Because the market for teachers is controlled by monopolies, namely the unions that have exclusive rights to represent teachers in each school district, American current public education system doesn't reward for performance and its rigid structure penalizes younger teachers by limiting pay increases for newer teaches while padding the salaries of those approaching retirement. It has precipitated costly and wasteful early retirement programs to induce the most experienced and highly paid teachers to retire. In addition, public employees are not easy to fire; protections of employee rights in state law and arbitration procedures usually discourage administrators from even trying to dismiss teachers. Tenure and protection rather than performance improvement are standards of employment.

Public educational institutions are governed by the related state and local government agencies and entities, which devour a significant amount of the education budget. The debate "more government — less government" related to the public education system speaks unequivocally in favor of less educational bureaucracy as a way to improve the system's efficiency and decrease education spending.

The inefficiency of the US K–12 education sector hampers investment and innovation. Although education is a huge part of the US economy, until recently it wasn't much of a real business. Revenues of for-profit and non-profit education organizations account less than 20% of the $780 billion spent on education. Since the public education system is the main consumer of their products and services, these organizations use strategies oriented on this specifics of the educational market, which include direct contacts with the government educational agencies and entities, as well as managing supporter relationships (e.g., using advocacy groups, politicians).

With the distinction between for-profit and non-profit organizations becoming increasingly irrelevant (working for a *non-profit* organization doesn't necessarily mean *not profitable*), to improve public education and decrease education spending it is important to understand what drives the education industry — improving student achievements, profit or both.

A government monopoly in the system of public education makes the prices for educational products and services, as well as their volume, highly dependent upon decisions of educational bureaucracy of all levels — federal, state, and local. The bureaucrats use taxpayers' rather than their own money, and the accountability problem remains unsolved. In the book, *Bat-*

tling Corruption in America's Public Schools (Northwestern University Press, 2003), New York University law professor Lydia G. Sega argues, "one impediment to reform that no one is seriously studying in the debate over how to improve public schools is systematic fraud, waste, and abuse." Her careful documentation of the pervasive corruption and waste in the nation's three largest school districts — New York City, Chicago, and Los Angeles — shows that incidents of corruption and mismanagement in the public schools occur frequently, often on a massive scale.

Despite all drawbacks of the US education system, the revenues of the for-profit and nonprofit organizations continue growing. Advances in information technology, including the Internet, gave rise to education services which simplified work of educators and made it possible for students to access additional information related to the subject matter in their study. These services, which simplify both teaching and learning processes are necessary to improve efficiency of the existing education system, and expenditures related to these services are justified. In contrast to the above-mentioned services, the tutoring, training and assessment services are the products of American failed system of public education. The assessment services are needed because of different curricula, requirements and measurement of students' performance in various schools. The tutoring and training services are the result of insufficient quality of education at many public schools. Cynics may say that the organizations involved in the tutoring, training and assessment services are interested in maintaining the status quo in education, since the lack of progress is their life support. Of course, this is not true. However, their profit-oriented mentality doesn't allow them to contribute efficiently to educational progress. By developing tests that contain questions requiring the knowledge of material, which is not taught in many schools, and promoting new educational "products", they take additional money from the US Department of Education on the related research and from students' pockets the money needed to pay for college education. But do these new products necessary contribute to improving K–12 education?

The AP tests offered by the College Board and Educational Testing Service deserve special attention. AP Exam Test Preparation Materials are published by the College Board, Princeton Review, Kaplan, Barron's, Research and Education Association (REA), and Wiley. This is a multimillion dollar business, which is accompanied by aggressive marketing. Students who took AP exams receive from the College Board the AP Scholar awards if they exceed on an average 3 on three or more AP exams; more prestigious awards are given to students who take more tests and receive higher grades. They are lectured that since "many schools ward college credit for good grades on AP tests," success on AP exams could save them and/or their parents a lot of money. This creates an impression that money rather than knowledge is the most important factor. To decide what should be covered in the AP course and what should be on the AP exam, the College Board appoints a development committee for each of 32 subjects in which AP exams are available. Does the College Board's administration understand that American failed system of public education has no qualified teachers to teach such a number of courses? Of course, it does understand. Does the College Board's administration think that American public schools are able to teach at the university level? Of course not. Since different universities have different requirements concerning the admissible level of knowledge, which allows a student to pass an exam, it is reasonable to ask on what level the AP exams are oriented. Usually, a university student's grade is based on several tests results. However, the College Board decided to simplify this procedure. The Fordham Foundation's report on the state of AP quality, which reflects the opinion of school teachers, misses the most important part of the program, AP exams — the life support of the College Board and ETS.

On the website *www.CollegeBoard.com* the following information can be found: "The free-response questions on the AP Exams are scored annually by approximately 6,000 Readers at various sites throughout the United States, to evaluate over five million essays, solutions to extended problems, audio taped responses, and works of art. Each response is reviewed by two independent readers who have no knowledge of the score assigned by the other. In the event of a scoring discrepancy between the readers, the booklet is referred to the Table Leader or Chief Reader for review. Sub-scores are not available (except for Calculus BC and Music Theory). The AP Program, at its discretion, does not share sub-score or diagnostic information at the student level with students, parents, schools or higher education institutions."

While the multiple-choice questions are checked by a computerized system, the free-response sections are evaluated mostly by school teachers hired to work several days with a huge load of reading material, and it is unlikely that high-level experts would participate for low pay. The ad *Apply to be an AP Reader* is constantly posted on the website *www.HigherEdjobs.com*.

Similar ads can be found on other education websites, in *Education Week*, etc. That is why it is reasonable to assume that the evaluation is accompanied by negligence and mistakes are inevitable. As a result, the College Board and ETS receive multiple parents' complaints to provide them with information on scores of separate test components.

Here is a case in point. A student with GPA = 4.0 (WGPA = 4.76), a participant in a special program for the best students, the APEX (Advanced Placement Experience) Scholars Program, which requires the students to take seven APEX-designated courses throughout their four years and pass six AP exams (apparently, this requirement is a result of the College Board's marketing efforts), was informed that she got 3 on the AP English Language and Composition exam, whereas her friend who had a C for English got a 5. The student's parents spent four months contacting the College Board and ETS (the president, vice-president, executive director of the AP program, a representative of the Test Taker Services division, and the associate general counsel) trying to receive information about the students' essays scores. Since this exam reflects the level of accumulated knowledge and doesn't require special preparation before the test, the mistake in evaluation was obvious. However, in violation of the principles imbedded in the *Family Educational Rights and Privacy Act,* this information was denied. The College Board's response stated that, "In grading the free response section, each question is read by a different reader....Some questions may be read a second time by a different reader." This contradicts to the indicated earlier statement about the evaluation procedure. The statement "The AP Program, at its discretion, does not share sub-score or diagnostic information at the student level with students, parents, schools or higher education institutions" violates fundamental education principles. Why deny students or parents access to the sub-scores (for the multiple-choice questions and essays) which are in the computerized system? No school teacher or college professor is allowed to hide test scores. In this case the "discretion" can be considered a deliberate action to cover up errors in the AP exam evaluation procedure. The AP program students take tests at their schools. There is no proof that their teacher's evaluation is less reliable than those based on AP Exams. Moreover, conspiracies surrounding the AP Exams sow doubt whether they evaluate students' knowledge better than the schools. It is questionable whether AP exams serve to improve the education system or are a smart initiative to enrich certain education services and production organizations.

Information for Reflection

It is a common rule that any student's evaluation is accompanied by an indication of his/her mistakes or it contains the scores for separate parts of the test so that the students can understand why they deserved a certain grade. Any student of any level (elementary, middle, and high school or college and university) can ask an instructor to explain his/her grade. In case a student is not satisfied with the explanation, certain complaint procedures are usually established. Surprisingly, this rule is ignored by the College Board and the Educational Testing Service administering AP tests, although the students who take the SAT handled by the same organizations receive their final score accompanied with the evaluation of the separate parts of the test. For example, the AP English Language and Composition exam consists of two components: the multiple choice section and the free-response section that includes three essays. Instead of reporting how all components of the test were evaluated, the College Board and Educational Testing Service offer to rescore the multiple choice section for $25 and to return the essays (without rescoring them) for $7. It looks like the College Board and Educational Testing Service educators lack elementary logic. How is it possible to offer to rescore something without indicating the initial score? Moreover, why are the scores of the test's separate components kept secret? The most persistent complainers receive a letter from the College Board (without any name and signature) which assures them that "all AP exams are evaluated by college professors and experienced AP teachers using a process designed to ensure fairness and accuracy." To unveil the secrecy around the AP tests, it is reasonable to ask: What is the quality of the testing procedure if its details are concealed? Should universities trust the AP test scores if the testing procedure violates elementary ethical norms?

One of the most difficult and hotly contested issues in public education is how and whether to fund it.

According to the "2008 Education at a Glance report of the Organization for Economic Cooperation and Development (OECD)", the United States ranks number one in all education spending and well above the OECD average for K–12 education. According to the Institute of Education Sciences of the ED, the United States ranked the highest among the G-8 countries, which represent the largest economies by nominal GDP, in terms of expenditure per student at the combined elementary and secondary education levels as well as at the higher education level. In 2003, expenditure per student for the United States was about $8,900 at the combined elementary and secondary education levels and about $24,100 at the higher education level. Both of these figures were higher than the corresponding figures for the five other G-8 countries reporting data, which ranged from about $6,500 in Germany to $7,700 in Italy at the combined elementary and secondary levels and from about $8,800 in Italy to $11,900 in the United Kingdom at the higher education level. All of the G-8 countries spent more per student at the higher education level than at the combined elementary and secondary education levels. However, all of the G-8 countries spent more money (in total dollars as a percentage of GDP) at the combined elementary and secondary education levels than at the higher education level, where student enrollment is much lower. The United States spent 4.1% of its GDP on elementary and secondary education, higher than the share of GDP spent on education at this level in Italy, Germany, and Japan. At the higher education level, the United States spent 2.9% of its GDP on education, higher than the percentage of GDP spent on education at this level than in any of the other G-8 countries. Considering education expenditure at all levels combined, the United States spent a higher percentage of its GDP on education (7%) than did any of the other G-8 countries. Now this expenditure reached 9%.

According to Department of Education data, the ED's budget in 1979 was $14.5 billion. Today, its budget has grown six fold. As indicated in a US Census Bureau report of 2008 (see also Chapter 12, the data from the report of 2006), school districts in the United States spent an average of $9,138 per pupil in fiscal year 2006, an increase of $437 from 2005. In 2006, public school systems received $521.1 billion in funding from federal, state and local sources, a 6.7% increase over 2005. State governments contributed the greatest share of funding to public school systems (47%), followed by local sources (44%) and the federal government (9%). Total expenditures reached $526.6 billion, a 6% increase. Total school district debt increased by 8.5% from the prior year to $322.7 billion in fiscal year 2006. School district spending per pupil was highest in New York ($14,884), followed by New Jersey ($14,630) and the District of Columbia ($13,446). States where school districts spent the lowest amount per pupil were Utah ($5,437), Idaho ($6,440) and Arizona ($6,472).

However, as we know, students' achievement at the end of their public education career has not kept pace with these huge investments. In the last 30 years, the United States has doubled per-pupil spending in real dollars — but with zero results. Student achievement levels at the end of high school have not improved since then. Graduation rates since 1970 have actually declined. Math and reading scores of 17-year-olds have not improved in 40 years. How much does America need to spend on public education?

There is no any guarantee that more than $147 billion in federal "education stimulus" injected by President Obama through the *American Recovery and Reinvestment Act* of 2009 will improve performance of the United States education system. It is an open question how much money should be spent on education. Like the investment strategy, the education financing policy depends on allocation of resources. Additional spending is unlikely to produce better outcomes without properly chosen priorities, without a deep understanding why the previous efforts failed.

Information for Reflection

Inefficiency of American public education system induced those who believe in the power of a market economy to apply some market principles to transform the existing bureaucratic system of public education with 3 million teachers and 5.6 million total employees into a competitive educational marketplace with teachers and schools competing to provide the best education at the lowest cost. The CEO of Apple Steve Jobs argues that if the money spent by government per student was given to every parent as a tuition grant, then parents could decide which schools and which teachers to choose for their offspring. Free-market competition will spur innovation, improve the quality of education and drive bad schools (and bad teachers) out of business, while good teachers and schools will be greatly rewarded.

It is strange that the talented CEO doesn't understand that free-market forces act efficiently near the so-called equilibrium mode. The transient mode from the current state government-controlled education system to the market-oriented educational system would be painful for both teachers and students. In this case, shock therapy is unacceptable. Moreover, usually the market allows only strong participants to survive. Education is for everybody.

Nevertheless, school choice, as an element of a market approach, should be considered as a useful step for restructuring the system of elementary and secondary education; it can help to locate bad schools, bad teachers, and bad administrators, and get rid of them.

Time and time again, the debate over funding is divided according to party lines or reform approaches. The end result of this short-sighted partisan bickering is that opportunities to make real change are missed. One side of the political spectrum is prone to saying that throwing money at public education doesn't solve anything. The other side of the funding debate is often accused of wanting to spend money on untested or frivolous programs without any kind of accountability or requirements for measurable outcomes. The government has pumped a lot of money into the system, including schools in poor states and districts, and it continues pumping. Has increased spending on education improved students' performance? Has it solved all the problems in schools? The above material answered these questions. At a time when education spending is at an all-time high and students' achievement levels are alarmingly low, it is impossible to expect that simply adding still more money to the public school system can produce significant improvement.

Of course, a reasonable counter argument is that the money hasn't been distributed properly. School systems that are financed and regulated on the national level, for example in countries such as France, Germany and Japan, are able to maintain a relatively uniform school environment regardless of the values and economies of local communities. Those who bring this type of example to defend the necessity of increased federal funding miss the important fact that the countries mentioned, which have national control over education, have allocated funding appropriately partially by mandating highly competitive standardized examinations. Students' achievements, i.e., the result of the government investment in education, determine, in part, the distribution of funds among local regions and schools. In such a huge country as the United States, most the states look like separate countries, and their obligation is to spend money on education wisely. If the state education systems worked efficiently, there would be no need for a centralized governmental body such as the US Department of Education. Unfortunately, in reality, different governors interpret the national education policy differently, although their speeches concerning high education standards sound similar. Being unable to fund education themselves, the states ask for help from the federal government and promise, in return, rosy results. As mentioned in Chapters 6 and 12, to achieve such results the state departments of education lower their standards. We described the educational mess created in the country, with different curricula not only within states but also within districts, various grading systems, various teachers' certification processes, etc. As shown in Chapter 12, the only way to make order in the public education area is to increase the role of the US Department of Education, which must determine the education policy and establish high education standards, curricula and tests related to basic subjects, which are obligatory for all states, and direct federal funds to states according to educational progress in these states. Does that require an increase in the staff of the Department of Education? Not at all. Now the ED acts mostly as a distributor of grants supporting various initiatives promoted and/or supported by influential groups, organizations, and politicians. Even as the richest country in the world, America can't squander money. No country has so many educational organizations as the US feeding at the ED's trough and taking advantage of the existing educational mess. The properly restructured ED, which would work with several highly professional educational organizations, responsible for curricula and testing, and which would stop wasting money on so-called research with obvious results, can significantly decrease federal spending on education. Accountability should not be just a popular word. It must be a real measure of educational progress.

Information for Reflection

To defend the constantly increasing education spending advocates of the current education policy don't forget to remind their opponents that while ED's programs and responsibilities have grown substantially over the years, the Department itself has not; with a planned fiscal year 2010 level of 4,199, ED's staff is 44% below the 7,528 employees who administered Federal education programs in several different agencies in 1980, when the Department was created (see www2. ed.gov/about/overview/fed/role.html). However, it is also necessary to indicate that the above number existed only one year. In his first year as president, Ronald Reagan decreased the ED's staff to 6,488. In 1983, the ED had 5,288 employees and in 1989 the ED's staff consisted of 4,696 employees, which is close to its current level. Educational bureaucrats chose statistics showing that the ED is a very small department compared, for example, to the Department of Defense or the Department of Energy. However, they forgot to compare the 14 billion dollars ED's budget in 1981 with the 64.9 billion dollars budget in 2009 and the main budget components (elementary and secondary education — 5.5 and 36.6 billion, postsecondary education — 7.1 and 21.6 billion, and the so-called others that include research, assessments, etc. — 1.4 and 5.8 billion, respectively).

For many years Americans have seen new Acts, reorganizations, additional spending, but no real positive results. As mentioned earlier, in 2002 the Institute of Education Sciences (IES) with four centers was created within the ED "to provide rigorous evidence on which to ground education practice and policy." The goal of its Research Center (NCER) is to support "rigorous research that addresses the nation's most pressing education needs, from early childhood to adult education." Do the above quotes from the ED's website reflect reality? The analysis of the 2009 "rigorous research" grants answers this question. Among the ED's grant topics one can find Middle and High School Reform; National Assessment of Educational Progress. But these topics were not awarded in 2009. However, 2.3 million dollars award was given to the proposal "Evaluating the Efficacy of Enhanced Anchored Instruction for Middle School Students with Learning Disabilities in Math," 0.5 million — to the project "School Leader Communication Model," 1.4 million — to the project "A Multi-Part Intervention for Accelerating Vocabulary Acquisition through Inductive Transfer." Why does the IES spend millions of dollars on dubious projects which have no direct and important impact on educational progress? The awarded projects should be considered by the National Science Foundation, which is the funding source for approximately 20% of all federally supported basic research conducted by America's colleges and universities and which has experts to evaluate their scientific importance. Maybe this is the reason why some politicians speak openly about abolishing the ED. Of course, these radicals demonstrate their ignorance. But it is obvious that the US Department of Education should squeeze its staff and prove its efficiency.

Let us dream and transfer ourselves in the better future, when the US Department of Education skipped its philanthropic function as, a money distributor, and became a real education policy maker. Its work power didn't increase. Instead, it shrank in size. Offices of the Secretary, the Deputy Secretary and the Under Secretary become smaller. Budget Office stops giving money to various educational organizations supporting dubious research. Such funding is provided mostly by the National Science Foundation and by the SBIR program, i.e., similar to what the Department of Energy or the Department of Defense do. The Institute of Education Sciences and Office of Elementary and Secondary Education play the main role in implementing education policy. They are responsible for preparing annual tests in the basic subjects (English language, mathematics, and science) for middle and high schools (by using their own experts or altogether with the leading education service organizations). The tests are designed in a way, so that they evaluate the students' basic knowledge in accordance with the established requirements. In addition, an optional part of the tests (especially, for tenth-twelfth graders) provides supplementary information on students' intellectual ability, which can be used to offer them higher level courses and which can be used by college admission offices to choose the brightest students. The evaluation is based on an identical clear system of points and grades. The established high education standards and reliable information about student achievement make unnecessary many existing testing and tutoring services, and their qualified workforce is used more efficiently in classrooms. The tests are sent to the state departments of education, which are responsible for their implementation. The exams' results are processed by the district departments, sent to the state departments, which, in turn, provide the ED with truthful information on the students' achievements. This reliable feedback enables the ED to develop strategy and take measures to improve the educational process in separate states and formulate requirements the state authorities must abide by. Financial help is given only to those states which follow the requirements and demonstrate progress in education outcomes. The money is given mostly for construction or reconstruction of schools and information technology equipment;

and its usage is rigorously controlled. The information on the students' achievements enables the ED to formulate more precisely the education research policy which will create a real competition of ideas concerning how to improve further education in the country. Financial discipline allows the ED to reduce its budget by stopping feeding hundreds of various educational organizations.

The functions of the reorganized ED's are simple and clear. It must be smaller and its activity should be focused mostly on core subjects. All other subjects, programs and actions related to these subjects can be resolved and should be resolved on local levels. The ED shouldn't spend money in vain. The ED should formulate precisely educational requirements and check how they are followed by states. The states which don't perform in accordance with the requirements should lose the federal financial aid and should be known to the public, so that people of these states can force their officials to do better their job or choose the new more efficient leaders. Public awareness is the most important factor. But the public shouldn't be misinformed and fooled by empty phrases and promises. The ED must be a real education policy maker and judge.

Assuming that Americans do establish the above-indicated high education standards, develop curricula for basic subjects, and work out the sophisticating testing system, can all these measures guarantee the expected educational progress? The positive answer can be only if these measures are accompanied by money directed to schools and by the decreased size of educational bureaucracy. We described the disproportional sizes of the boards of educations of various states which translate into the swollen educational bureaucracy. Information technology is the bitterest enemy of bureaucracy. As mentioned earlier, the regular national basic subjects standard tests can decrease the size of local educational departments, i.e., decrease states' money spent on education. It is difficult to get rid of bureaucratic thinking accompanied by long and expensive bureaucratic procedures. For example, the ED's report says, "Developing the assessment instruments — from writing questions to analyzing pilot-test results to constructing the final instruments — is a complex process that consumes most of the time during the interval between assessments. In addition to conducting national pilot tests, developers oversee numerous reviews of the assessment instrument by NAEP measurement experts, by the National Assessment Governing Board, and by external groups that include representatives from each of the states and jurisdictions that participate in the NAEP program." ("The Nation's Report Card: An Overview of Procedures for the NAEP Assessment" (NCES 2009–493) US Department of Education. Institute of Education Sciences. National Center for Education Statistics. Washington, DC: 2009.) It is difficult to imagine that experts in separate subjects need such a complicated procedure to prepare a test. Fighting bureaucracy means to decrease the unnecessary state and federal educational staff. Establishing high education standards means to get rid of unqualified teachers, which is not simple since most of educational workforce has trade unions' support.

Information for Reflection

On 14 February 2009, the Detroit Free Press reported that the US Secretary of Education Arne Duncan "loses sleep over 'the poor quality of education' Detroit children are receiving." He had reason to. A February 2009 Brookings Institution report found that Detroit Public Schools (DPS) was the worst overall major urban district, and the only one whose performance fell between 2000-2007. This caused the district to lose its place as a first-class district for state funding and opened the door for more charter schools to open up in the city. Nevertheless, this fact didn't embarrass the Detroit Federation of Teachers (DFT). It emboldened the DFT to demand a 15.6% pay increase for the highest income teachers, pointing out that they're making less than their counterparts in the suburbs. (The median total compensation, including all benefits, for the Detroit Public Schools is $70,046, while the median teacher pay in the tri-county area is $76,100.) A prolonged strike was averted primarily because DFT understood that a strike would encourage more children to leave the district for suburban schools of choice and charter schools, so that more DPS traditional public schools would be closed (29 schools is planned to close in 2009 to help cut into a $300 million budget deficit) resulting in layoffs and program cuts.

Such measures as *School Choice* and *Charter Schools Act* target indirectly teacher unions and educational bureaucracy. If poorly performing schools start losing students, their doors will be closed. When parents are able to send their children in non-unionized charter schools, fewer students will attend unsatisfactory functioning traditional public schools and, as a result, their funding will be diminished and they can face a possible closure. The charter schools are overwhelmingly supported by parents. A Gallup poll of September 1992 showed 70% overall support for *School Choice*, with 86% support among blacks, and 84% among Hispanics. Minorities well understand that poorly performing schools keep them in an underclass. The above-mentioned shows that the released market mechanism can bankrupt poorly performing schools, so that the local government will be forced to stop their life-support. This is a way, maybe not the best one, to get rid of bad teachers and school administrators. Unfortunately, the above "medicine" is expensive and can be considered as a temporary measure to move forward the process of improving the system of public education. The establishment of a single national system of education standards, tests, and curricula for the basic subjects accompanied with the regulations allowing the competition among the educational workforce and providing the job opportunity only for those who satisfy certain requirements — only under these conditions the United States system of public education can produce the expected results.

The empathized necessity of the increased governmental control over education doesn't mean that the author is an advocate of the nanny state. Vice versa. I strongly believe that the government has no right to control our lives and, moreover, it must not make decisions for us and in our place. Each individual succeeds by establishing certain goals and by doing everything necessary to achieve them. The government is unable to do that for us.

But there are overall goals, which are larger than our own (irrespective of how ambitious we are), where the government involvement is necessary. The government's first obligation is to protect its citizens. Nobody argues the necessity of sophisticated armed forces. National security also depends on the education level of its population. The educated young generation is America's second line of defense. The government involvement in education shouldn't be interpreted as micromanagement. There is no need to destroy the existing educational structure. It should be only modernized to work more efficiently, as we have explained.

By investing money in the public education system, Americans expected to benefit from that. This is the goal of any investment. But what have they received in reality? The US high school dropout crisis poses one of the greatest threats to the nation's economic growth and competitiveness. Nationwide, 7,000 students drop out every day and only about 70% of students graduate from high school with a regular high school diploma. Two thousand high schools in the US produce more than half of all dropouts, and a recent study suggests that in the 50 largest cities only 53% of students graduate on time. Children raised in extremely uncomfortable surroundings, poor and minority children, attend these so-called "dropout factories" at significantly higher rates. Of course, the government cannot legislate decent parenting. However, the mentioned schools are part of the problem as well. Young persons without high education are unable to perform properly at a decently paid job. They pay low taxes or don't pay any taxes at all. They become society's dead weight.

If the US public schools and universities don't provide American children with proper knowledge of mathematics, physics, and other important scientific disciplines, the future generation will not be able to compete with the world workforce. Without decent elementary knowledge of mathematics many school graduates apply to universities to get a degree in liberal arts. As a result, the American public education system prepares too many "talkers" and too few who are able to create something useful for society. It is natural that many persons who earned, for example, a degree in political science, are unable to find a job in this area, and they are forced to make a living in absolutely different areas. Usually, their salaries are not high. With higher education diplomas, they expect to be paid like scientists and engineers in manufacturing companies, research centers, etc. But their desire is at odds with reality, since no business will pay much if you are not an expert. Bitterness and dissatisfaction color their lives.

This is a risk built into the capitalist system, the system that in a short period of time transformed the United States into a superpower. The US education system is guilty of not producing the right workforce to build on its technical and scientific progress. (The schools and society in general fail to foster in children a love for mathematics and science; no one, not even the universities, manages the number of people entering various fields in the liberal arts.)

Now the country is experiencing a severe economic crisis. The national debt is huge. A great British physicist, Ernest Rutherford, the father of nuclear physics, wrote: "We haven't the money, so we've got to think." Maybe this is the best recommendation to educators, parents and politicians, to everyone who cares about the future of their country.

Appendix 1. Post-World War II American Nobel Prize Laureates

The list below contains the names of American post-World War II Nobel Prize laureates in physics, chemistry, physiology or medicine and economics, i.e., in the most important fields determining technological progress and high living standards.

In Physics:

2009 George Smith (University of Pennsylvania, University of Chicago).

2006 John C. Mather (Swarthmore College, University of California, Berkeley).

George F. Smoot (Massachusetts Institute of Technology (MIT)).

2005 Roy J. Glauber (Harvard University).

John L. Hall (Carnegie Institute of Technology).

2004 Hugh D. Politzer (University of Michigan, Harvard University).

Frank Wilczek (University of Chicago, Princeton University).

2002 Raymond Davis Jr. (University of Maryland, Yale University).

2001 Eric A. CornellCornell (Stanford University, MIT).

Carl E. Wieman (MIT, Stanford University, University of Chicago).

2000 Jack S. Kilby (University of Illinois at Urbana-Champaign, University of Wisconsin-Milwaukee).

1998 Robert B. Laughlin (University of California, Berkeley; MIT).

1997 Steven Chu (University of Rochester, University of California, Berkeley).

William D. Phillips (Juniata College , MIT).

1996 David M. Lee (Harvard University , University of Connecticut, Yale University).

Douglas D. Osheroff (California Institute of Technology, Cornell University).

Robert C. Richardson (Virginia Tech, Duke University).

1995   Martin L. Perl (Brooklyn Polytechnic University, Columbia University).

Frederick Reines (Stevens Institute of Technology , New York University).

1994   Clifford G. Shull (Carnegie Mellon University, New York University, MIT).

1993   Russell A. Hulse (Cooper Union, University of Massachusetts, Amherst).

Joseph H. Taylor Jr. (Haverford College, Harvard University).

1990   Jerome I. Friedman (University of Chicago).

Henry W. Kendall (Deerfield Academy, Amherst College).

1989   Norman F. Ramsey (Columbia University).

1988   Leon M. Lederman (City College of New York, Columbia University).

Melvin Schwartz (Columbia University).

1983   William A. Fowler (Ohio State University, California Institute of Technology)

1982   Kenneth G. Wilson (Harvard University, California Institute of Technology).

1980   James W. Cronin, (Southern Methodist University, University of Chicago).

Val L. Fitch (McGill University, Columbia University).

1979   Sheldon Glashow (Cornell University, Harvard University).

Steven Weinberg (Cornell University, Princeton University).

1978   Arno A. Penzias (City College of New York, Columbia University).

Robert W. Wilson (Rice University, California Institute of Technology).

1977   Philip W. Anderson (Harvard University).

John H. Van Vleck (Harvard University).

1976   Burton Richter (MIT).

1975   Ben R. Mottelson, (Purdue University, Harvard University).

James Rainwater (California Institute of Technology, Columbia University).

1972   John Bardeen (University of Wisconsin, Princeton University).

Leon N. Cooper (Columbia University).

John R. Schrieffer (MIT, University of Illinois at Urbana-Champaign).

1969   Murray Gell-Mann(Yale University, MIT).

1968   Luis W. Alvarez (University of Chicago).

1965   Julian S. Schwinger (City College of New York, Columbia University).

Richard P. Feynman (MIT, Princeton University).

1964   Charles H. Townes (Furman University, Duke University, California Institute of Technology).

1961   Robert Hofstadter (City College of New York, Princeton University).

1960   Donald A. Glaser (Case Institute of Technology, California Institute of Technology).

1959   Owen Chamberlain (Dartmouth College).

1956   William B. Shockley (California Institute of Technology, MIT).

John Bardeen (University of Wisconsin).

Walter H. Brattain (Whitman College, University of Oregon, University of Minnesota).

1955   Willis E. Lamb (University of California, Berkeley).

Polykarp Kusch (Case Western Reserve University, University of Illinois).

1952   Edward M. Purcell (Purdue University, Harvard University).

1946   Percy W. Bridgman (Harvard University).

In Chemistry

2010   Richard F. Heck (University of California, Los Angeles).

2009   Thomas Steitz (Lawrence University, Harvard University).

2008   Martin Chalfie (Harvard University)

2006   Roger D. Kornberg (Harvard University, Stanford University).

2005   Robert H. Grubbs (Columbia University).

Richard R. Schrock (University of California, Riverside; Harvard University).

2004   Irwin A. Rose (Washington State University ,University of Chicago).

2003   Peter Agre (Augsburg College, Johns Hopkins University).

Roderick MacKinnon (University of Massachusetts, Boston; Brandeis University, Tufts University).

2002   John B. Fenn (Berea College, Yale University).

2001   William S. Knowles (Harvard University, Columbia University).

Karl B. Sharpless (Dartmouth College, Stanford University).

2000   Alan J. Heeger (University of Nebraska, University of California, Berkeley).

1997   Paul D. Boyer (Brigham Young University, University of Wisconsin-Madison).

1996   Robert F. Curl, Jr. (Rice University, University of California, Berkeley).

Richard E. Smalley (Hope College, University of Michigan, Princeton University).

1995   Frank S. Rowland (Ohio Wesleyan University, University of Chicago).

1993   Kary B. Mullis. (Georgia Institute of Technology, University of California, Berkeley).

1990   Elias J. Corey (Massachusetts Institute of Technology).

1989   Thomas Robert Cech (Grinnell College, University of California, Berkeley).

1987   Donald J. Cram (Rollins College, University of Nebraska, Harvard University).

1986   Dudley R. Herschbach (Stanford University, Harvard University).

1985   Herbert A. Hauptman (City College of New York, Columbia University). Jerome Karle (City College of New York, Harvard University, University of Michigan, Ann Arbor).

1984   Robert B. Merrifield (Pasadena Junior College, University of California, Los Angeles).

1981   Roald Hoffmann (Columbia University, Harvard University).

1980   Paul Berg (Pennsylvania   State University, Case Western Reserve University).

Walter Gilbert (Harvard University, University of Cambridge).

1979   Herbert C. Brown (University of Chicago).

1976   William N. Lipscomb, Jr. (University of Kentucky, California Institute of Technology).

1974   Paul J. Flory (Manchester College, Ohio State University).

1972   Christian B. Anfinsen, Jr. (Swarthmore College, University of Pennsylvania, Harvard University).

Stanford Moore (Vanderbilt University, University of Wisconsin).

William H. Stein (Columbia University, Harvard University).

1966   Robert S. Mulliken (MIT, University of Chicago).

1965   Robert B. Woodward (MIT).

1961   Melvin E. Calvin (Michigan Tech University, University of Minnesota).

1960   Willard F. Libby (University of California, Berkeley).

1955   Vincent du Vigneaud (University of Illinois, Rochester University).

1954   Linus Carl Pauling (Oregon State University, California Institute of Technology).

1952   Edwin Mattison McMillan (California Institute of Technology).

Glenn T. Seaborg (University of California, Los Angeles; University of California, Berkeley).

James B. Sumner (Harvard University).

John H. Northrop (Columbia University).

Wendell M. Stanley (Earlham College, University of Illinois).

In Physiology or Medicine

2009   Carol Greider (University of California, Santa Barbara; University of California, Berkeley).

2007   Mario R. Capecchi (Antioch, Harvard University).

2006   Andrew Z. Fire (University of California, Berkeley; MIT)

Craig C. Mello (Brown University, Harvard University).

2004   Richard Axel (Columbia University, Johns Hopkins University).

Linda B. Buck (University of Washington, Seattle University of Texas, Dallas).

2003   Paul C. Lauterbur (Case Institute of Technology, University of Pittsburgh).

2002   Robert H. Horvitz (MIT, Harvard University).

2001   Leland H. Hartwell (California Institute of Technology, MIT).

2000   Paul G.Greengard (Hamilton College, Johns Hopkins University).

1998   Robert F. Furchgott (University of North Carolina, Northwestern University).

Louis J. Ignarro (Columbia University, University of Minnesota).

Ferid Murad (DePauw University, Case Western Reserve University).

1997   Stanley B. Prusiner (University of Pennsylvania).

1995   Edward B. Lewis (University of Minnesota , California Institute of Technology).

Eric F. Wieschaus (University of Notre Dame, Yale University).

1994   Alfred G. Gilman (Yale University, Case Western Reserve University).

Martin R. Rodbell (Johns Hopkins University, University of Washington).

1993   Phillip A. Sharp (University of Illinois).

1992   Edwin G. Krebs (University of Illinois, Washington University at St. Louise).

1990   Joseph E. Murray (College of the Holy Cross, Harvard University).

Donnall Thomas (University of Texas at Austin, Harvard University).

1989   John M. Bishop (Gettysburg College, Harvard University).

Harold E. Varmus (Amherst College, Harvard University, Columbia University).

Gertrude B. Elion (Hunter College, New York University).

George H. Hitchings (University of Washington).

1986   Stanley Cohen (Brooklyn College, Oberlin College, University of Michigan).

1985   Michael S. Brown (University of Pennsylvania).

Joseph L. Goldstein (Washington and Lee University, University of Texas).

1983   Barbara McClintock (Cornell University).

1981   Roger W. Sperry (Oberlin College, University of Chicago).

1978   Daniel Nathans (University of Delaware, Washington University at St. Louis).

Hamilton O. Smith (University of Illinois at Urbana-Champaign, University of California, Berkeley; Johns Hopkins University).

1977   Rosalyn S. Yalow (Hunter College, New York University, University of Illinois).

1976   Baruch S. Blumberg (Union College in Schenectady, Columbia University).

Carleton Gajdusek (University of Rochester, Harvard University).

1975   David Baltimore (Swarthmore College, Rockefeller University).

       Howard M. Temin (Swarthmore College, California Institute of Technology).

1972   Gerald M. Edelman (Ursinus College , University of Pennsylvania).

1971   Earl W. Sutherland, Jr. (Washburn University, Washington University at St. Louis).

1970   Julius Axelrod (College of the City of New York, New York University).

1969   Alfred D. Hershey (Michigan State University).

1968   Robert W. Holley (University of Illinois at Urbana-Champaign, Cornell University).

       Marshall W. Nirenberg (University of Florida, University of Michigan, Ann Arbor).

1967   Haldan K. Hartline (Lafayette College, Johns Hopkins University).

       George Wald (New York University, Columbia University).

1966   Peyton Rous (Johns Hopkins University).

1962   James Watson (University of Chicago, Indiana University).

1959   Arthur Kornberg (College of the City of New York, University of Rochester).

1958   George Beadle (University of Nebraska, Cornell University).

       Edward Tatum (University of Chicago, University of Wisconsin).

       Joshua Lederberg (Columbia University, Yale University).

1956   Dickinson W. Richards (Yale University , Columbia University).

1954   John F. Enders (Yale University, Harvard University).

       Thomas H. Weller (University of Michigan at Ann Arbor, Harvard University).

       Frederick C. Robbins (University of Missouri, Harvard University).

1950   Edward C. Kendall (Columbia University).

       Philip S. Hench (Lafayette College, University of Pittsburgh).

1946   Hermann J. Muller (Columbia University).

In Economics

2010   Peter A. Diamond Diamond earned (Yale University, MIT).

       Dale Mortensen (Willamette University, Carnegie Mellon University).

       Elinor Ostrom (University of California, Los Angeles).

       Oliver E. Williamson (MIT, Stanford University, Carnegie Mellon University).

       Paul Krugman (Yale University, MIT).

       Eric S. Maskin (Harvard University).

       Roger B. Myerson (Harvard University).

2006   Edmund S. Phelps (Amherst College, Yale University).

2005   Thomas C. Schelling (University of California, Berkeley; Harvard University).

2004   Edward C. Prescott (Swarthmore College, Case Western Reserve University, Carnegie Mellon University).

2003   Robert F. Engle III (Williams College, Cornell University).

2002   Vernon L. Smith (University of Kansas, Harvard University).

2001   George A. Akerlof (Yale University, MIT).

       Joseph E. Stiglitz (Amherst College, MIT).

2000   James J. Heckman (Colorado University, Princeton University).

       Daniel L. McFadden (University of Minnesota).

1997   Robert C. Merton (Columbia University, California Institute of Technology, MIT).

1995   Robert E. Lucas Jr. (University of Chicago).

1994   John F. Nash Jr. (Carnegie Mellon University).

1993   Robert W. Fogel (Cornell University, Columbia University, Johns Hopkins University).

       Douglass C. North (University of California, Berkeley).

1992   Gary S. Becker (Princeton University, University of Chicago).

1990   Harry M. Markowitz (University of Chicago).

       Merton H. Miller (Johns Hopkins University).

       William F. Sharpe (University of California, Los Angeles)

1987   Robert M. Solow (Harvard University).

1986   James M. Buchanan Jr. (Middle Tennessee State College, University of Tennessee, University of Chicago).

1982   George J. Stigler (University of Washington, Northwestern University, University of Chicago).

1981   James Tobin (Harvard University).

1980   Lawrence R. Klein (Los Angeles City College, University of California, Berkeley; MIT).

1979   Theodore W. Schultz (South Dakota State College, University of Wisconsin).

1978   Herbert A. Simon (University of Wisconsin-Madison, University of Chicago).

1976   Milton Friedman (Rutgers University, Brown University).

1972   Kenneth J. Arrow (City College of New York , Columbia University).

1971   Simon Kuznets (Columbia University).

1970   Paul A. Samuelson (University of Chicago, Harvard University).

Appendix 2. A Hypothetical Curriculum for Basic Subjects

Education in the United States is highly de-centralized, and the federal government is not heavily involved in determining curricula or education standards. This gave rise to a huge number of different school curricula. They are different not only in schools of various states but also in schools of the same districts.

As an advocate of an identical curriculum for basic subjects (English language, mathematics, and science) in all American public schools, here the author offers a hypothetical curriculum for these subjects, which he developed analyzing the curricula of a wide variety of schools. Additional useful information about existing curricula can be found on the following websites: *www.homeschoolacademy.com*; *www.musthighschool.com*; *www.linkslearning.org*; *www.coreknowledge.org/CK/about/index.htm*.

The author believes that it is impossible to ignore English grammar when teaching an English language course, just as it is impossible to avoid offering a physics course, although many schools do that. Science courses presents a mixture of various disciplines (physics, chemistry, life science, earth science). In elementary school, the science class includes only basic facts, without details, and doesn't require a teacher who knows the area well. Moreover, it is difficult for young students to concentrate on one specific topic for the whole academic year, so that it is useful for a variety of scientific topics to be taught by one teacher. However, it's hard to believe that middle school students can get deep knowledge if the same person is teaching, for example, Newton's laws and the human digestive system. It's better if, during the academic year, science courses in middle school consist of material related only to two disciplines, each subject being taught by a specialist in that specific area, i.e., by two, rather than one, teachers. Taking into account the fact that some courses are taught at various levels of difficulty, the hypothetical curriculum focuses on the basic level (usually, the lowest acceptable level of difficulty).

The curriculum of higher level courses, designed for motivated students, can be developed by teachers together with local education authorities. That is why the curriculum outlined below does not contain, for example, a pre-calculus course. Since high school students need to earn only 3 credits in science, the author has recommended the following courses: physics, chemistry (or biology), and computer science. Computers have become a part of our lives, and everyone in the new generation should understand how computers work, how to use existing applications, and how to develop their own.

FIRST GRADE

ENGLISH

In English, first graders are taught mainly how to read. They should learn the following:

Reading and Comprehension

- identify letter sounds in words, blend letter sounds to make words, sound out short words, etc.
- read simple stories and beginning reader books and discuss the readings
- read aloud with someone outside the school at least ten minutes daily

Writing

- write brief compositions (e.g., letters, short stories)

Spelling

- correctly spell dictated words
- know simple spelling rules

Grammar and Usage

- know simple capitalization rules
- make the plural form of nouns by adding s
- use periods, question marks, and exclamation points at the end of sentences

MATHEMATICS

In mathematics, first grade students learn addition and subtraction, practice with small numbers, and become familiar with simple fraction. They should:

Numbers and Number Systems

- know the concept of a set, identify items that belong to a set, recognize and extend simple patterns
- read, write, count (forward and backward) and compare (more or less) numbers from 0 to 100; compare quantities using the symbols ‹,›, and =
- learn about place value (ones, tens, hundred)
- learn what simple fractions (1/2,1/3, and ¼) represent
- make and read simple bar graphs and pictographs

Geometry

- identify and draw basic plane figures (square, rectangle, triangle, and circle) and identify solid figures (cure, cone, sphere)

Measurements

- take simple measurements of length, weight, volume, and temperature using standard units; tell time to the half hour

Applications

- learn relative values of penny, nickel, dime, and quarter; demonstrate how to get the same amounts of money with different combination of coins

SCIENCE

First grade science students learn how to conduct simple equipment and tools to gather data, how to observe, measure, connect, record and report data, and to classify living and nonliving objects. They should do the following:

- make observations to build an understanding of the needs of living organisms (plants, animals)
- make observations to build an understanding of earth materials (soil, rocks) and their properties
- classify solids according their properties (color, shape, size, texture, hardness)
- classify liquids according their properties (color, ability to float or sink in water, tendency to flow)
- observe mixtures (solids with solids, liquids with liquids, solids with liquids)
- make observations to build an understanding of motion of objects and equilibrium

SECOND GRADE
ENGLISH
In English, second graders continue learning how to read.
Reading and Comprehension
- read words and stories and beginning reader books and discuss the readings
- answer who, what, why, how, and what if questions about reading
- retell stories and explain in their own words what they learned
- read outside the school at least fifteen minutes daily

Writing
- write letters, brief stories, and small compositions (with the beginning, middle, and end)
- how to use paragraphs

Spelling and Vocabulary
- review spelling rules
- how to use dictionary to check word meanings and spelling
- some types of contractions (e.g., don't) and abbreviations (e.g., Mr., Ms.)

Grammar and Usage
- subjects and predicates in simple sentences
- information about nouns and how to make the plural form of nouns
- initial information about verbs, present and past tenses, and how to change from present to past tense
- about adjectives and forms that end with *-er* and *-est*
- how to use commas in dates and addresses
- use periods, commas, question marks, and exclamation points in sentences

MATHEMATICS
In mathematics, second grade students practice adding and subtraction and begin studying multiplication. They also study properties of some basic shapes and use simple graphs.

Numbers and Number Systems
- read, write, order, and compare whole numbers up to 1,000
- locate whole numbers on a numeric line
- identify even and odd numbers, place values, round numbers to the nearest ten
- make and read simple charts and bar graphs
- identify patterns; determine the core of a pattern; extend patterns

- learn how to add and subtract two- and three-digit numbers; use addition to check subtraction
- practice multiplying single-digit numbers by 1, 2, 3, 4, 5
- recognize simple fractions

Geometry
- learn properties of basic shapes; identify lines of symmetry and create simple symmetric figures; measure perimeters of squares and rectangles

Measurements
- measure, estimate, and compare objects by size, quantity, weight, and capacity

Applications
- read and write money amounts using the symbols $ and ¢ and the decimal point
- learn how to write the time and the date

SCIENCE

Building on the concepts introduced in first grade, students study topics such as:

- seasons change and how it affects living things
- understand the life cycle (birth, growth, reproduction, death) and conditions for development (food, air, space)
- basic life cycles of some plants and animals (survey of plants, survey of animals)
- the water cycles (evaporation, condensation, precipitation)
- understand weather conditions (temperature, wind direction, wind speed, precipitation) and use common tools to measure weather (wind vane, anemometer, thermometer, rain gauge); observe and record weather changes over time
- the sun as the source of light and warmth; understand how energy from the sun warms the land, air, and water
- identify three states of matter (solid, liquid, gas); observe changes in state due to heating and cooling of common materials

THIRD GRADE
ENGLISH
Reading and Comprehension
- orally summarize the main ideas of reading texts

- ask and answer who, what, why, how, and what if questions about reading texts
- learn to use a book's table of contents and index
- read outside the school at least twenty minutes daily

Writing

- write letters, brief stories, small compositions, etc.
- learn letter-writing conventions (e.g., heading, salutation, closing)
- practice writing paragraphs with topic sentence, central idea, and supporting details

Spelling and Vocabulary

- practice regularly at spelling and vocabulary enrichment
- learn to use prefixes (e.g., *re*, *un*, *dis*) and suffixes (e.g., *er*, *less*, *ly*)
- learn some common abbreviations (e.g., US., NY, MD, ft, Dr..)

Grammar and Usage

- identify subjects and predicates in sentences
- identify and use declarative, interrogative, imperative, and exclamatory sentences
- learn possessive nouns
- learn how to use articles (a, an , the), nouns, pronouns, verbs, adjectives, and adverbs in sentences
- know how to use period, question mark, exclamation point, comma (in dates, addresses, series, after *yes* and *no*), apostrophe (in contractions and possessive nouns)

MATHEMATICS

Third grade students should learn multiplication and division facts and practice basic operation with whole numbers. They continue learning about geometric shapes and measurements, how to tell time, use the calendar, and handle small quantities of money. They should be able to do the following:

Numbers and Number Systems

- read, write, order, and compare whole numbers up to 999,999; recognize place value of each digit
- learn the concept of negative numbers; locate positive and negative whole numbers on a numeric line
- learn Roman numerals I,V,X and combinations of them
- find the sum (up to 10,000) of two whole numbers; find the difference between two whole numbers less than 10,000

- understand multiplication and division as opposite operations; use multiplication and division symbols
- use calculator to find sums, differences, products, and quotients
- solve problems with more than one operation
- recognize, read, compare and equate simple fractions; read and write decimals to hundredth

Measurements

- measure, estimate , and compare objects by size , quantity, weight, and capacity; make measurements using standard units; learn some relationship between units

Geometry

- identify polygons and congruent shapes

Applications

- solve simple problems involving time, money, temperature, length, weight, and capacity
- work with data and construct bar graphs and pictographs

SCIENCE

Third graders continue learning how to conduct an investigation and analyze the results, using various equipment and working in teams. They study topics such as:

- understanding of the concepts of sound (how sound is produced by vibrating objects and vibrating air columns; how the frequency can be changed by altering the size and shape of a variety of instruments
- how sound travels in waves (through solids, liquids, and gases)
- understand how the human ear detects sound by having a membrane that vibrates when sound reaches it
- how light travels (observe that light travels in a straight line until it strikes an object and is reflected and/or absorbed); difference between transparent and opaque objects
- basic structure of solar system (sun, stars, planets, universe, earth, moon and beyond)
- earth's place in solar system (e.g., orbits the sun; rotates every twenty four hours)
- phases of the moon (observe and record the change in the apparent shape of the moon from day to day over several months and describe the pattern of changes)
- solar and lunar eclipses

- understanding of the structure and function of major systems of the human body (e.g., skeletal, muscle, digestive, circulatory, excretory)
- the ecosystem; the organism and its environment
- learn about living things and their environments (observe and measure how the quantities and qualities of nutrients, light, and water in the environment affect plant growth; observe and describe how environmental conditions determine how well plants survive and grow in a particular environment)
- how changes in environment (e.g., food supply) and by man-made changes (e.g., industrial waste) affect ecosystems

FOURTH GRADE
ENGLISH

Fourth graders should be able to do the following:

Writing and Comprehension

- write summaries, descriptions, letters, stories, poems
- identify the purpose of the writing and/or a text; defining a main idea;
- practice writing using well organized paragraphs, with a clear idea, an introduction, and conclusion
- use various sources (e.g., encyclopedias, magazines) to write short reports
- learn how to create a bibliography

Spelling and Vocabulary

- practice regularly at spelling and vocabulary enrichment
- practice using synonyms and antonyms
- learn more prefixes (e.g., *im, non, pre. mis*) and suffixes (e.g., *ily, able, ment, ful, ness*)

Grammar and Usage

- identify subject and predicate in sentences; understand subject-verb agreement
- use declarative, interrogative, imperative, and exclamatory sentences
- know the following parts of speech and how to use them: nouns, pronouns, verbs, adjectives, adverbs, conjunctions, interjections
- know how to use period, question mark, exclamation point, comma, apostrophe, quotation marks

MATHEMATICS

In mathematics, fourth grade students continue to practice multiplication and division with whole numbers, and gain an initial knowledge of lines, angles, circles and plane figures. They should be able to do the following:

Numbers and Number Systems

- operate with up to six digit numbers (read, write, use expanded notation, round to the near 10, 100, 1000, 10000, 1000000)
- add and subtract four-digit numbers
- study multiplication and multiply by two- and three-digit numbers
- identify multiples and factors of a given number; common multiples and factors of two given numbers
- study division and divide by one- and two-digit numbers
- learn fractions (proper and improper) and mixed numbers
- illustrate the concept of a set as a whole in using fractions
- operations with fractions (change improper fractions to mixed numbers, put fractions in lowest terms, compare fractions
- operations with decimals (read, write, and compare decimals; read and write decimals as fractions; round decimals to nearest tenth or hundredth
- read and write fractions of a number line

Geometry

- identify horizontal, vertical, intersecting, parallel, and perpendicular lines; locate the lines of symmetry in given shapes
- describe similarities and differences of shapes having 3,4,5,6, and 8 line segments; classify shapes by self-selected criteria and describe the classification scheme; identify and name polygons (3,4,5,6, and 8 sides)

Measurements

- understand the basic idea of measurement; measure and record lengths (including perimeters) and capacities; learn basic measurement equivalence and make simple conversions
- measure, record, and estimate weight; learn measurement equivalence and make simple conversions

Applications

- solve simple problems involving money and time

SCIENCE

In science, fourth grade students continue learning about various phenomena of the natural or material world, such as:

- interdependence of organisms and their environment (how all living and nonliving things affect the life of a particular animal; how animals of the same kind differ in some of their characteristics and possible advantages and disadvantages of this variation; how behaviors and body structures help animals survive in a particular habitat; how humans and other animals can adapt their behavior to live in changing habitats)

- basic concept of atoms; structure of atoms (protons, electrons, neutrons)
- basic properties of matter (e.g., concepts of mass, volume, and density)
- magnetism and electricity (observe and investigate the influence of magnets on all materials made of iron and on other magnets; law of magnetic attraction)
- electricity as the flow of electrons; electric current and circuits (parallel and series)
- conductors and insulators of electricity
- how magnetism can be used to generate electricity (design and test an electric circuit as a closed pathway including an energy source, energy conductor, and an energy receiver)
- the ability of electric circuits to produce light, heat, sound, and magnetic effects
- the earth and its changes (earth's layers; earthquakes; volcanoes; how the continents and oceans and mountains were formed; weathering and erosion; weathering and soil formation; surface water and ground water; glaciers)
- the role of the water cycle and how movement of water over and through the landscape helps shape land forms; the wearing away and movement of rock and soil in erosion and in forming canyons, valleys, meanders, and tributaries

FIFTH GRADE

ENGLISH

In English, fifth graders proceed to literary knowledge. They should be able to do the following:

Writing and Comprehension

- write summaries, descriptions, letters, stories, poems, etc
- use different resources (e.g., newspapers, glossaries, the Internet) in writings
- practice writing using well organized paragraphs, with a well defined idea, an introduction, and conclusion; support main points with good examples, make references

Spelling and Vocabulary

- practice regularly at spelling and vocabulary enrichment

- learn more prefixes (e.g., anti, *co, semi*) and suffixes (e.g., *ist, ish, tion*)

Grammar and Usage
- identify subject and predicate in sentences; use correct subject-verb agreement
- use declarative, interrogative, imperative, and exclamatory sentences
- know the following parts of speech and how to use them: nouns, pronouns, verbs, adjectives, adverbs, conjunctions, interjections
- learn pronoun-antecedent agreement
- use correctly punctuation studied in earlier grades and expand it (e.g., commas used with appositives and appositive phrases)

MATHEMATICS

Fifth grade students practice addition, subtraction, multiplication, and division with decimals and fractions, learn ratios and percentages, learn about polygons and various types of angles.

Numbers and Number Systems
- read and write numbers through billions
- use exponents to express related factors and convert exponential notation to whole numbers
- multiply 2-, 3-, and 4- place factors times 2-place factors
- divide 3- and 4- place factors by multiples of 10
- study prime numbers and find the greatest common factor and least common multiple; use rules of divisibility for 2,3,5,6,9, and ten and use these rules to identify prime numbers
- study percentages and find fraction, decimal, percent equivalents
- put fractions in lowest terms
- add, subtract, multiply and divide with fractions and mixed numbers
- add, subtract, and multiply with decimals; divide decimals by whole numbers; round decimals; write them in expanded form; place them on number line

Geometry
- identify and draw acute, obtuse, right, and straight angles
- identify and draw equilateral, right, and isosceles triangles
- identify the bases, heights, vertices, sides, and diagonals of polygons
- compute areas of squares, triangles, rectangles, and parallelograms
- find area of composite figures by dividing them into known standard figures

- identify arc, chord, radius, and diameter of a circles; compute circumferences of circles

Probability and Statistics

- find averages (means) for a given data sets

Measurements

- practice measuring with different units (e.g., *ft*, *lb*, *gal*, *min*, *sec*)
- present a given amount of time in various units (e.g., *min*, *sec*)

Applications

- construct patterns to explore the concept of ratio; solve problems regarding speed as a ratio of distance and time

SCIENCE

Fifth grade students continue examining various phenomena and learning some models which help to explain them. Fifth graders study the following topics:

- structures and properties of cells
- parts of cells (e.g., membrane, nucleus, cytoplasm); differences in plant and animal cells; cells without nuclei (e.g., bacteria); single-celled organisms
- organization of cells into tissues, organs, and systems
- basic structure of vascular and nonvascular plants; mechanism of plant reproduction; photosynthesis in plants
- main parts of flowers and their functions
- structure of the atmosphere (e.g., troposphere, stratosphere, mesosphere, ionosphere)
- air movement and pressure; cold and warm fronts; thunderstorms, tornadoes, hurricanes
- formation of various types of clouds and their relation to weather
- how global atmospheric movement patterns affect local weather
- the influence of geographic conditions on weather and climate
- the muscular system (e.g., voluntary and involuntary muscles)
- the skeletal system (e.g., skeleton, spinal column, rib cage)
- the circulatory system (heart, role of red and white cells)
- the respiratory system (e.g., lungs, oxygen-carbon dioxide exchange)
- the digestive system (e.g., intestines, salivary glands)
- excretory system (e.g., kidney, bladder}
- the nervous system (e.g., spinal cord, nerves)
- structure of the eye (e.g., cornea, iris, pupil) and ear (ear canal, eardrum) and how they work

SIXTH GRADE

ENGLISH

In English, sixth graders should demonstrate deeper reading skills and understanding of literature. They should be able to do the following:

Writing and Comprehension

- write essays, summaries, descriptions, letters, stories, poems, etc
- write an essay that requires gathering information, taking notes, and preparing bibliography
- practice writing letters

Speaking, Spelling and Vocabulary

- practice regularly at spelling and vocabulary enrichment
- participate in group discussions
- give a presentation before the class

Grammar and Usage

- identify independent and dependent clauses
- identify and use simple, compound, complex, and compound-complex sentences
- learn about the active and passive voices
- study correct use of troublesome words (e.g., well, good; like, as; who, whom)
- use correctly punctuation studied in earlier grades and expand it (e.g., commas used with appositives and appositive phrases)

MATHEMATICS

Sixth graders should be competent operating with positive and negative numbers, fractions and decimals, working with ratios, proportions and percentages; in geometry they should learn and use formulas to find the perimeters, areas, and volumes. They should be able to do the following:

Numbers and Number Systems

- solve problems with prime numbers; squares and square roots; greatest common factors; least common multiples
- learn about exponents; identify powers of ten up to 10^6
- solve problems involving ratios and proportions
- solve problems with percentages
- add, subtract, multiply, and divide with fractions, decimals, and mixed numbers
- present fractions as decimals, decimals as percents, percents as fractions, etc.

Algebra
- solve simple equations with one variable

Geometry
- identify congruent sides, angles and axes of symmetry in various plane figures
- find perimeters and areas of various plane figures
- find volumes of rectangular solids
- find the circumferences and areas of circles
- graph simple functions

Probability and Statistics
- determine probability of an event
- for a given set of data determine the mean, median, range and mode
- make histograms and tree-diagrams

Measurements
- learn prefixes used in metric system and convert units within the US system and within the metric system

SCIENCE

In the sixth grade science program, students learn to observe and analyze through hands-on experiments and gain further insight into how scientists understand our natural world. They should learn about physical science and earth science. Major topics of study include:

- concept of speed and acceleration (Speed = Distance/Time; Acceleration = Speed Change/Time)
- concept of force; examples of force (e.g., gravity); Newton's laws (Force = Mass x Acceleration)
- concept of work (Work = Force x Distance)
- concept of energy as the ability to do work
- kinetic and potential energy
- concept of power (Power = Work/Time)
- different forms of energy (mechanical, heat, chemical) and their sources
- renewable and non renewable sources (fossil fuels, nuclear energy, hydro energy, alternate energy resources, energy from wind, solar energy, geothermal energy)
- transformation of energy
- physical changes in matter caused by as a result of energy changes
- study of chemical and physical properties of matter (determine and measure experimentally: boiling point, melting point, density, and solubility; demonstrate understanding that chemical and physical properties de-

termine a substance's identity; compare common metals, nonmetals, and metalloids by name, symbol, and characteristics; relate density to mass and volume)

- fossils as a record of earth's past life
- how fossils are formed; types of fossils (mold, cast, trace, true-form)
- history of life on earth (origin of life on earth, evidence for change over time)
- natural selection; modern views of evolution; the origin of new species

SEVENTH GRADE

ENGLISH

Seventh graders' assignments in English include more difficult reading texts and frequent writing exercises.

Writing and Comprehension

- write descriptive essays, book reports, summaries, stories, poems, etc
- write well organized nonfiction and research essays

Speaking, Spelling and Vocabulary

- practice regularly at spelling and vocabulary enrichment
- participate productively in group discussions
- give a presentation before the class

Grammar and Usage

- learn preposition phrases (e.g., adjectival and adverbial)
- learn subject-verb agreement with compound subjects
- learn about subject and object complements, as well as complements of verbs, nouns and adjectives
- learn participle, gerund, infinitive and practice with sentences containing these verbal forms
- learn about different types of clauses (independent, dependent, noun, adjective, and adverb)

MATHEMATICS

Seventh graders expand their knowledge of geometry and learn some material from theory of probability and statistics.

Numbers and Number Systems

- learn order of operations, and apply it to expressions with whole numbers and decimals
- learn and apply distributive and associative properties in operations with signed mixed numbers, fractions, and decimals
- compare numbers using the symbols $<, >, =, \leq, \geq$

Algebra
- study basic algebraic equations; solve simple equations with one variable

Geometry
- calculate surface areas and volumes of three-dimensional objects (e.g., right prisms, cones, cylinders, spheres)
- study and build plane figures that possess symmetry
- learn about vertical, congruent, complementary, supplementary, adjacent, corresponding, alternate interior, and alternate exterior angles and their properties
- know and use formulas to calculate areas of plane figures
- plot points on the Cartesian coordinate plane and determine their coordinates
- calculate the distance between two points on the Cartesian coordinate plane
- learn proportions and how to solve problems using proportions

Probability and Statistics
- interpret statistical data from tables and graphs
- use line graphs, bar graphs, circle graphs , and histograms
- determine probabilities of events
- for a given set of data determine the mean, median, range and mode

SCIENCE

Seventh graders spend substantial time focusing on chemistry and the elements of biology. Major topics of study include:
- atoms, molecules, and elements; how molecules are formed from atoms;
- how chemical bonds are formed; how ionic, metallic, and covalent bonds form
- periodic table
- chemical reactions, how reactions are described by equations (e.g., $HCl + NaOH = NaCl + H_2O$)
- the conservation of matter (in chemical reactions, the number of atoms stays the same no matter how they are arranged, so their total mass stays the same)
- law of conservation of energy and matter
- chemistry of living systems
- cell theory; cell organelles; diffusion/osmosis/active transport; photosynthesis/respiration; the cell cycle
- cell division (asexual and sexual reproduction)

- how traits are passed from one generation to another
- chromosomes and genes
- DNA codes; heredity; how DNA makes new DNA
- the processes of the reproduction and heredity of organisms
- distinguish genes as sections of DNA molecules that carry the genetic code for inherited traits:
- the concepts of homozygous and heterozygous traits
- cells interaction with their environment; homeostasis; an organism's growth and repair processes
- genetic changes (e.g., adaptation, mutation, extinction)
- theory of natural selection (trait variation, speciation)
- bacteria, fungi, protists, and viruses

EIGHTH GRADE

ENGLISH

In English, assignments include reading high-quality literature and analyzing books, articles from newspapers, etc., in class and in their homework.

Writing and Comprehension

- write descriptive essays, book reports, summaries, stories, poems, etc
- write well organized nonfiction and research essays
- practice drafting and revising writings

Speaking, Spelling and Vocabulary

- practice regularly at spelling and vocabulary enrichment
- participate productively in group discussions
- give a presentation before the class

Grammar and Usage

- learn, review, and practice using colons, semicolons, commas, parentheses, hyphens, dashes, italics, and apostrophes
- examine misplaced modifiers
- learn about parallel structure in sentences and practice with such sentences

MATHEMATICS

In mathematics, eighth graders focus mostly on introductory algebra and elements of geometry. They should know the following:

Algebra

- simplify expressions by using the number properties and combining like terms
- know integer exponents , the multiplication property of exponents

- learn how to use scientific notation
- solve simple algebraic equations
- factor algebraic expressions
- translate word problems into equations and solve them
- study inequalities and solve simple inequalities
- understand what a function is and learn linear functions
- use concepts of slope and intercepts when operating with linear functions and linear equations

Geometry

- study the concept of perpendicular
- study various types of triangles and their properties; know the Pythagorean theorem
- study translations and rotations of plane figures

Probability and Statistics

- calculate frequencies from data; build charts, graphs and tables indicating frequencies

SCIENCE

Eighth graders students strengthen their knowledge in subjects considered earlier. They study the following topics:

- basic electrical parameters
- how to measure electric potential, current, and resistance
- electromagnetic radiation and light (light waves; radio waves, x-rays, gamma rays)
- the electromagnetic spectrum
- properties of waves (e.g., amplitude, frequency, wavelength)
- refraction and reflection (e.g., effects of concave and convex lenses)
- characteristics of sound waves (frequency range)
- generation of sound waves (transverse and longitudinal waves)
- travel of sound waves through different medium
- geological history of earth; characteristics of earth's crust, mantle, outer and inner core
- plate tectonics; how plates move on the earth's surface
- main reasons and characteristics of earthquakes
- main reasons and characteristics of volcanoes
- minerals (identifying minerals and crystals, classification of minerals)
- rocks (igneous, sedimentary, and metamorphic)

NINTH GRADE

ENGLISH

In English, ninth graders study of the contents of language and literature, focusing on the writing process and improving their language skills.
The course includes:

- spelling (focusing on etymology, connotation and denotation)
- literature study (literary devices, features of poetry; short story, the novel
  and drama; and American and British literature survey)
- writing instruction (review grammar; sentence structure; verb forms and
  types; phrases and clauses; sentence reduction and expansion)
- instruction on the five-paragraph composition, the essay, the research
  paper, speech writing, and creative writing
- writing assignments as a means of application and assessment on a variety
  of topics

MATHEMATICS

The Algebra 1 course provides tools and develops ways of thinking that
are necessary for solving problems in a wide variety of disciplines such as
science, business, and fine arts. It includes the following topics:

- the basic structure of real numbers
- algebraic expressions and functions
- linear equations and functions
- inequalities
- linear systems
- quadratic and polynomial equations and functions
- data analysis and elements of probability and statistics

SCIENCE

The Chemistry course contains a more detailed and rigorous presentation of basics of chemistry than it was in middle school. It includes topics
such as:

- structure of the atom; atomic number and atomic mass
- element location on the periodic table; groups of elements in the periodic
  table; position of an element in the periodic table relating to its chemical
  reactivity; trends in the periodic table (ionization energy, electronegativ-
  ity, relative sizes of ions and atoms)
- Rutherford's nuclear atom
- Einstein's explanation of the photoelectric effect
- quantum theory of atomic structure

- Bohr's model of the atom
- Planck's relationship
- chemical bonds between atoms in molecules
- stoichiometry (balanced equations; definition of the mole; molar and atomic masses; masses of reactants and products in a chemical reaction; oxidation and reduction reactions; balancing oxidation-reduction reactions)
- acids and bases (properties of acids, bases and salt solutions; strong and weak acids and bases; pH scale, tests and pH in acid-base reactions)
- gases (applying the gas laws to relations between the pressure, temperature, and volume; kinetic theory of gases; Dalton's Law of Partial Pressures; Graham's Law to describe diffusion of gases)
- chemical solutions (definitions of solute and solvent; temperature, pressure, and surface area — their affect the dissolving process; concentration of a solute in terms of grams per liter, molarity, parts per million and percent composition)
- rates of chemical reactions; chemical equilibrium
- thermodynamics and physical chemistry (endergonic and exergonic chemical processes)
- introduction to organic chemistry and biochemistry (formation of large molecules and polymers; amino acids as building blocks of proteins)

TENTH GRADE

ENGLISH

Tenth graders continue studying of the contents of language and literature focusing on the writing process and improving their language skills. The course includes:

- vocabulary words list, spelling
- literature study (fiction and nonfiction, poetry; short story, the novel and drama; essays, articles and speeches)
- writing instruction (review grammar; sentence structure; verb forms and types; phrases and clauses; sentence reduction and expansion)
- study of the various types of newspaper articles and techniques for writing them
- detailed instruction in essay writing and the research paper process
- writing assignments as a means of application and assessment on a variety of topics

MATHEMATICS

The Geometry course refines students' knowledge and formalizes their understanding of geometric concepts. More complicated problems and new material are included. Tenth graders should know the following:

- congruence and similarity
- the Pythagorean theorem
- parallel and perpendicular lines
- circle chords, secants, tangent segments; angle and side measures (e.g., degrees, radians)
- coordinate geometry; vectors; transformation of coordinates
- how to determine surface area and volumes of solids

SCIENCE

The Physics course is the study of the physical world, more detailed and rigorous than in middle school. It includes topics such as:

- mechanics (Newton's three laws of motion; linear motion; circular motion; forces, momentums; energy; gravitation; center of gravity; projectile motion, satellite motion)
- waves (light; sound; radiation; reflection, refraction, diffraction and interference)
- electricity and magnetism (Ohm's law; Faraday's law)
- thermodynamics (heat transfer; the effect of heat on motion; thermodynamics laws)
- elements of atomic and nuclear physics (atom, atomic nucleus, radioactivity, fission and fusion)

ELEVENTH GRADE

ENGLISH

In English, students continue studying the contents of language and literature focusing on the critical reading and improving their writing skills. The course includes:

- reading, writing and evaluating different genres carefully assigned to expose students to noble ideals and writing techniques that equip students to craft strong sentences and paragraphs,
- vocabulary words list
- literature study (fiction and nonfiction, poetry; short story, the novel and drama; essays, articles and speeches)
- writing instruction (review grammar)

- study how to address literary concepts such as cause and effect, logic, premises, comparison and contrasts
- detailed instruction in essay writing and the research paper process
- writing assignments as a means of application and assessment on a variety of topics

MATHEMATICS

Algebra 2 extends students' ability to model and solve real-world problems. Topics include the following:

- complex numbers; operations with complex numbers
- symbolic manipulations; computer algebra systems
- functions and their properties (linear, quadratic, polynomial, exponential, logarithmic, and rational functions)
- sequences and series
- matrices
- systems of equations

SCIENCE

The Biology course contains some materials studied in middle school. Its main topics are:

- the science of biology
- the chemistry of life, the biosphere, ecosystems and communities (homeostasis, organization, metabolism, growth, adaptation, response to stimuli and reproduction)
- cell structure and function
- elements of biochemistry
- membrane transport mechanisms
- photosynthesis, cellular respiration, cell growth and division
- protein synthesis
- mitosis and meiosis
- DNA and RNA
- classical genetics
- molecular genetics
- inheritance; evolution; classification and the diversity of life

TWELFTH GRADE

ENGLISH

The twelfth grade studies a variety of texts, including traditional works of literature. Students should develop practical and persuasive forms of

communication, their own voices as writers and speakers, and combine literary study with writing. They study topics such as:
- what constitutes good literature
- examples and analyses of the best literature from various writers and literary periods of British and American literature
- how to evaluate a writer's style and technique and find reading of classical
  works enriching and enlightening
- writing assignments (write summaries, comparisons, contrasts, sketches,
  and evaluations)

MATHEMATICS

Statistics and Consumer Mathematics is an integrated course which
contains topics necessary for making decision in the everyday life. Students should be able to apply their mathematical knowledge to solve such
problems. Some problems require an elementary knowledge of statistics.
Twelfth graders study topics such as:
- averages (mean, weighted mean, median, mode); frequency distribution
- central tendency; standard deviation
- graphs (bar graphs, line graphs, picture graphs, and circle graphs)
- word problems containing percents (e.g., changes in the prices of mer-
  chandise or stocks, cost of living or unemployment, decrease in expenses
  or net profit)
- simple interest; present value; maturity value (problems with the borrowing and lending of money)
- compound interest; interest compounded daily; present value (problems
  with the borrowing and lending of money; bank accounts; annuities)
- multiple payment plans
- distribution of profits and loss

SCIENCE

The Computer Science course introduces students to the fundamental
concepts of computer programming. Students will become familiar with the
structure of iterative computer programs while also developing an appre-
ciation for object-oriented design and programming. The course includes
the following topics:
- the history and development of the computer including an overview of the
  computer itself, its peripherals, and a brief overview of networking and
  computer languages

- the study of standard algorithms and typical applications; data structures; data abstraction and both linked structures (e.g., arrays and records) and non-linked structures
- programming methodology; the development of computer programs that correctly solve a given problem
- basics of the Java programming language (or C++ language)
- a student-designed final project

Afterword

As this book was being written, the 2009 national testing results became available. They show that the average score in mathematics at grades four and eight increased 27 and 21 points, respectively, over seventeen years. In other words, compared to 1990 they increased only about 20%, without noticeable changes from 2005, and are still low (in 2009, the average math scores of fourth- and eighth-graders are, respectively, 240 and 283 compared to 213 and 262 in 1990); the average reading scores of fourth- and eighth-graders were, respectively, only 4 points higher than in 1992 and 2 points higher than in 2005. Education reform is making no headway.

As parents, we try to help our children to succeed in school. We share their success and painfully react to their failure. Usually, we are informed locally: we obtain information about schools in our area and about teachers. However, most of us know little about the US education system; we are uneducated concerning education itself. Maybe that is why we agree with everything we hear from politicians about education and how to improve it. Maybe that is why we humbly accept our constantly increasing state and local taxes.

Parents, more than anyone else, are interested in improving education. Parents are a powerful force that can make a difference. Only they can press politicians to step forward with realistic proposals. Only they can press state and local leaders to improve their work.

Americans have learned a great deal from the achievements of others. For years now, they have been keenly aware of many deficiencies in their education system. The industrial success of countries like Japan and South Korea has confirmed the importance of an advanced education system and the role of central government in policy planning. That is why there is a ray of hope. But how long can Americans live on hope? There is a distinction between hope and expectation. It's high time to expect decisive actions from our government to reform the system of education. The author hopes that his book helps bring us closer to such reform.

INDEX

A

academic freedom, 183-184

accountability, 41, 45, 49, 60, 68-69, 73-74, 78, 83, 127, 131-132, 134-135, 160-163, 167, 170-171, 174, 177, 183, 202, 208, 210

accreditation, 48, 173, 176

achievement, 7-8, 11, 22, 28-31, 41, 43, 46-47, 58, 60, 63-66, 68-69, 73, 84-86, 112, 114, 124, 132, 136, 141, 145-146, 149-150, 152-154, 158, 160-162, 164, 167, 169-171, 207, 209, 211

ACT test, 86-87

Acts,

American Recovery and Reinvestment (ARRA, 2009), 57, 207

Bilingual Education (1967), 56

Charter School Act (1992), 66, 73, 131-137, 166, 201, 213

Civil Rights (1964), 56

Department of Education Organization, 40, 58

Education Professions Development (EPDA, 1967), 57

Education Sciences Reform (2002), 63

Educational Television (1962), 56

Elementary and Secondary Education (ESEA, 1965), 20, 56

Family Educational Rights and Privacy (FERPA, 1974), 57

Fair Labor Standard (1938), 19

Goals 2000: Educate America (1994), 22, 60, 115

Higher Education (HEA, 1965), 56, 64

Impact Aid (1950), 55

Improving America's Schools (IASA, 1994), 60

Individuals with Disabilities Education (IDEA, 1991), 2, 5, 15, 57, 75, 77, 99, 120, 125, 139, 141, 158, 230, 232-234

Land-Grant (1862), 54

Lanham (1941), 55

Morrill (1862, 1890), 54

National Defense Education (NDEA, 1958), 55-56

National Skills Standards (1994), 61

No Child Left Behind (NCLB, 2001), 11, 63, 65, 68-69, 72-73, 83, 85, 101, 120, 132, 142-145, 149-150, 157, 167-168

School-to-Work Opportunities (1994), 61, 95

Smith-Hughes (1917), 54

administration, 17, 26, 45, 47, 56, 67, 73, 75-77, 94, 110, 119, 132, 151-152, 161-162, 170, 175-176, 185, 189, 198, 204

Advanced Placement (AP) program, 81-83, 92, 128, 155, 195, 203-206

American Association of Educators (AAE), 74

American Association of School Administrators (AASA), 47

American Association of Teachers (AFT), 47-48, 71-73, 102

American College Testing Program, Inc. (ACT), 10-11, 13, 15, 17, 19-20, 22, 40, 50, 54-58, 60-68, 70-73, 83, 85-87, 89, 95, 107, 110, 112-115, 120, 132, 142-143, 145, 148-150,